nd April,1953

or your letter
orry that
k to me
luck

magnificent
art to the
e to keep
rking very
mised one
, for Charterhall
to have either
ans are not

g that there will
M. cars are
July, and we
ust Charterhall,

ar Bryan,

Than   so much for your letter a
            s delighted to have.
oklet

Di
e Wor
ma
h a
s

BRITISH RACING MOTORS LIMITED

DIRECTORS:
PETER BERTHON
RAYMOND MAYS
A. G. B. OWEN
B. F. W. SCOTT

Designers & Constructors of B.R.M. Racing Cars
UNDER THE COMPLETE CONTROL OF THE BRITISH RACING MOTOR RESEARCH TRUST

TELE
BOURNE

BOURNE
LINCOLNSHIRE

7th February last,   I have
                                      ill
                                      ke

Raymond Mays

EASTGATE HOUSE
BOURNE
LINC

BOURNE 17

t 1947 I had a short
o one of Raymond Sommer's
tis in Grand Prix (Rather
dn G.P.s !)
inally see the wonderful
d it looks exactly th
I had it. How nice to
a Talbot and not a
do not want to point
photograph of it but

Road.

hank you ver
d to hear fr
or your good

We are hoping
e present B.R.
hough they may

To Bryan
I
F1 World
BRM (1956 &
nearly hill
disillusione
retiring fro

Raymond Mays'
Magnificent Obsession

www.veloce.co.uk

Hubble & Hattie

BATTLE CRY!

For post publication news, updates and amendments relating to this book please visit
www.veloce.co.uk/books/V4786

First published in August 2015 by Veloce Publishing Limited, Veloce House, Parkway Farm Business Park, Middle Farm Way, Poundbury, Dorchester DT1 3AR, England. Fax 01305 268864 / e-mail info@veloce.co.uk / web www.veloce.co.uk or www.velocebooks.com.

ISBN: 978-1-845847-86-9 UPC: 6-36847-04786-3

Raymond Mays'
Magnificent Obsession

VELOCE PUBLISHING
THE PUBLISHER OF FINE AUTOMOTIVE BOOKS

CONTENTS

BIBLIOGRAPHY

All my Races, Stirling Moss and Alan Henry
Autosport
Behind the Scenes, Louis T Stanley
Bits and Pieces, Prince Birabongse of Thailand
BRM, Raymond Mays and Alan Henry
BRM: The Saga of British Racing Motors, Doug Nye with Tony Rudd
Classic Cars
Classic & Sports Car
Famous Racing Cars, Doug Nye
Formula One Through the Lens, Nigel Snowdon
Grand Prix! Mike Lang
Grand Prix Showdown! Christopher Hilton

History of English Racing Automobiles, The, David Weguelin
History of motor racing, The, William Boddy and Brian Laban
Monaco Grand Prix, The, Alex Rollo
Mon Ami Mate, Chris Dixon
Motor Sport
Murray Walker's Formula One Heroes, Murray Walker and Simon Taylor
Poetry in Motion, Tony Brooks
Split seconds, Raymond Mays
Winners, Brian Laban
Winning is not enough, Jackie Stewart

The three Mark I V16 BRMs of Froilán González, Ken Wharton and Reg Parnell line up for the start of the Goodwood Trophy Race, September 27, 1952.

TELEPHONE:
BOURNE 327-328

BRITISH RACING MOTORS LIMITED

DIRECTORS:
PETER BERTHON
RAYMOND MAYS
A. G. B. OWEN
B. F. W. SCOTT

Designers & Constructors of B.R.M.Racing Cars
UNDER THE COMPLETE CONTROL OF THE BRITISH RACING MOTOR RESEARCH TRUST

BOURNE
LINCOLNSHIRE

My whole life has been given up to the development of racing cars, and actually racing them. I was the originator of the E.R.A., which won so many races both in England and on the Continent.

. After the war I was the instigator of the B.R.M. project. The idea at the back of my mind in starting this was to try to produce a national racing car which could uphold British prestige throughout the world in International Grand Prix events.

"A unique record compiled by a genuine enthusiast"

– Louis T Stanley

"Bryan Apps' enthusiasm, knowledge and skill as an artist have produced a unique record of two great motor racing marques. As someone who is old enough to have watched the legendary ERA single-seaters in their pre-World War II glory days, and who similarly watched their BRM successors – from the ambitious V16 to the World Championship winners – I warmly welcome his tribute to the Constructor achievements of Raymond Mays."

– Murray Walker

ACKNOWLEDGEMENTS

Thanks are due to all the professional journalists and photographers who have created a complete record of motor racing from its earliest years. Also to Stirling Moss, Sir Jackie Stewart and Tony Brooks for their invaluable contributions to my account of the BRMs in this book.

Thanks also to Michael Apps, Geoffrey Wright, Colin Simmons, Grant Wells and Jacqueline Nichols.

INTRODUCTION

Raymond Mays was a quintessentially English gentleman, whose primary object in life was to develop and race fast cars. His earliest successes enabled him to fund this consuming interest through the patronage of Zenith Carburettors, Englebert Tyres and Lodge Plugs, and this defined his motor racing career. In the 1920s, Brooklands and Shelsley Walsh were his happy hunting grounds, and both Bugatti and Mercedes-Benz were anxious to offer him cars with which he could further both his reputation and theirs. In the 1930s, Victor Riley gave him the 1½-litre 12/6 chassis and engine which became the basis of the legendary White Riley, from which Humphrey Cook funded the production of the famous ERAs. Through this project, Raymond Mays and others enhanced Britain's prestige on the motor racing circuits of Europe.

An indispensable ingredient of Mays' early success was his ability to gain the help of young men of outstanding technical ability, such as Amherst

Left: Foreword, written by Raymond Mays for the author, June 1952.

Raymond Mays.

"Such stuff as dreams are made on." From a 1950 Dunlop advertisement prior to the car's debut.

Villiers and Stewart Tresilian, who were able to coax the maximum power from his machinery. After the Second World War, Raymond Mays' lifelong interest became a magnificent obsession, and he threw all his energy into building an all-British Grand Prix racing car, which would achieve what the ERAs had already done in voiturette races. No less than 200 British firms responded to his appeal to get onboard with this ambitious project. One man, Alfred Owen, who was later knighted, stood by him throughout the bad times until 1962, when a BRM driven by Graham Hill won the World Championship, and beyond.

In *BRM, Ambassador for Britain*, produced by the *Daily Express* on the eve of the car's debut, Basil Cardew wrote: "I gather they find the BRM develops such a tremendous turn of speed that it calls for new tactics in motor racing. Its enormous unleashed power seems to shorten the corners, and the drivers have to watch their revolution counters ceaselessly to check distance for gear changing and braking. This, of course, is not only handsome testimony to the force of the engine but also to the highly developed semi-soft springing and splendid steering."

Raymond Mays lived through exciting times. After winning an important race at the Nürburgring in prewar Nazi Germany, he smuggled his prize money out of the country by concealing it in the exhaust pipe of his ERA. In 1953 he drove his fearsomely loud V16 BRM along the public roads from Brackley, in flagrant breach of countless highway regulations, to arrive at Silverstone just in time for it to race. During the 1959 Italian Grand Prix Alfred Owen's sister, Jean Stanley, with commendable resourcefulness, snatched the helmet from a policeman's head in order to prevent Raymond Mays being forcibly, and quite unreasonably, arrested for being in a prohibited area. By the time the pursuing policemen caught up with the abandoned helmet, Jean was nowhere to be seen.

My interest in Raymond Mays and his determination to build a world-beating British racing car was sparked by seeing the flame-red Italian 4CLT Maserati of Reg Parnell cross the line at Goodwood well ahead of the more elderly British ERAs in 1949. Mays' enthusiasm was infectious, and his obsession soon became mine. At school, I doodled BRMs on exercise books during lessons, and the girls would say in exasperation: "You and your BRM!" When, contrary to the school rules, I pinned a photograph of the BRM on the class notice board, the master let it remain. (Could he have been a covert enthusiast?)

I decided to compile a scrapbook of newspaper cuttings about the BRM, beginning with its very first race in 1950. There proved to be a plentiful supply of cuttings from both newspapers and magazines for my book, as the BRM constantly made the headlines, though often for the wrong reasons. Undaunted by the setbacks and disappointments which afflicted the project, and never wavering in my support, I posted my BRM scrapbook to Raymond Mays in June 1952, and what he wrote for that fifteen-year-old schoolboy has become the foreword to this book.

After Rubery Owen bought BRM in 1953, Alfred

The target: Juan Fangio in the all-conquering Italian Alfa Romeo.

Owen wrote a foreword for the second edition of my scrapbook, and this also appears here. A third foreword was written for me by David Brown, Chairman and Managing Director of Aston Martin and Lagonda, who was a member of the original British Racing Research Trust. In addition to this, I have included my correspondence with Raymond Mays at pivotal times over the years that followed.

My wife and I met Raymond Mays for the first time at Eastgate House in Bourne, Lincolnshire, on August 17, 1963, after setting out from Southampton in our Morris Minor for a camping holiday in Scotland. He met us at the door and warmly invited us into his home. Tall, distinguished and, as always, impeccably dressed, he immediately put us at our ease and soon got down to the serious business of motor racing, with many entertaining anecdotes about the BRM and his beloved ERAs. He spoke of his exceptionally successful career as a racing driver before taking us to see his vast glass-fronted cabinets, which were crammed full of the most impressive trophies which he had won in the 1930s. He then led us to the workshop next door where there was an amazing assembly of virtually every model of BRM that had ever been produced, including Graham Hill's World Championship-winning car.

We needed no encouragement to stay much longer than we had anticipated before setting off again to complete the first leg of our journey to Scotland. Eventually, by the light of the car's headlights and in torrential rain, I pitched our primitive ridge tent in a field just outside York, at the end of a day I will never forget.

This book includes a complete history of ERA and BRM, with some of the fascinating letters I received over the years from Ken Richardson, Rivers Fletcher, Tony Rudd, Sir Stirling Moss, Sir Jackie Stewart, Juan Fangio and many others. When I showed the original scrapbooks to the Stanleys at Old Mill House, Trumpington in 1990 Louis wrote in them: "A unique record by a genuine enthusiast." He signed it, and Jean added her name, too.

Bryan Apps

PART ONE

Prewar

B G Apps

1.1

Eastgate House, Bourne

AUGUST 1, 1899

Raymond Mays was born in the market town of Bourne, Lincolnshire, on August 1, 1899. An only child, he was Christened Thomas Raymond, and Eastgate House remained his home all his life. His father, Tom, was the head of T W Mays & Son, which traded in wool, fertiliser and tanned hides, and this gave him the funds to indulge his interest in high-performance cars, and to employ a mechanic to prepare them for him to race.

As Raymond was growing up, motor racing in the UK mostly took the form of hillclimbs and speed trials. There *was* the famous banked racing circuit of Brooklands, but this was intended for the more serious racing motorist, prepared to risk life and limb high up on its famous banking. Tom Mays was content with the other events, which offered excitement enough, and were a sufficient test of both men and machines. None of this was lost on Raymond, who watched the mechanic as he worked under the bonnet of his father's 30/98 Vauxhall in the garage alongside the house, anxious to help. He liked to sit beside the mechanic when he opened the cars up along the flat Lincolnshire roads, and he accompanied his father whenever he pitted his skill against the rest in competitions. The most renowned of these events was the Shelsley Walsh Hillclimb in the heart of the Worcestershire countryside which, dating from 1905, consisted of 100 yards of narrow country lane, ascending along a tortuous route to 100m in height. It was the dream of every competitor to lower the record for the Shelsley Walsh climb, and this simple aspiration grew in Raymond's mind until it became a magnificent obsession to produce a British racing car capable of beating all comers in Grand Prix races on the most prestigious Grand Prix circuits of Europe.

As a boy, Raymond went to Oundle School. Here he met Charles Amherst Villiers, who

Eastgate House, Bourne.

shared his interest in high-performance cars. This interest was further stimulated by Raymond's correspondence with Laurence Pomeroy Sr, designer of the 30/98 Vauxhall, who he met when his father took him to the Vauxhall works. Pomeroy patiently replied to these letters, which were full of questions about his cars. Mays' wrote in *Split seconds* that "... Laurence Pomeroy gratified the curiosity of a small boy with patience and understanding."

Tom took his son to a race meeting at Brooklands where he watched A J Hancock drive the Vauxhall KN, so named because, like cayenne pepper, it was made of hot stuff!

In 1918 Raymond served briefly in Germany and France as a Grenadier Guards officer with the Army of Occupation, before going to Christ's College, Cambridge, to study engineering. There he met up again with Amherst Villiers, now a brilliant engineer who tuned fast cars. The two spent much of their time in Cambridge developing and racing a Speed Model Hillman, given to Ray by his father, and which he regarded as the outstanding 1½-litre sports car

of the day. Amherst would prove to be invaluable to him in later years.

'Quicksilver'

The 1½-litre Hillman, having been tuned by Amherst, enabled Raymond to win a hillclimb organised by the Cambridge University Automobile Club. After this initial success, the two stripped the Hillman's engine and had a light, racing body constructed for the car. Amherst, who had gained experience with aero engines at Farnborough, knew how to obtain yet more power from the Hillman's engine. The 'works' car, which was driven by George Bedford, was called Mercury, so Ray called his car 'Quicksilver', and had the name applied professionally to its pale blue sides. Blue mixed with battleship grey became Mays' colours.

He immediately established the fastest time of the day with this car in the Inter-Varsity hillclimb in Aston Clinton, and thus gained valuable publicity in the motoring press. It was just the beginning, but it led to his skill as a racing driver becoming more widely recognised, and he was able to enlist the

A youthful Raymond Mays.

Raymond Mays with the Speed Model Hillman
at the Kop Hillclimb.

help of Zenith, which invited him to try out a range of carburettors and find the one most suited to the car. In 1921, Mays took 'Quicksilver' to Brooklands, where he won his first race and finished second in his next. It provided an opportunity to meet some famous racing drivers, such as Malcolm Campbell and Henry Seagrave. He also met Humphrey Cook, who was to feature prominently in his life.

The Brescia Bugattis

By the time Raymond left Cambridge, his father's business had been badly affected by the recession, and he was told to spend a few months in Glastonbury learning the wool trade. He continued to have some involvement with the company up until the death of his father, after which he relied on managers to run it for him.

He never allowed the business to get in the way of his motor racing however, and, undaunted by

this first hurdle, Mays negotiated the exchange of his Hillman for a new Brescia Bugatti, with an agreement that the remaining £300 would be paid later. The Bugatti was repainted in his favourite pale blue, and he made the fastest time of the day at a meeting at Dean Hill. Further successes followed, and Englebert Tyres, Lodge Plugs and Speedwell Oil agreed to supply their products to him free of charge. Amherst Villiers reappeared to help develop the potential of the car, and Bugatti's agent in England agreed to supply free spare parts.

In 1923 Ray broke the record at Shelsley Walsh, beating all comers. This set him apart from the rest, and Ettore Bugatti invited him to Molsheim, where he offered to rebuild his Brescia and supply him with an additional car. Returning eventually to Bourne with the two Brescia Bugattis, Ray named his original car 'Cordon Rouge' and the new one 'Cordon Bleu', after Mumm's Brandy. Mumm sent

Raymond Mays at the wheel of 'Cordon Rouge' with Amherst Villiers.

Mays three dozen complimentary bottles in return for this recognition!

The two Bugattis were a great success. The highly-developed Bugatti engines were run in competitions on expensive alcohol fuel known as RD2, and the fuel tanks were fitted with two compartments so that two thirds of it could be filled with normal fuel for road use and the remainder with the more potent fluid for competition purposes. An additional 8mm cylinder packing became necessary for the car to run on normal fuel and this had to be removed before the switch was made to RD2. From the standard maximum of 4000rpm, Mays was able to extract in excess of 6000rpm from his developed engines. He swept the board with his two cars at the Spread Eagle hillclimb near Shaftesbury, and according to one reporter: "The wonder of the afternoon was Raymond Mays on his Brescia Bugattis. Several drivers made a number of changes of gears during the climb, but Mays appeared simply to put his foot hard down and let the engine roar on a low ratio from the foot to the summit. Mays again proved unbeatable."

After breaking his own record at the South Harting hillclimb the press reported: "The spectators stood back instinctively as soon as Raymond Mays was announced on the line. He was the star turn with his Bugatti, his driving being nothing short of marvellous, while he took the second bend with the nearside wheels in the air. It was a great effort and deservedly gave him premier honours."

The Caerphilly Mountain climb was next, where a broken axle shaft caused the nearside rear wheel to come off 'Cordon Bleu'. The damage was caused by the additional power from the car's engine, and stronger axle parts and shafts were fitted to remedy the problem. Improvements were constantly tried, and Mays secured a deal with Whitehead to supply its new front wheel brakes free of charge, in addition to contributing a fee of £500.

Raymond Mays with 'Cordon Bleu' losing a wheel during the 1924 Caerphilly Mountain hillclimb.

The Vauxhall TT, driven by Raymond Mays with riding mechanic, Peter Berthon, at Shelsley Walsh, September 1926.

An AC and a Tourist Trophy Vauxhall

At the end of 1924 Selwyn Francis Edge, the head of AC, loaned Raymond one of his cars for Amherst to supercharge and for him to race, with an aim to afford AC valuable publicity. To make way for this project, the Bugattis were sold. 'Cordon Bleu' went to the young and inexperienced Francis Giveen who, in spite of some tuition and words of caution from Ray, came off the road and seriously injured a number of mechanics at Kop. As a result, hillclimbs were no longer allowed on public roads.

Attempts to increase the power of the AC were plagued by overheating and cracks to its cylinder head. The experiment to supercharge the AC had failed, but Mays was also loaned a TT Vauxhall by Harold Clay with which to compete at Shelsley Walsh in 1926. Amherst held on grimly as his riding mechanic as he charged up the hill using every inch of the road to break the course record once again. Minutes later it was lowered even further by Davenport's GN.

Peter Berthon

Peter Berthon entered the scene in 1927 when he was a young flying cadet at RAF Cranwell. Whilst recovering from landing a Gloster Grebe upside down, he stayed at Eastgate House, moving in afterwards on a permanent basis. He left Cranwell to join the family business, but was more interested in Ray's motor racing ambitions and, with little formal engineering training, but a natural aptitude, he became fully involved in tuning and developing the cars.

The Targa Florio Mercedes

Mays' reputation as a racing driver grew, and in 1927 Mercedes-Benz offered him a 2-litre Targa Florio Mercedes to race throughout that season with works support. It was to this car that Peter Berthon first applied his engineering skills and he became Raymond Mays' racing mechanic. Stronger Terry valve springs and a clutch-operated supercharger were fitted, and the success of the modified Mercedes led the company to offer Mays a straight-eight-cylinder supercharged car of two litres, together with a complete team of mechanics. Sadly, its power only really came through over 5000rpm, rendering it unsuitable for hillclimbs like Shelsley Walsh. The car was also unmanageable at Brooklands, and required all of the track, but Ray managed a second in one race after starting the race from scratch. He later discovered that the

The Villiers Supercharge at Eastgate House.

other two examples of the car had both crashed and claimed the lives of their drivers.

The Villiers Supercharge and an Invicta

In 1928 Ray and Amherst jointly bought a 4-cylinder 3-litre TT Vauxhall from Humphrey Cook, of later ERA fame, which they had stripped down and rebuilt. A new two-seater body was constructed and sprayed light blue. Although the car already had a supercharger, a new, Roots-type supercharger was designed by Villiers, and new pistons were made with thicker crowns. In place of coil and battery ignition, Villiers introduced BTH magnetos. The chassis frame was strengthened and, at Amherst's suggestion, the then-novel arrangement of twin rear wheels was adopted to give greater traction. Mays, driving the now dubbed 'Vauxhall-Villiers,' returned to Shelsley Walsh to beat Davenport's GN and to establish the fastest time of the day. *The Motor* reported: "The outstanding feature of the day was the breaking of B D Davenport's record by Raymond Mays driving a 3-litre Vauxhall-Villiers supercharged special, the rear wheels of which were equipped with twin tyres ... Mays, who was for a long time the finest driver in this country in this class of competition, came back with a vengeance, and it can be said without fear of contradiction that it was the finest display of driving that has been seen for many a long day."

Raymond Mays in the Villiers Supercharge at Shelsley Walsh, with Peter Berthon alongside.

After this, Amherst turned his attention to supercharging Tim Birkin's Le Mans Bentleys, and Mays became the sole owner of the much-modified car, now known as the Villiers Supercharge. Its stable in Bourne was shared with a 4.5-litre white Invicta which was modified and tuned by Peter Berthon and Tom Murray Jamieson. Mays drove the Invicta at Brooklands in 1931, and passed an Alvis being driven over the top of the bank, fortunately without serious injury to its driver. The Invicta went on to finish second after starting from scratch, and set a new class record at 69.74mph. It was the fastest lap of any British sports car to date, and drew the following comment from *Autocar* magazine: "If Invictas can perform as well as Raymond Mays' car, surely a team of this make would do well in all road races."

At the end of 1930, and after further attempts to extract more power from the Villiers Special, a new crankshaft, timing gears, and supercharger were required, and both Shell and India Tyres agreed to sponsor the project.

At Skegness in 1931, Ray made the fastest time in the unlimited sports car class with the Invicta, and in the unlimited class with the Villiers. From its TT Vauxhall days the Villiers' brake horsepower had been increased from 125 to 300, and the time came at last for it to be tried at Brooklands. Mays and Berthon discovered that, at 150mph on the

The White Riley at Brooklands in 1933 with Raymond Mays at the wheel. From the right are Murray Jamieson and Peter Berthon.

Byfleet Banking, extreme vibrations caused the car to become unmanageable and their vision to be seriously impaired. They reluctantly decided that the car could only be used for sprint races, and concentrated on the Invicta.

At Shelsley Walsh in 1932 Mays made one last attempt to break the record with Villiers, but broke its crankshaft. Luckily, he also had the Invicta, in which he gained a new sports car record. The Invicta, which was owned by India Tyres, was later sold to Humphrey Cook, and work concentrated on repairing the stricken Villiers. When this was done Ray achieved the fastest time of the day at Shelsley Walsh, but by this point he and Peter Berthon had already begun to develop a 1½-litre racing car based upon a Riley.

The White Riley

In 1933 Mays persuaded Victor Riley that, with the help of Peter Berthon, he could modify one of his cars by adding a new aluminium cylinder head and supercharger, and with this lower the record at Shelsley Walsh. It was currently held by Hans Stuck's Austro-Daimler and, if successful, the project would gain invaluable publicity for Riley. As a result he was loaned a 1½-litre Riley 12/6 chassis and engine and given £300 to help with the development of the car. Berthon was joined by Murray Jamieson, who designed the supercharger. The two also modified the block, built a new crankshaft and cylinder head, and strengthened the chassis, axles and gearbox. The car was finished in off white with 'Mays blue' leather seats. In the book *Split Seconds,* Raymond

Mays, on course to break the record at Shelsley Walsh with the White Riley, September 1933.

prophetically saw the Riley as "... the foundation stone for the future creation of a real British racing car which would challenge the world."

At its first trial, the new car reached an impressive 8000rpm before its supercharger drive sheared. As promised, Mays exceeded the Shelsley record with the White Riley, although Whitney Straight improved on his time later the same day with his 3-litre Grand Prix Maserati.

At Brooklands, the White Riley excelled in its first race, until Mays had to coast in with it – it had a broken distributor arm. Later that day it broke the 1½-litre course record on the Mountain circuit at 74.69mph. Prince Bira of Siam watched

Mays driving the White Riley on the banking at Brooklands, and wrote in *Bits and Pieces* of Mays "... flinging his white machine round the bend as if he was banking steeply with a Hurricane plane. The exhaust note of that car very much resembled that to which I was to grow accustomed two years later."

Some thought had been given to the production of a team of White Rileys to compete in Voiturette races, but at the end of the season Humphrey Cook wrote to Raymond, suggesting that a team of 1½-litre single seater racing cars based on the Riley might be built, and it was from this that the ERA was to emerge.

Raymond Mays about to break the record.

1.2

English Racing Automobiles Ltd

Following the success of the White Riley, Humphrey Cook met Raymond Mays and Peter Berthon to discuss the possibility of building a team of 1½-litre single seater Voiturette racing cars with Riley-based engines. The three agreed to produce English cars capable of taking on the Italian Maseratis and Alfa Romeos in Europe, and English Racing Automobiles Ltd was registered on November 6, 1933. It was financed by Humphrey Cook, and both Raymond Mays and Peter Berthon became directors, receiving wages of £250 per year. Mays was to be the team's principal driver, with Cook driving a second car. Berthon became race manager, and Ken Richardson the chief test driver.

A small factory was built in the grounds of Eastgate House, and Victor Riley agreed to manufacture any additional mechanical parts that would be required.

Reid Railton of Thomson and Taylor, based at Brooklands, designed and built the chassis having been responsible for John Cobb's Napier Railton, while Murray Jamieson worked on further modifications to the Riley engine and its supercharger. Two panel-beating brothers named George and Jack Gray drove up from Emsworth in Hampshire each day to hammer out the cars' bodies. The original badge, incorporating a rising sun with the letters E, R and A, was designed by Gordon Crosby.

It was during this time that Raymond's father died after a long illness. In spite of his understandable reservations, he had been proud of his son's achievements, and Ray regretted that his father would not witness the unveiling of the first single seater English road racing car ever to be built.

1934

The first ERA, designated R1, was to have made its debut in the Mannin Beg Race for 1½-litre cars around the streets of Douglas on the Isle of Man, but, after arriving on the back of its double decker Leyland transporter, the car had to be withdrawn before the race because of major handling problems. Modifications were carried out back at Bourne which resulted in softer springs and revised steering. At Brooklands for the Empire Trophy Race, its main oil pipe broke on the starting line. After a delayed start, and in spite of a puncture and a holed silencer, which claimed another precious twenty minutes, the car performed well. By its next outing, the Dieppe Grand Prix, the car was sporting the famous ERA badge with its three interlinked circles. Mays was forced to retire during the race because of a broken valve rocker.

Two ERAs were entered for the BARC August meeting at Brooklands. Cook won the Second Esher Handicap in the 1100cc R2, while Mays, driving the 1½-litre R1, finished second to a 2-litre Bugatti. He also broke the White Riley's lap record at 76.31mph and, with R1, won the appearance prize for the smartest turnout, wearing blue silk monogrammed overalls. In addition, Cook and Mays broke the standing start kilometre records for the course.

Mays recorded that the 1100cc car had a deeper exhaust note and exceptional torque at low revs. In September he established the fastest time of day at Shelsley Walsh in the first 2-litre ERA, beating Whitney Straight's 3-litre Grand Prix Maserati and, in the month that followed, he won the 100 miles Nuffield Trophy Race at Brooklands from Richard Seaman's MG Magnette. That October, Ray came second in the Brooklands Mountain Championship Race to Straight's Maserati, and he also broke the World Record for a standing start kilometre at Brooklands.

Encouraged by the success of the ERAs, Cook decided that a limited number should be produced for sale. A 1100cc model was bought by the South African Pat Fairfield for £1500, and a 1½-litre went to Richard Seaman for £1700. This car, which had a strengthened chassis, was the first of the B Types. The price of a 2-litre model was £1850.

1935

For 1935 four Bedford transporters were supplied by Vauxhall, and additional sponsorship was gained from Shell and Dunlop. Modifications were made to the suspension, and a new chassis crossmember was introduced to the cars, which were to be known as B Types. Larger capacity radiators were fitted, as well as larger fuel tanks, which gave the car's rear ends their iconic shape. An experimental 1100cc engine was fitted with a Zoller supercharger for the Mannin Beg Race in Douglas, Isle of Man, and Mays also supercharged his black Riley Kestrel for road use.

Raymond Mays with R1 at Brooklands in 1934, when the car had a vertical windshield mount and an earlier silencer.

Cook won the first race of the year at Brooklands in March in the R1; also winning his class at the Inter Varsity Speed Trials at Syston Park with the same car. Seaman came second to Martin's 2300cc Bugatti in the 25 mile Handicap Race at Donington Park in April, and Cook, again in R1, finished second in the Brooklands British Mountain Handicap Race later that month. In May, Mays achieved the fastest time of the day at Shelsley Walsh in the 2-litre R3. Then came the Isle of Man Mannin Beg Race, run over 202 miles, which Mays led until his oil pipe fractured, leaving Fairfield to win in another ERA.

On June 16 the three works A Type ERAs, together with Dick Seamen's privately-entered B Type, competed in the 1500cc Eifelrennen for 1½-litre cars, over 170 miles of the famous Nürburgring in Germany. In order to familiarise himself with the challenging fourteen mile course, Mays drove his new, much loved 3½-litre Bentley saloon at speed around the circuit before and in-between official practice sessions, both by day, and with the help of its headlights and twin spot lights by night.

During the race he established the fastest lap in the 1500cc R3A, and eventually won in spite of having to pump up his fuel whenever possible, and fierce competition from Seaman. Immediately after winning, he was lifted out of his car by German

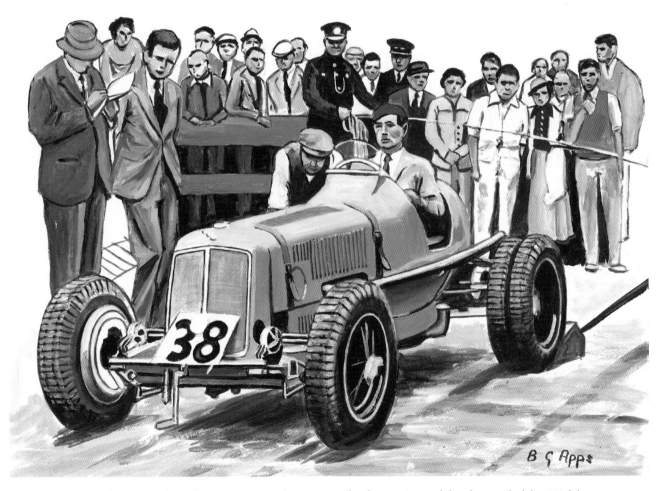

Raymond Mays in the 2-litre ERA R4B, about to set the fastest time of the day at Shelsley Walsh on September 28, 1935, matching his record of 39.6 seconds.

Raymond Mays in the 1½-litre ERA R1, at the same Shelsey Walsh meeting, before going up the hill in 40.4 seconds to record the second fastest time of the day.

stormtroopers, before having a laurel wreath placed around his neck while the band played the British National Anthem. Ruesch finished second in his Maserati, followed by the ERAs of Tim Rose-Richards, Dick Seaman, who had lost precious seconds in his pit, and Humphrey Cook. When the German authorities ordered the four not to take their prize money out of the country, they rolled the bank notes up and concealed them at the further end of their cars' exhaust pipes!

The organisers were so impressed by Mays' performance and his ERA that they invited him to compete in the German Grand Prix the following month. Two 2-litre car cars were to be driven by Mays and von Delius, but the German driver wrote off his car in practice after spinning off the track and into a solitary tree, which saved him from a drop of 100ft along that section of the circuit.

On race day, the field included the mighty Mercedes-Benz and Auto Union teams, which, naturally, outclassed the tiny British car. Fumes from the exhausts of the German cars stung Ray's eyes like tear gas, but he persevered and, as agreed, handed his car over to von Delius halfway through the race, after 2hrs 40min. Shortly after this, the failure of a main bearing caused the ultimate retirement of the car.

My dear friend, Manfred von Brauchitsch, held a

clear lead until the last lap, when a rear tyre on his Mercedes burst, allowing Tazio Nuvolari to claim his hard fought place as winner.

Two works ERAs were entered for the Prix de Berne – which immediately followed the Swiss Grand Prix on the Bremgarten circuit in August – one for Mays and the other for an ex-Auto Union driver called Leiningen. Both cars suffered mechanical failures, but the privately-entered ERAs of Dick Seaman and Prince Bira finished second and third: Hans Stuck's 5-litre Auto Union could not be caught.

In the course of the year, Seaman's ERA won races in Pescara and Brno, Czechoslovia, in addition to the numerous successes achieved in England by the other drivers, such as Mays putting up first and second fastest time of the day at Shelsley Walsh with R3 and R1 in September.

Also in 1935, Prince Chula of Siam bought R2B for his cousin Prince Bira's 21st birthday. Bira named it 'Romulus' and had it finished in 'Bira blue,' with a small white mouse painted on its side. He always spoke to his cars in their garage before going to bed, and invariably had a word with them during the course of a race.

1936

Prince Chula bought a second ERA for Bira, which he called 'Remus,' while Dick Seaman sold R1B to Manly-Colegrave after buying Earl Howe's 1927 1500cc Grand Prix Delage. At Bourne, ERA sought to obtain a higher boost from its Zoller superchargers than was possible with the Roots type designed by Jamieson. The Zollers were found to be less effective at low revs, but more potent at over 4000rpm. This brought its own problems by causing great stress to other components.

Bira entered 'Remus' for the Opening Meeting of the BARC at Brooklands on March 14, and finished in fourth place. He went on to win the Prince Rainier Cup Race at Monaco on April 11, with ERAs also finishing in second, third and fifth places. Bira also won the JCC International Trophy Race at Brooklands with 'Romulus,' managing to pass Mays just before the finishing line.

Seaman's newly modified Delage arrived at Donington for the Meeting on May 9, to win the ten lap Handicap race for cars up to 5000cc. He also won the 200 Mile Light Car Race at Brooklands, with ERAs taking the next five places. Two new 6CM Maseratis driven by Count Trossi and Tenni led five ERAs across the line in the 114 mile Eifelrennen, and Mays and Cook had the works cars painted black for the Prix de Berne, hoping that this might change their fortunes. However, it was Seaman in the Delage who won, followed by three ERAs.

At Shelsley Walsh the ERAs came into their own again, with Mays making the fastest time of the day with his 2-litre, and second fastest with his 1.5-litre car. Mays' season was rounded off by his winning the Brooklands Mountain Championship Race during the BARC's Autumn Meeting in the 2-litre R12B. After a typically slow 'Zoller' start, Mays led Ruesch's 4-litre Alfa Romeo, and a number of other 3-litre Alfas and Maseratis, across the line. He also won the Siam Challenge Trophy, for which only ERAs were eligible.

Mays and Cook decided that, at the end of the season, cars would no longer be built for private entrants, so that more time could be given to the works cars.

As an aside, in the 1970s I bought a 1936 Riley Adelphi, had it lovingly resprayed and rechromed, and relished its points of contact with the ERAs!

1937

The new 6CM Maseratis were less powerful than the ERAs, but had the advantage of independent front suspension, so, this year, ERA produced its C Type. This adopted an independent, paid-for front suspension design from Dr Porsche. It required a new front end for the chassis, and softer rear springs with adjustable hydraulic shock absorbers. At the same time, the engine was made more reliable with stronger connecting rods, designed by Peter Berthon. Murray Jamieson and draughtsman Harry Munday also joined ERA on a full time basis. Dick Seaman who had been given a place in the works Mercedes-Benz Team, sold his Delage to Prince Chula.

2.11.99

Dear Bryan

Excuse the informality but I can't go on calling you Revd.! Thank you for your letter and the news that you propose to paint a picture of the ERA with twin Arnott superchargers which is in fact the same car (R6B) which I drove in the 1938 Grand Prix at Donington. The manufacturers of the superchargers asked me to carry out the experiment and provided the superchargers. It was not a success as it was too hot for the pistons which kept getting melted, and so we reverted to the normal Roots blower.

It is difficult to remember for certain what the colours were and sometimes one of the ERAs that I drove was painted grey for a time. However, on looking at all the photographs that I have, I am pretty certain that both the cars and my helmet were painted navy blue and the chassis was a silver-grey. The wheels must have been blue as well. What a pity that colour photography had not come in!

I hope that you and Kath are both well. I seem to remember that when I saw you at Southbourne you had not been well.

We are both fine and I have had cataract operations in both eyes with enormous success so that I can now see colours as they should be.

With very best wishes to you and Kath

Yours ay
Ian Connell

Letter from Ian Connell about the twin superchargers.

An incendiary device!
Ian Connell's twin Arnott supercharged ERA R6B at Crystal Palace,
August 14, 1937.

The first race of the year was the South African Grand Prix, and it was won by Fairfield driving the R4A. The Auto Unions of Delius and Rosemeyer took the first two places in the Grosvenor Grand Prix in Cape Town, followed by the ERAs of Earl Howe and Fairfield. Fairfield also won the Rand Grand Prix and the Farewell Race. Ian Connell, whom I came to know in later years, finished second, driving the R6B in the Swedish Winter Grand Prix, which was run on ice using spiked tyres! Back in the UK, Mays won the British Empire Trophy Race at Donington Park with the R4C.

An ERA won the Coronation Trophy Race at Crystal Palace, and took the first five places in the RAC Light Car race on the Isle of Man. Mays made the fastest time of the day at Shelsley Walsh in the R4C, and won the Picardy Grand Prix on June 27 in the same car ahead of two 6CM Maseratis. ERAs took the first three places in the Albi Grand Prix, and 'Romulus' won the London Grand Prix at Crystal Palace, with Ian Connell finishing in second place.

Connell brought his ERA to Crystal Palace with an extended bonnet which concealed twin Arnott superchargers. He wrote to me about it in 1999: "The manufacturers of the superchargers asked me to carry out the experiment and provided the superchargers. It was not a success, as it was too hot for the pistons, which kept melting, and so we reverted to the normal Roots blower." The JCC International Trophy Race at Brooklands was won by Mays.

ERAs took the first four places in the Prix de Berne, and at Phoenix Park in Dublin Mays won the 1500cc Scratch Race, with Band leader Billy Cotton coming third in his newly acquired R1B. The Grand Prix Mercedes-Benz and Auto Union Teams dominated the Donington Grand Prix on October 2. Bernd Rosemeyer won the 80 lap race in his C Type Auto Union, and Manfred von Brauchitsch was second in his W125 Mercedes. The ERAs of Earl Howe, Arthur Dobson and Robin Hanson were unclassified, and Raymond Mays retired on the 51st lap due to brake failure. The ERAs of Brian Martin and Peter Whitehead retired earlier because of engine failures. After this, Bira won the Imperial Trophy Race at Crystal Palace on October 9 with R2B, and Mays ended his season by winning the Siam Trophy at Brooklands on October 16 with R12C.

1938

In 1938 the ERAs had to face stronger opposition from the Italian teams. The dominance of Auto Union and Mercedes-Benz in Grands Prix made the companies determined to succeed in the lesser voiturette races. They produced the 158 Alfa and the 4CL Maserati while, from Stuttgart, came the fabulous W165 Mercedes-Benz, which won the Tripoli Grand Prix on its first, and only, outing.

Raymond Mays' ERA R4C, having been overtaken by Hermann Lang's W125 Mercedes at Donington, October 2, 1937.

Prince Birabongse Bhanudej Bhanubandh – 'Bira' in 'Romulus' at Crystal Palace in May 1938 before the car's wheels were painted yellow.

Mays' C Type ERA became a D Type with further modifications to the chassis, suspension and brakes and, when the new 3-litre supercharged Formula was announced, Mays and Cook regarded it as a test bed for a future Grand Prix car.

The Grosvenor Grand Prix was won by Earl Howe from the 4CL Maseratis of Piero Taruffi and Count Johnny Lurani. Prince Chula bought the R12C for Bira to drive, and it was named 'Hanuman'. 'Remus' was sold to Tony Rolt, and Bira won the Coronation Trophy Race at Crystal Palace in 'Romulus'. Mays arrived at Donington Park for the British Empire Trophy Race with R4D, but retired during the race due to brake failure. Bira won the Campbell Trophy Race at Brooklands and the Cork International Race at Cork with 'Hanuman'. Mays finished in second place with R4D in the JCC International Trophy Race at Brooklands, but at that meeting Murray Jamieson, who was spectating, was killed when a V12 Delage ploughed into the crowd. It was a huge setback to ERA's future plans.

Rolt won two races at Donington Park in May with R5B, and Mays established the fastest time of the day at Shelsley Walsh with R4D that same month. Numerous successes followed: Bira won the Nuffield Trophy Race at Donington Park, in which five ERAs were amongst the first eight finishers, and The ERAs of Mays, Rolt and Connell took the first three places in the Coronation Trophy Race, also at Donington.

The new Grand Prix ERA appeared at Donington on July 20 for private trials – it had yet to be shown to the public. It looked more like a Grand Prix Mercedes than an ERA!

In September Mays set the fastest time of the day at Shelsley Walsh in R4D. He also won Brooklands Mountain Championship Race in R4D.

The Donington Grand Prix on October 22 brought the German teams back to England with the latest 3-litre cars. Tazio Nuvolari won the race with his D Type Auto Union, Hermann Lang and Dick Seaman were second and third in W154

Bira with 'Hanuman' in the Campbell Trophy Race at Brooklands in 1938.

Mercedes, Hermann Muller fourth in another D Type, and Manfred von Brauchitsch fifth in another W154. The works ERAs didn't compete, but the privately-entered B Type ERAs of Arthur Dobson, Billy Cotton/Wilkie Wilkinson and Ian Connell/Peter Monkhouse finished in the next three places, six laps behind. Many years later, Ian Connell told me that, even though the ERAs were unable to keep up with the German cars, they had the consolation of being awarded the Team Prize as ERA was the only team to finish the race. He agreed with me that they also had the best vantage point from which to watch the Mercedes-Benz and Auto Unions!

At the end of the year Cook was presented with a cheque for £200 by the ERA Supporters Club, to help with the Grand Prix Project. The appeal was run by Rivers Fletcher.

Ian Connell's ERA being pursued by Bernd Rosemeyer's Auto Union at Donington in 1938.

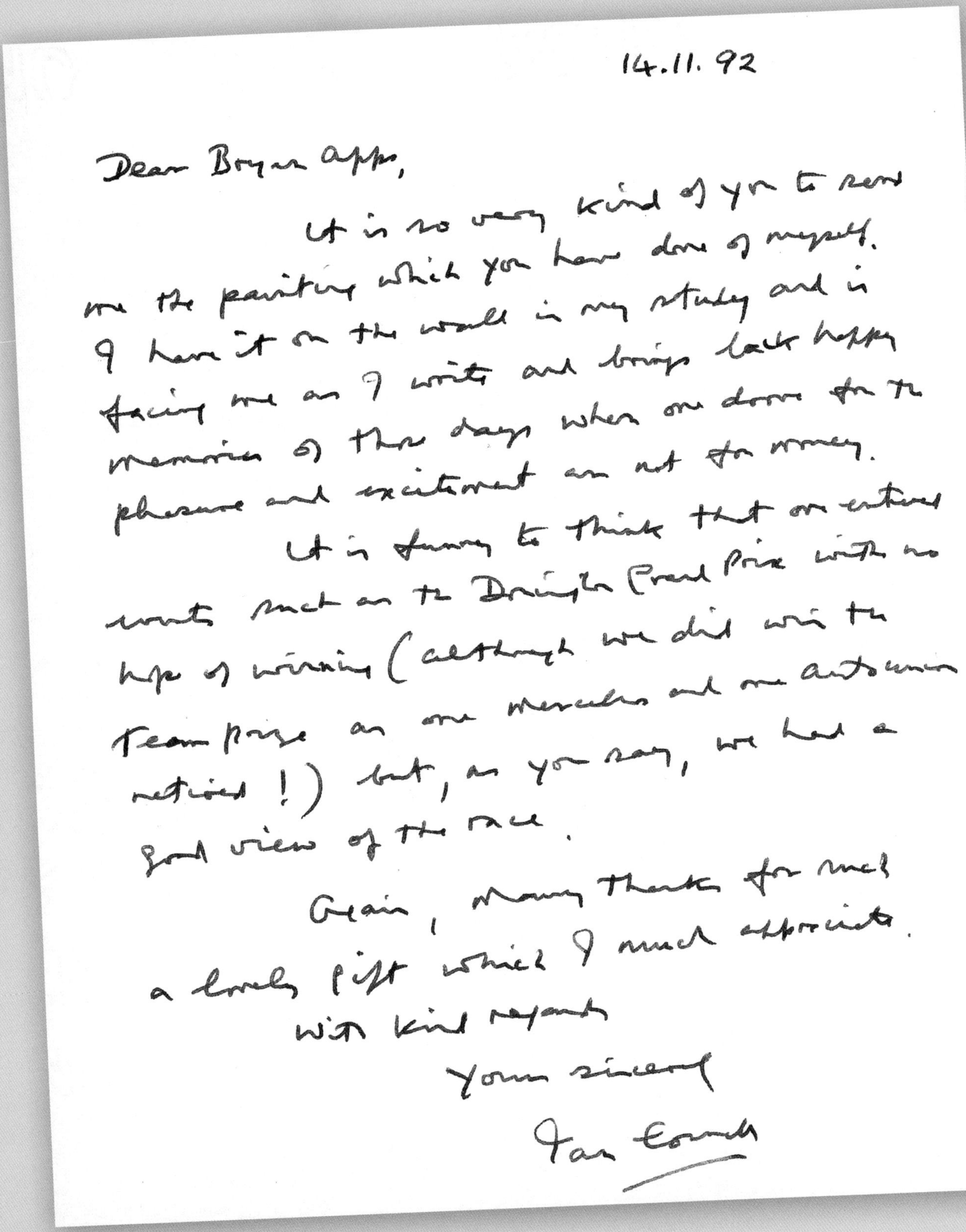

14.11.92

Dear Bryan Apps,

It is so very kind of you to send me the painting which you have done of myself. I have it on the wall in my study and is facing me as I write and brings back happy memories of those days when one drove for the pleasure and excitement and not for money.

It is funny to think that one entered events such as the Donington Grand Prix with no hope of winning (although we did win the Team Prize as one Mercedes and one Auto Union retired!) but, as you say, we had a good view of the race.

Again, many thanks for such a lovely gift which I much appreciate.

With kind regards

Yours sincerely

Ian Connell

Letter from Ian Connell concerning the 1938 Donington Grand Prix.

We had a lovely time last month when Wilkie Wilkinson and I were fêted at Donington on the 60th Anniversary of the 1938 British Grand Prix as we are the only drivers in the race still living. I displayed your painting of me being passed by Nuvolari who won the race. The actual ERA (R6B) that I drove was produced as a surprise for me.

Ian

Bryan Apps

Season's Greetings

and best wishes for christmas and the New Year to you and Kath

from

Ian Connell

The message in a Christmas card from Ian Connell, in which he tells me that he displayed my painting when he was invited to the 60th anniversary celebration of the 1938 Donington Grand Prix.

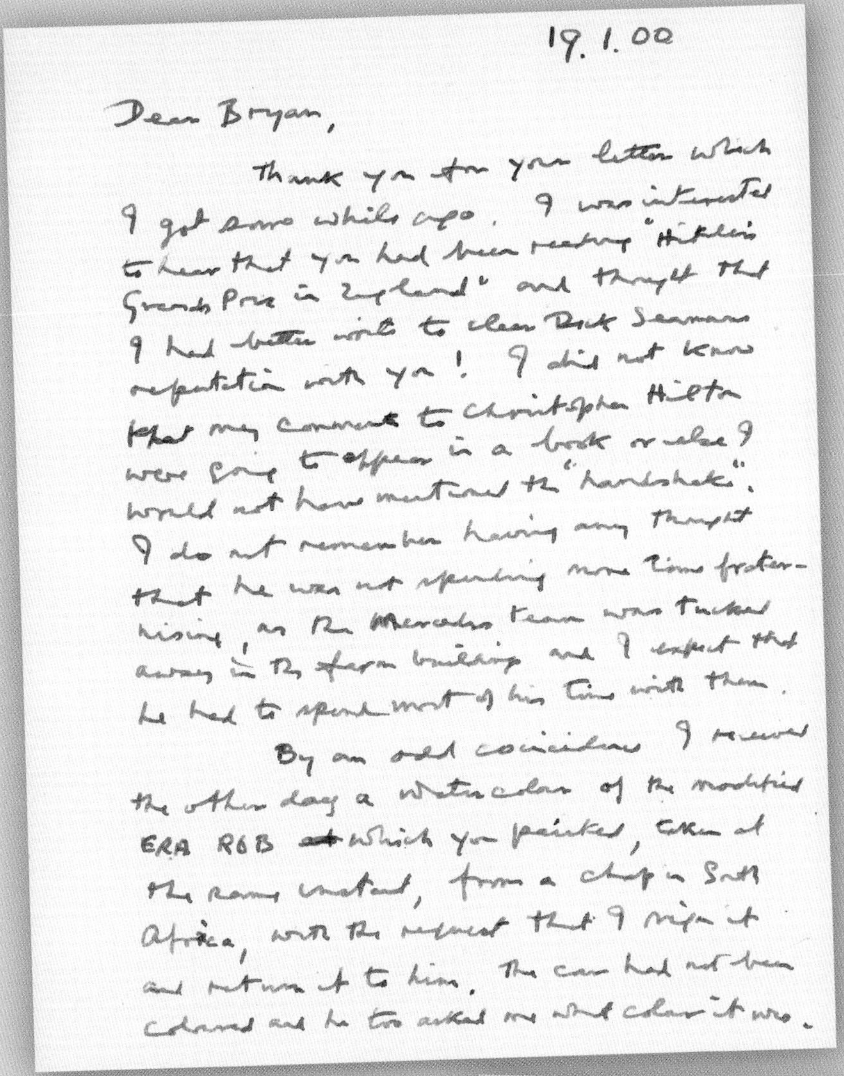

19.1.00

Dear Bryan,

Thank you for your letter which I got some while ago. I was interested to hear that you had been reading "Hitler's Grands Prix in England" and thought that I had better write to clear Dick Seaman's reputation with you! I did not know that my comments to Christopher Hilton were going to appear in a book or else I would not have mentioned the "handshake". I do not remember having any thought that he was not spending more time fraternising, as the Mercedes team was tucked away in the farm building and I expect that he had to spend most of his time with them.

By an odd coincidence I received the other day a watercolour of the modified ERA R6B which you painted, taken at the same instant, from a chap in South Africa, with the request that I sign it and return it to him. The car had not been coloured and he too asked me what colour it was.

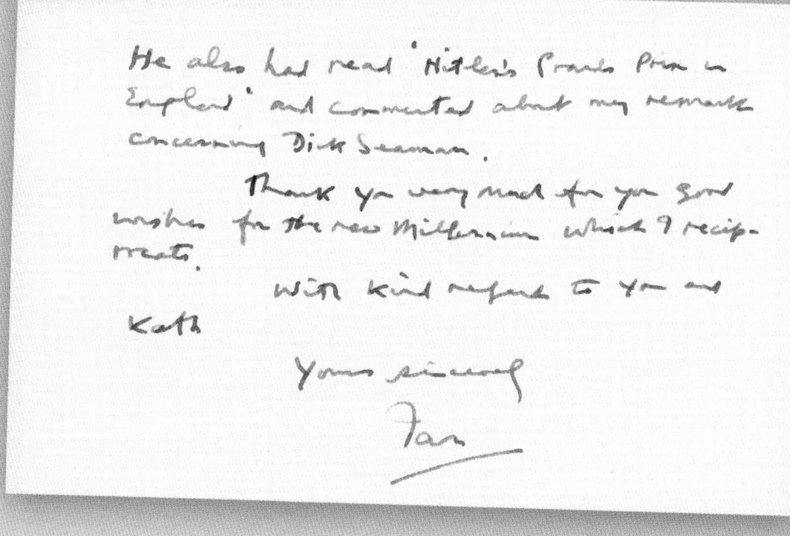

He also had read "Hitler's Grands Prix in England" and commented about my remarks concerning Dick Seaman.

Thank you very much for your good wishes for the new Millennium which I reciprocate.

With kind regards to you and Kath

Yours sincerely
Ian

In his letter, Ian Connell absolves Dick Seaman from having a weak handshake, and also from the charge that he was unsociable!

'The Raymond Mays'

In 1938 a 90hp sports car called 'The Raymond Mays' was announced by Shelsley Motors Ltd, a company led by Mays himself. The car was to cost £450, and have a V8 engine produced by the Standard Motor Company. A sports saloon model was to be followed by a drophead coupé and an open sports car. Sadly, none of these cars ever materialised.

1939

Despite the growth in support for ERA Ltd, Cook announced in 1939 that the financial support he provided would have to decrease, as the personal cost had become too great to maintain.

There were calls for state aid from ERA supporters, and the British Motor Racing Fund was established to offer Cook some much needed financial support so the cars could continue to race. It only managed to raise £1000, though, and on May 26, Cook announced the closure of the ERA works at Bourne, and he and Mays went their separate ways.

Mays took Peter Berthon and Ken Richardson with him, officially resigning from ERA Ltd on May 24, two days before Cook's announcement.

Mays said that they parted on good terms, and he bought R4D from Cook, together with a 1500cc and a 2-litre engine with the germ of the BRM project already forming in his mind. In *Split Seconds* he wrote: "Fortunately Humphrey and I had known each other so long that, despite marked differences in temperament, we were able to preserve a perfectly amicable, almost affectionate, personal relationship, even when in business we could not see altogether eye-to-eye."

6CM Maseratis took the first three places in the South African Grand Prix, but ERAs continued to flourish in British events. The Brooklands Road Championship Race was won by Dobson driving the R4D and, while Bira won the JCC International Trophy Race at Brooklands in a 3-litre Maserati, ERAs took five of the first ten places. After previous tests at Donington, the E Type Grand Prix car, known as the GP1, was now put through high speed tests by Mays at Brooklands, where some problems with its cylinder head were discovered. Regardless, Mays recorded that the GP1 was 11 seconds faster than his best lap with the ERA 4RD.

Bira won the RRC Sydenham Trophy Race at Crystal Palace with 'Romulus,' now sporting a blue body with yellow chassis and wheels.

Aubrey Barratt took charge of the GP1 Project while Mays won the RRC Crystal Palace Cup race with R4D and established a new lap record. GP1 appeared at Rheims, where it was timed by Mercedes-Benz at 172mph on the finishing straight. The louvres had to be enlarged along the bonnet for greater cooling, and the car was withdrawn from the race when its piston rings began to break up. Mays had been invited to drive the new single seater 4½-litre unsupercharged Talbot in the French Grand Prix at Rheims, but during practice and again in the race, its fuel tank split. He also took his ERA over to France to compete in the Albi Grand Prix, but during the race it lost a wheel at high speed and he only managed to bring it safely to rest by using "... all of the track, and the banks and verges as well." Dobson led the race in GP1, until lap nine, when it spun into the straw bales and retired.

Mays had a runaway win in the Campbell Trophy race at Brooklands in R4D with its 2-litre engine

Raymond Mays competing in the French Grand Prix in the new works Darracq.

at 72.71mph, 13.4 seconds ahead of Bira's Maserati. He stayed at Brooklands after the race to make an attempt on the Campbell course record. On August 8, 1939, nine days before the war began, he broke the record at 77.79mph. It was a record that would never be broken.

GP1 and GP2 were promised for the Donington Grand Prix on September 30, but by this time war had been declared, and all motor racing ceased.

Raymond Mays returning down the hill at Shelsley Walsh.

Signed photograph of Ian Connell with his 4CLT Maserati at Shelsley Walsh in 1946.

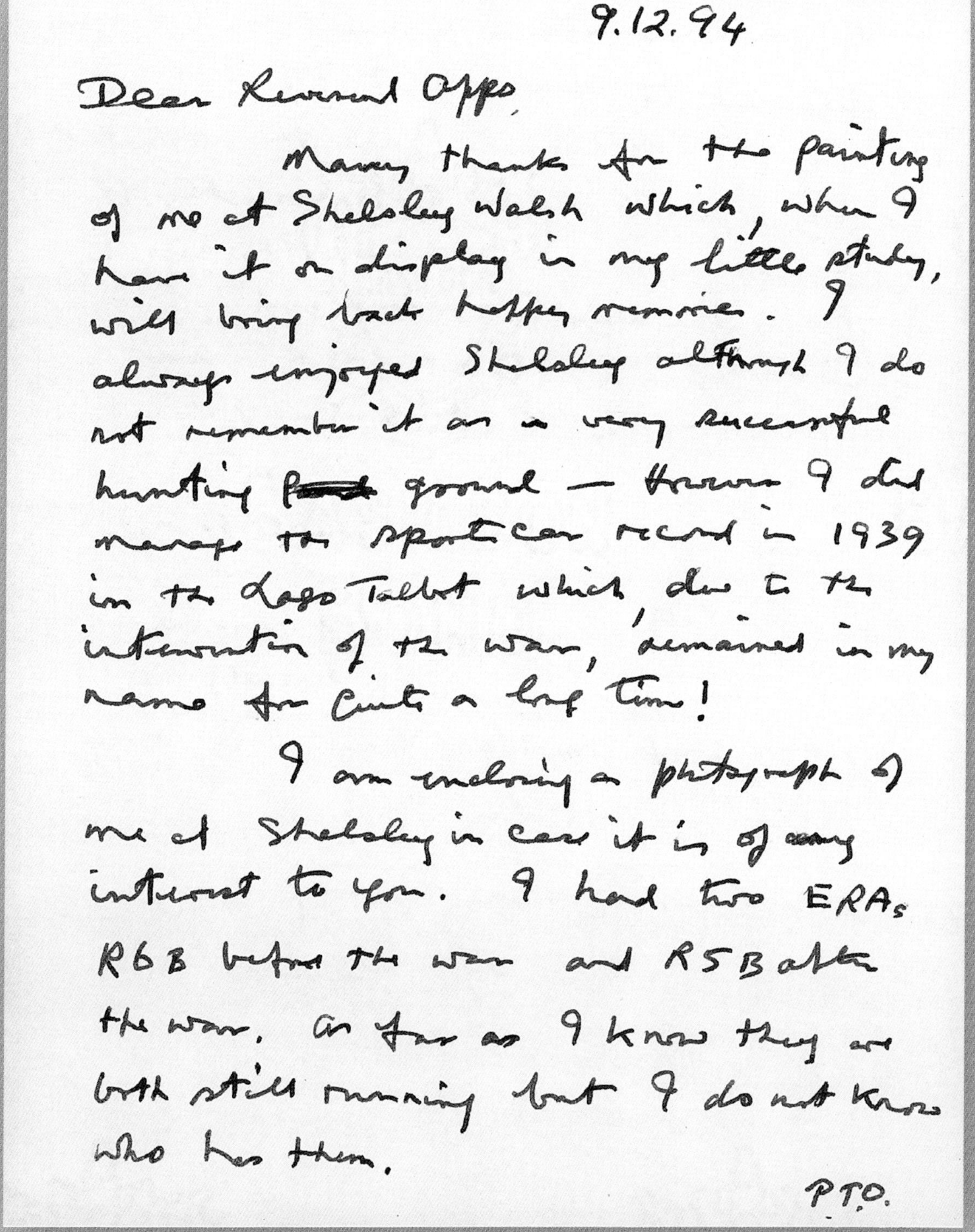

9.12.94

Dear Reverend Apps,

Many thanks for the painting of me at Shelsley Walsh which, when I have it on display in my little study, will bring back happy memories. I always enjoyed Shelsley although I do not remember it as a very successful hunting ~~ground~~ ground — however I did manage the sport car record in 1939 in the Lago Talbot which, due to the intervention of the war, remained in my name for quite a long time!

I am enclosing a photograph of me at Shelsley in case it is of any interest to you. I had two ERAs R6B before the war and R5B after the war. As far as I know they are both still running but I do not know who has them.

P.T.O.

Letter from Ian Connell about Shelsley Walsh.

In about 1947 I had a short season driving one of Raymond Sommer's 4CLT Maseratis in Grand Prix (Rather different to modern G.P.s!)

I occasionally see the wonderful Lago Talbot and it looks exactly the same as when I had it. How nice to have it called a Talbot and not a Darracq! I do not want to part with any of my photographs of it but if you are keen to replace yours I could arrange for a copy to be made.

I hope you will have a happy, and no doubt busy(!), Christmas and that the New Year will bring all you wish for

Yours sincerely

Ian Connell

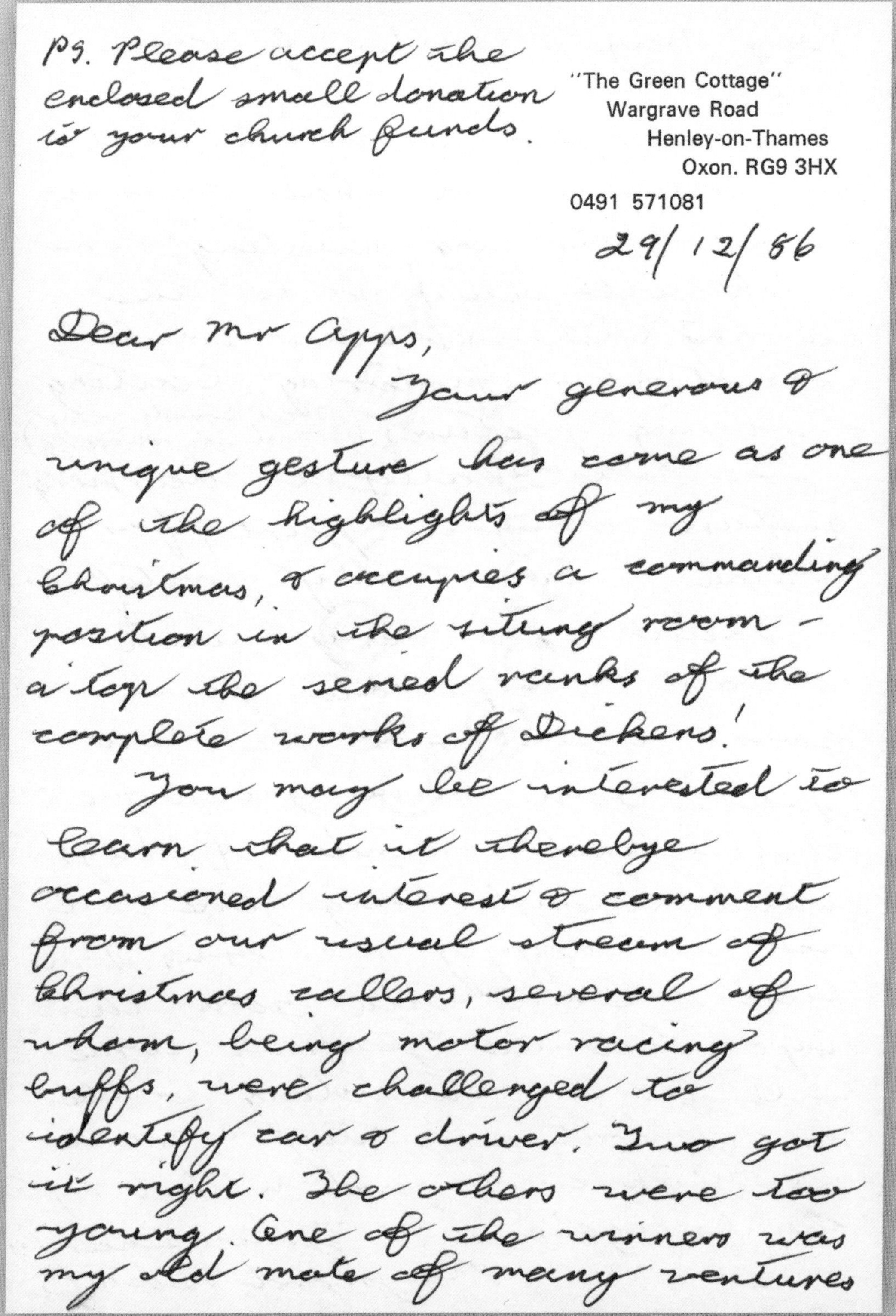

P.S. Please accept the enclosed small donation to your church funds.

"The Green Cottage"
Wargrave Road
Henley-on-Thames
Oxon. RG9 3HX

0491 571081

29/12/86

Dear Mr Apps,

Your generous & unique gesture has come as one of the highlights of my Christmas, & occupies a commanding position in the sitting room - atop the serried ranks of the complete works of Dickens!

You may be interested to learn that it thereby occasioned interest & comment from our usual stream of Christmas callers, several of whom, being motor racing buffs, were challenged to identify car & driver. Two got it right. The others were too young. One of the winners was my old mate of many ventures

Letter from the famous broadcaster Raymond Baxter, regarding the painting of Raymond Mays at Shelsley Walsh.

Tony Mays. I wonder if you knew him.

But apart from all that, the concensus was that it is a clever & striking painting, & one which will duly go to the library with my other small collection of motoring, boating & flying pictures. (that sounds very grand. It's not really)

It was really a charming gesture on your part, for which I am truly grateful.

Thank you very much, & may I reciprocate your good wishes for the New Year? You have given me a delightful reminder of days which, though long gone, are rich in happy memories. I'm sure I share with you the hope that the years to come will be as rewarding to the next generation as they were to us. With every good wish & my thanks again

Yours sincerely
Raymond Baxter

Raymond Mays driving R4D at Shelsley Walsh
in June 1948.

F R Gerard's ERA R14B sandwiched between
T C Harrison's ERA R8C and Reg Parnell's 4CLY
Maserati during the British Empire Trophy race in
Douglas, Isle of Man, June 15, 1950.

Bob Gerard on his way to second place in the 1949
British Grand Prix.

Firstly, most sincere apologies for being such a dilatory correspondent. Sadly Joan had a severe nervous breakdown when we evacuated our home after 32 years and had to compress ourselves into a flat, and - we have been battling with it for nearly two years and she is still in + out of hospital at Northampton.

I am most appreciative of your excellent paintings. The latter one showing Cuth. myself + Reg Parnell struck a very strong chord in memory as the positioning of the cars appears odd. It is at Parkfield Corner, the first, some ¼ mile down hill from the start — Cuth got a flier + led all of us away with so much enthusiasm that he is in fact departing straight on down Bray Hill with all wheels locked, while Reg + I are positioning to turn right round Parkfield as intended. Later in the race it got very slippery there + I did same thing, losing about 30 secs - luckily by then the lead was adequate to remain in front!

- We still retain racing interest, being part sponsors of a local driver with Ralt/VW in 'B' Class Formula 3. He does not aim to become an 'ace' + thoroughly enjoyable without being too serious, though only got to three meetings in 86 as have had ops for sciatica, cataract + prostate - personal life is now much more comfortable!! With kindest regards

To Bryan Apps.

With

BEST WISHES for CHRISTMAS

and the NEW YEAR

from

Joan + Bob Gerard.

Message in a Christmas card from Bob Gerard, in which he explains the position of his car during the British Empire Trophy race.

PART TWO

British Racing Motors 1950-1962

2.1

The V16 BRM

BRITISH RACING MOTORS LTD

Raymond Mays, Peter Berthon and Ken Richardson had parted company from ERA in 1939. They established Automobile Developments Ltd with a view to building a 1½-litre supercharged car which would be capable of taking on the W165 Mercedes-Benz and the 158 Alfa Romeo. Knowing that the German and Italian teams had the advantage of state aid, Mays hoped that his project would attract financial support from the British Government and Motor Industry. The Second World War put these plans on hold, but in March 1945 Mays was quick off the mark in writing to all the key leaders of industry outlining his plans. The basic design had been established, and Mays stressed the benefits that would be accrued by British firms if the car proved successful. Oliver Lucas, of Joseph Lucas Ltd, and Alfred Owen, of Rubery Owen, both expressed interest, and offered £1000 each on behalf of their firms, plus the free manufacture of components. After this, Sir John Black, Managing Director of the Standard Motor Company, donated a cheque for £5000, and Rolls-Royce agree to produce the car's centrifugal supercharger. Mays estimated that, in addition to gifts of £25,000, the firms also agreed to a further £25,000 worth of support in terms of component manufacture.

The mood of the first generation of BRM supporters is best exemplified by the following

Raymond Mays, the racing motorist.

Peter Berthon, who was, in large measure, responsible for the design of the V16 BRM.

The Maltings next to Eastgate House, which was to house BRM's machine shop and drawing office.

comment from Alfred Owen, which Raymond Mays recorded in his book *BRM*: "This project of yours is important because it is impossible to know where pioneer work like this will lead us. Do you realise, for instance, that it is hardly an exaggeration to say that we owe the existence of this country to Lady Houston? When the Government refused to build machines to fly for the Schneider Trophy, she came forward and put the money down. The research that went into building the Supermarine seaplane which won the trophy outright, led, as you know, to the development of the Rolls-Royce Merlin engine and the Spitfire fighters."

Eric Richter, who had been the key draughtsman at ERA, joined Mays from the very beginning, and with Berthon worked on the design of a 16-cylinder engine which would develop in the region of 500bhp at 12,000rpm.

The British Motor Racing Research Trust

In 1947 the British Motor Racing Research Trust was established to promote, support and finance Mays' project. It consisted of broadcaster Donald McCullough; Alfred Owen of Rubery Owen; Bernard Scott of Lucas; Tony Vandervell of Vandervell Products; David Brown of Aston Martin; Percy Bilton of Vigzol; Denis Flather; Captain J C Hopcraft; R Salter-Bache, and A C Burdon, all of whom

possessed power and influence in the British Motor Industry. It was agreed to call the car the 'British Racing Motor,' or 'BRM,' and Sir Stafford Cripps, the Chancellor of the Exchequer, offered what help he could, short of a financial subsidy. Harry Mundy, the Technical Director of *The Autocar* magazine, and Frank May, who had been a draughtsman at ETA, joined the staff, and later on so did Stuart Tresilian whose input as an engineer would prove to be invaluable. Component manufacture began, but more slowly than the situation required. Much of the work was subcontracted, and priority had to be given to the recovery after the war. Soon, some 200 British firms were involved in the manufacture of the BRM, and an attempt was made to streamline the process by coordinating it at Rubery Owen in Darlaston. The first engine was produced in December 1949, and the Air Ministry made Folkingham airfield near Bourne available for testing the car. Ken Richardson was appointed chief mechanic and test driver.

The car was unveiled to the press on December 15, 1949, at Folkingham. Mays had warned that it was far too early to go public, but, apart from Alfred Owen, most members of the Trust were anxious that the unveiling should not be delayed. Mays demonstrated the BRM on the perimeter track, and the unmistakable scream of its supercharger

The P15 BRM in its original form.

operating on its 16 cylinders was heard for the first time.

Project 15 described

The P15 was small and low compared to its competitors; its propeller shaft being offset to enable the driver to sit close to the track – I would discover just how low for myself years later. Its chassis was similar to that of the prewar Grand Prix Mercedes-Benz or Auto Union, and it had trailing arm, independent suspension at the front, a de Dion semi independent suspension at the back, and oleo-pneumatic struts at both ends.

A five-speed gearbox transmitted the enormous power which the 135 degree V16-cylinder engine produced. It was boosted by twin overhead camshafts and a two stage centrifugal supercharger, which was perhaps better suited to an aircraft engine than that of a car. The engine could achieve 11,000rpm if its driver was able to cope with the excessive wheel spin. The driver's greatest problem was that the V16's enormous power only came through at high revs, and then with an alarming rush, so the car tended to be slow out of corners. Not surprisingly, Juan Fangio proved to be most successful in taming the monster.

Great Expectations! A 1950 Lucas advertisement.

My scrapbook

The moment I first heard of Raymond Mays' ambition to produce an all-British Grand Prix racing car, I was captivated by his vision, and decided to keep a scrapbook to record the car's progress, cutting out every reference to the BRM I came across in newspapers and motoring magazines.

The car is demonstrated at Silverstone in 1950

The BRM was shown to the public on May 13, 1950, at the British Grand Prix meeting at Silverstone, where it was inspected by King George VI and Queen Elizabeth. Raymond Mays completed three laps with the car, its pale apple green colour echoing that of the prewar works ERAs, and the high pitched scream of its engine drawing the applause of the crowd.

The BRMA

The British Racing Motors Association was formed on the same day by A F Rivers Fletcher, who I came to know in later years. My brother David and I paid half a crown each to become members, and received chromium plated lapel badges which we wore with pride.

1950 *Daily Express* International Trophy Race

The debut of the BRM was to be the International Trophy Race at Silverstone on August 26, 1950, and the *Daily Express* produced an attractive booklet entitled *BRM Ambassador for Britain* to celebrate the occasion. It described the BRM as "Britain's greatest racing car," and contained in a double-page spread an artist's impression of the car streaking down the finishing race to glory. I included in my a small newspaper cutting which declared that "... the two BRMs making their first appearance, which will carry the good wishes of thousands of spectators, must feel at the moment like debutantes before the ball." Another cutting included the entry list in which Raymond Mays, Reg Parnell, Raymond Sommer and Peter Walker were all listed as BRM drivers. In the event, only one car made it to Silverstone, and it was to be driven by the French ace Raymond Sommer. Arriving too late for practice, the car had to start at the back of the grid, and I heard on the wireless Raymond Baxter's report that the BRM moved only two inches on the starting line before its driveshaft broke. Previously, the shaft had successfully coped with countless starts!

Derisive onlookers tossed coins into the car's cockpit, and the press immediately turned against it. *The Sunday Pictorial* wrote: "Four years, eighteen men and £160,000, much of it in half crown subscriptions, went to build a car that would not start." It all had to be painfully recorded in my book.

The author's dilapidated copy of *BRM: Ambassador for Britain*.

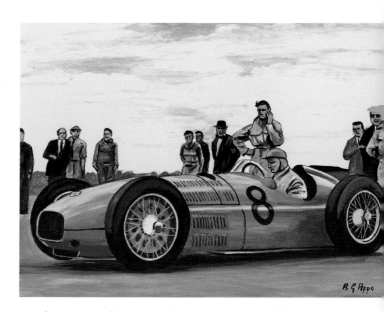

A disappointed Raymond Sommer after the failure of the BRM at the start of the 1950 International Trophy Race at Silverstone.

The Goodwood Meeting: 30 September 1950

"BRM wins: 'This car is a world-beater'
TRIUMPH FOR THE GREEN STREAK"*

It was in this way that the *Sunday Express* announced the success of Reg Parnell in winning the Woodcote Cup at 78.5mph and the Goodwood Trophy at 82.48mph the following month. The race commentator at the course had exclaimed: "It's tremendous! I've never seen such speed in my life. Britain has a world-beater!" The reality was that they were very short races, and heavy rain prevented the high speeds necessary to really test the car. Prince Bira came second in both races in his blue and yellow 4CLT Maserati, followed by ERAs.

After his wins, Parnell said: "It is the most wonderful car I have ever driven, and that was the

Ken Richardson taking the BRM from the paddock to the wet circuit at Goodwood for Reg Parnell to drive.

Reg Parnell driving to victory in the rain at Goodwood.

best ride I have ever had. The acceleration was terrific and I felt I had a lot in reserve." It probably felt and sounded as though it was going extremely fast!

The Barcelona Grand Prix: October 29, 1950

Next came the Spanish Grand Prix at Peña Rhin on October 29. Ray thought it was too early to subject the cars to this test, but Tony Vandervell managed to overrule him. Two cars for Reg Parnell and Peter Walker were despatched in their Austin transporters, accompanied by a travelling Commer workshop which had been contributed by the Midland Automobile Club in recognition of Mays' achievements at Shelsley Walsh. There were three works Ferraris in this non-championship race for Alberto Ascari, Dorino Serafini and Piero Taruffi, and the two BRMs were fourth and fifth in practice. After a slow start, Parnell overtook seventeen cars to catch up with the third Ferrari by the end of the first lap. He retired on lap three due to a supercharger failure. Walker held fifth place until retiring after 35 laps due to an oil leak. The race was won by Ascari at 94mph.

The race was deemed by many to have been a humiliating failure, and Tony Vandervell bought a 1½-litre supercharged Formula 1 Ferrari to go motor racing by himself. It was noted afterwards that the BRMs were slow to pick up speed out of corners, and that their engines had to be kept above 7000rpm. They were difficult to handle, and engine failures during high speed tests after the race resulted in them being withdrawn from the Grand Prix of Europe at Rheims.

Ken Richardson's secret tests

I came upon some interesting cuttings about secret tests, carried out after the Spanish race by Ken Richardson at Silverstone, when "... driving to instructions, and with at least 1000 of the 12,000 revolutions per minute in hand, he rounded the circuit in electrifying fashion." The report suggested "... a Parnell or a Bira could have beaten the Alfa Romeo record."

Peter Walker manfully pressing on during the 1950 Peña Rhin Grand Prix.

Reg Parnell.

It would prove to be the V16 BRM's only World Championship race: Reg Parnell during the 1951 British Grand Prix.

Savour the moment! Reg Parnell's BRM leading Alberto Ascari's Ferrari, albeit about to be lapped.

Froilán González makes history by beating the Alfa Romeos at last, gaining Ferrari's first World Championship win.

1951

The British Grand Prix at Silverstone: July 14, 1951
In 1951, Tony Rudd joined BRM from Rolls-Royce to work on the supercharger and to become the assistant team manager.

The next race was the British Grand Prix, and a newspaper recorded that Reg Parnell had flown to Silverstone after work had continued under floodlights all night at Bourne in an effort to get two cars to arrive, too late for practice but in time for the scrutineering.

"Our problem cars gain places"

This was the measured verdict of the *Sunday Express* after Reg Parnell and Peter Walker had finished fifth and seventh in spite of being badly burned by heat from the BRM's exhaust pipes. The report continued: "The problem BRMs DID get to Silverstone, and DID race yesterday after all. And 50,000 spectators saw them hold their own in the British Grand Prix against 18 of Europe's fastest aces and cars."

It was to prove the only occasion that the V16 BRM would ever compete in a World Championship race. The problem of heat in the cockpits only came to light during the race because, previously, the cars had never been driven continuously for more than fifty miles. Walker nearly passed out in the closing laps, and both drivers were in need of medical attention after the race. The cars' radiator cowls had been cut back before the race in an attempt to reduce the heat. Raymond Mays said afterwards: "This wonderful performance has given us a new lease of life. We told our drivers to limit their revs. We still had a few in hand. I am very happy." Froilán González' Ferrari won the race at 95.61mph and made history in beating the Alfa Romeos.

MONZA.

TWO BRMs ARE TO RACE IN ITALY

TWO B.R.M. cars will race in the Italian Grand Prix at Monza on September 16. Mr Raymond Mays, originator of the £200,000 B.R.M. venture, announced yesterday. Reg Parnell will drive one of them.

He got the low green car up to 182 miles an hour—the fastest it has ever shown.

Italy's top race may give BRM man his chance

By KAY PETRE, Daily Graphic Motoring Correspondent

FOR three years a lean man of 40 has nursed the £200,000 B.R.M. cars through their teething troubles, driven them for hundreds of test miles—and had an ambition to drive one in a race.

He is Ken Richardson, B.R.M. test driver and chief mechanic.

And his ambition may be fulfilled on September 16. Two B.R.M.s have been entered for the Italian Grand Prix at Monza.

Reg Parnell is nominated as number one driver. But no one has been named for the second car.

Ken Richardson

An official said last night that the second driver's name was being kept secret. My forecast is that it will be Richardson.

1,000-mile hustle

After competing in the Ulster Tourist Trophy race at Dundrod yesterday, young Londoner Lesley Johnston made a 1,000-mile car-and-air dash to Italy to be in reserve as a B.R.M. driver for the races at Monza. Britain's B.R.M. No. 2, driven by Ken Richardson, lapped at 112 m.p.h. in the speed trials. An Alfa-Romeo averaged 125 m.p.h.

After mechanics had worked all night to lower the gear ratios, 40 - year - old Ken Richardson took it out for practice lapping.

Taking a stiff corner, he tried to change down into third gear, but the selectors jammed, and he was left in no gear at all.

Without the engine to act as a brake, the car drifted off the track into the straw bales.

The bump was not serious, but the front of the car was dented.

Meanwhile Reg Parnell in the other B.R.M. was going splendidly. He put in a lap at 2mins. 2secs., which is within 2secs. of the lap record.

Italian experts are openly forecasting that the 1½-litre B.R.M.s, which cost £200,000 to build, will be in the first three in Sunday's 300-mile race.

MONZA CIRCUIT

START. DOUBLE-BEND.
1¼ MILE STRAIGHT.
DOUBLE-BEND.
¾ MILE STRAIGHT.

NEXT YEAR OPPOSITION MAY COME FROM MERCEDES.

SNEERS AS BRM CARS FLOP AGAIN

THE B.R.M.s' challenge to the supremacy of continental racing cars resulted in another humiliating failure yesterday.

Both entries were withdrawn from the Italian Grand Prix at Monza with gear-box trouble a few hours before the race.

The announcement, made through loudspeakers, brought a wave of sneers from the 100,000 spectators, who had expected a tough British-Italian contest.

Almost in tears

Reg Parnell, who was to have driven one of the £200,000 B.R.M.s, was almost in tears.

"Well, it can't be helped," he said. "It's better for things to go wrong before the race than during it.

"This is just one of those scurvy tricks fate plays from time to time."

Reg Parnell sits at the wheel of one of the "world beater" BRMs as a mechanic starts up the engine for a practice run.

Said Raymond Mays, "father" of the B.R.M.: "It is one of the biggest blows we have had. The race experience to-day would have been invaluable.

"There is only one thing for us to do to save the name of British motoring.

"We shall stay here with one B.R.M. car, the gearbox of which will be put in order before Tuesday, and we shall engage drivers of international fame now assembled at Monza.

"They will drive the B.R.M. the same distance and under the same conditions as prevailed in the Grand Prix to-day, and we hope it will do even better than the cars of Italy's great motoring industry did."

Record beaten

That means beating the average speed of 115.5 m.p.h. with which Alberto Ascari, the Italian ace, won the race in a Ferrari.

He set up a new record for the 313-mile course.

Frolian Gonzales (Argentina), also in a Ferrari, was second and Giuseppe Farina (Italy), in an Alfa-Romeo, third.

Reg Parnell noticed the gear-box trouble when he brought the No. 1 B.R.M. back to the pit after a final practice run.

The trouble in the other B.R.M. was discovered about the same time by Hans von Stuck, the German appointed to partner Parnell because Ken Richardson was refused R.A.C. permission to drive in the race.

B.R.M. "uncertain"

Mr. Raymond Mays has told the British Automobile Racing Club that although the B.R.M. (Britain's racing car) has been provisionally entered for Goodwood next Saturday, it cannot be said for certain whether the car will start.

THE "MOTOR" SPEAKS WELL OF THE B.R.M. REFERING TO THE SECOND LAP "THE B.R.M. WOULD HAVE SHONE AGAINST ITALY.

ALSO. "THE ITALIANS WERE IMPRESSED BY THE B.R.M.s TESTS.

What the papers said: A page from my BRM scrapbook.

The Italian Grand Prix: September 16, 1951

The Italian Grand Prix followed next and Kay Petre, the famous *Daily Graphic* Motoring Correspondent, announced that test driver Ken Richardson was to be given an opportunity to drive the second BRM at Monza, as Peter Walker was still recovering from his Silverstone burns. Unfortunately, Ken damaged his car amongst the straw bales, its selectors having jammed as he tried to change down into third gear for a bend. Consequently, the cars were withdrawn from the race, and they made the front pages for the wrong reasons again.

"SNEERS AS BRM CARS FLOP AGAIN"

It was described as a humiliating failure when both entries had to be withdrawn before the race after the gearbox faults came to light. Parnell said: "Well, it can't be helped, it's better for things to go wrong before the race than during it. This is just one of those scurvy tricks fate plays from time to time."

Raymond Mays added: "There is only one thing for us to do to save the name of British motoring. We shall stay here with one BRM car, the gearbox of which will be put in order before Tuesday, and we shall engage drivers of international fame now assembled at Monza. They will drive the BRM the same distance and under the same conditions as prevailed in the Grand Prix today, and we hope it will do even better than the cars of Italy's great motoring industry did."

According to my scrapbook, *The Motor* reported that "... the Italians were impressed by the BRM's tests." Tony Rudd later said everyone at BRM was furious about the cars being withdrawn on the grounds of safety and believed that they would have given a good account of themselves. It would have been a second precious opportunity for the cars to perform in a World Championship race.

Keeping his promise (see letter, opposite), Ken Richardson sent me the signed photograph of him testing the BRM at Folkingham.

Ken Richardson

Many years later, Ken Richardson wrote to me about his experiences with the V16 BRM:

"Knysna"

Dear Revd. Bryan,   4·6·88

Thank you very much indeed for the painting, it is terrific, it is so nice to hear from someone, that was so genuinly interested, in the B.R.M.

Personally, I think it was a terrific car for it's day. as did Fangio, whom I knew very well, as you probably know I drove it for thousands of miles during it's development. & every day, I did on the test circuit straight it would easily reach 180 miles per hour. and on one lap a Monza, I pulled - 12,000 revs. which. with the ratio we had, was a speed of 203 Miles per hour, these are the press. never get told, of this kind of news, as it is obviously between the driver and the pit Manager, and even if they did. wouldn 'juggle it to suit there own press.

The photo copies you have sent me. written by Kay Petre is not correct, but I do not blame Kay. as she was not at monza, and would probably get her information, over the phone, Regg's time is correct, but I was lapping 2/3 seconds faster, which. was official timing and given to the press, and of which we have the write up. over

however that is in the past now.
but I am always interested to
hear from people such as
youself. persons that are genuinly
interested.
I am getting my son
to make a copy of the original
B.R.M the actual car I drove
at Monza which I will sign
for you and post at a later
date he being on Holiday at
the moment so please be a
little patient with me, but be
assured you will recieve it
in the near future.

Kindest regards.

Ken Richardson

The BRMs were held at Monza after the race for high speed tests, and I recorded in my scrapbook that Juan Fangio broke the lap record by 13 seconds. Also that Juan Fangio, Stirling Moss and possibly Froilán González would drive for BRM in 1952. Another report claimed: "Stirling Moss, just back from tests in Italy: 'I have complete faith in the car and the organisation.'" However, Sir Stirling Moss told me later that the V16 BRM had no chance of ever being successful, because its power only came through at very high revs when the sudden rush was unmanageable. He also believed that they were mistaken in repeatedly testing engines to destruction without allowing time to find solutions to their problems. A major factor was that the project was being run by a committee. The BRM entries for the 1951 Spanish Grand Prix Barcelona were withdrawn, and Alfred Owen, whose constant support was a tower of strength to Raymond Mays, said: "It is much more in the interests of the BRM that we should have cars that are unquestionably reliable. Barcelona must not interfere with what we are doing at Monza."

A small cutting in my scrapbook reports that the "... crack Italian race driver Piero Taruffi," was invited to drive the BRM in 1952 and that he said: "The BRM is a good car and its performance has improved."

Late in 1951 I also recorded news of a BRM Mark II. At about the same time I came across an article by Professor von Eberhorst, who had been the Racing Director of Auto Union in the 1930s. He wrote that the "... BRM had been forced into competition in an unripe state by virtue of the publicity given and the exaggerated expectations aroused." He emphasised the need for the closest co-operation between the drawing office, machine shop, test bench and proving ground.

Picture Post published an article in its December issue entitled: 'SCRAP THE BRM?' Illustrated by an artist's impression of the car being dropped from an aircraft into an ocean with weights around its axles.

1952

The Albi Grand Prix : June 1, 1952
Sadly, time had run out for the V16 BRM. Raymond

Mays couldn't assure the race organisers that the BRM would be able to consistently match the Ferraris throughout the year and so it was decided that all the World Championship Grands Prix in 1952 would be for 2-litre unsupercharged Formula 2 cars. However, Juan Fangio and Froilán González arrived at Albi to drive the BRM in a race for Formula Libre cars, and they would contend with the works 4½-litre Ferrari of Alberto Ascari. Listening to the race commentary on a French radio station, I heard that the BRMs led the race, which was run over 34 laps and for 190 miles, and broke the lap record before they failed.

Fangio and González were first and second in practice with Louis Rosier's 4½-litre Ferrari, which had been 11 seconds slower than the leading BRM, alongside them on the starting grid. After a poor start, González rapidly climbed through the field so that he had only Fangio ahead of him at the end of the first lap. He broke the lap record at 107.65mph

The Maestro: Juan Fangio.

Fangio leading at Albi at speed for as long as his engine held.

100 ton steel. The working stress of the stud in position is about 40 tons.

"Thereafter began an extraordinary series of stud failures, most of them breaking off short with the engine not even running. Two failed on the test bed, before it had been run. These failed in the water space, so we had all the studs rust-proofed, to avoid corrosion. One more, rust proofed, failed in one of the two cars on the way to Albi, and was found when the car was pushed out of the van. Fresh studs were made at Bourne in 70 ton steel and flown out to Albi. However, the original studs were fitted very tightly in the crankcase involving great difficulty in removal and in some cases, damage to threads. All studs were now replaced by the original 65-70 ton material, in which no failure has ever taken place, produced by the most reliable and fool-proof processes we can find."

but was out on lap six in a cloud of smoke and steam. Fangio's race was also over on lap 16, due to another broken cylinder head stud.

The privately-entered Ferraris of Rosier and Chico Landi came first and second respectively.

The headline in one paper the next day read as follows:

"BRMs LEAD – BUT THEN IT'S DISASTER
THEY FAILED AGAIN, THOSE SQUAT LITTLE BRMs WITH WHICH WE HOPED TO BEAT THE MOTOR RACING WORLD. BUT IT WAS A NEW KIND OF FAILURE, ALMOST GLORIOUS."

The BRMA issued *Bourne Viewpoint* to its members on June 30, 1952, penned by Raymond Mays over six closely-written A4 pages:

"A serious trouble occurred at Albi, and probably lost us the race after Fangio had built up a considerable lead with the greatest of ease. This was the failures of cylinder head holding down studs.

"Some months ago we had discovered that the cylinder head joint rings were showing signs of hammering, as if the heads were bouncing up and down. This we attributed to the progressive increase of power that had gone on for some time. The remedy was to tighten the predetermined torque loading on the cylinder head studs, which we did by about 30%. At the same time we strengthened the material of the studs from 68 tons to approximately 100 tons, using the finest and toughest known

The Ulster Trophy Race: June 7 1952

The two BRMs were sent to Ulster for Juan Fangio and Stirling Moss to drive as Raymond Mays was anxious to fulfil his commitment to the organisers. However, following Albi, neither car was in raceworthy condition. Stirling Moss experienced clutch failure, overheating and a detached gearlever knob during his four brief laps while Fangio retired from third place because of a blocked fuel filter. Sir Stirling Moss wrote to me years later that "... the 16-cylinder BRM was probably the best sounding worst car I ever drove. The 4-cylinder was great."

I write to Raymond Mays

It was after the Albi Grand Prix that I posted my scrapbook to Raymond Mays, asking him to write a foreword for it. The following was his reply:

True to his word, Raymond posted the book

BRITISH RACING MOTORS LIMITED

Designers & Constructors of B.R.M. Racing Cars

UNDER THE COMPLETE CONTROL OF THE BRITISH RACING MOTOR RESEARCH TRUST

Bryan G. Apps.
43 Fair Oak Road.
Bishopstoke.
Eastleigh.
Hants.

BOURNE
LINCOLNSHIRE

10th June, 1952

Dear Bryan,

 Thank you for your most interesting letter of 9th and for sending your B.R.M. book. I cannot tell you how much I admire this book and the way in which you have arranged it, and I am very pleased indeed to send you a little Foreword for it. I hope you will excuse this being typewritten but, as you can imagine, I am terribly busy, and also, after all the work and disappointment, I am very tired. The result of Albi and Dundrod, after all the months of preparation, was a crushing disappointment, but we are still hoping that by our showing later in the year at Silverstone and Boreham we may be able to justify our efforts and the faith of our good friend. We are aiming at re-establishing confidence so that we may be able to go ahead with the building of a car for the new Formula.

 With many thanks for your good wishes, and I am so glad to know of all your interest in the project.

 Yours sincerely,

 Raymond Mays!

P.S. I am so pleased with your book that I should like to keep it for a day or two to show to my co-directors. I will send it back with the Foreword quite safely at the beginning of the week.

Far left: Raymond Mays' letter, in which he agreed to write what was to become the foreword to this book.

The signed photograph of Raymond Mays driving the BRM in 1952.

Below: A letter from Juan Fangio, (translation overleaf).

back to me with his foreword and a signed photograph of himself at the wheel of the car.

The day after the disastrous race in Ulster Juan Fangio crashed while driving a 2-litre Maserati in France. It meant that he would not race again that year.

A letter from Juan Fangio

Fangio wrote the following to me from Buenos Aires in 1985:

In the latter half of 1952 Raymond Mays had a great struggle to persuade people to keep faith in the BRM. I included in my scrapbook a major magazine article he had written with the heading:

"So far a flop – but wait and see!"

He ended with the words: "So far the cars have never

Juan Manuel Fangio

Señor
Rev. Bryan Apps
All Saints'Vicarage
14 Stourwood Road
Southbourne
Bournemouth
BH6 3QP
I N G L A T E R R A

Av. Caseros 2967-1° Dpto. 15
Tel. 91-9143

Dirección Postal:
Mercedes-Benz Argentina S.A.
Casilla Correo Central 3390
Buenos Aires

Buenos Aires, 5.9.85

De mi mayor consideración:

Recibí con satisfacción su atenta carta del 16.8.85 con la pintura suya del Alfa Romeo 159 cuando corrí el Gran Premio en Inglaterra de 1951.

Le agradezco mucho su gentileza y es muy grato para mí comprobar que la gente aún recuerda mi campaña deportiva.

Corrí en Irlanda con BRM y a raíz del accidente que tuve en Monza en 1952, quedó cancelado mi contacto con esa marca. En aquel entonces aún le faltaban algunas cosas al coche, que tenía gran potencia. Quizá influyó también la turbina fija. Después los turbos evolucionaron mucho, como todos sabemos.

Al reiterarle mi reconocimiento por su atención, le saludo muy cordialmente,

Dear Sir,

It is with great pleasure that I received your kind letter of 16.8.85, together with your painting of the Alfa Romeo 159, when I raced in the 1951 British Grand Prix.

I really appreciate your kindness and am very grateful because you proved to me that people still remember my motor racing career.

I raced in Ireland with BRM, but as a result of the accident which occurred in Monza in 1952, my contacts with this team came to an end. At that time there were still some things missing, which had considerable power. Perhaps the fixed turbine had some influence. Turbo-engines have since improved a great deal, as we all know.

I am very grateful for your kindness.

Froilán González during his brief, but spectacular, drive at Silverstone in 1952.

been driven flat-out: they always had something in hand. We intend to have the cars driven really hard and long in practice before our next time out. And perhaps this time it will be our day. If it is not it will not be for the lack of trying."

Formula Libre Race at Silverstone: 17 July, 1952

The next outing was an 100 mile race at Silverstone which attracted Tony Vandervell's 4½-litre Ferrari Thin Wall Special driven by Piero Taruffi, a works 4½-litre Ferrari driven by Luigi Villoresi, and the privately-entered Ferraris of Chico Landi and Louis Rosier. The two BRMs were driven by Froilán González and Ken Wharton and the race was summed up by a newspaper headline: "One hundred thousand people at Silverstone yesterday leaped to their feet to see the lime green, snarling BRM, Britain's jinx car, battling the Italians for the lead in a big race. And

A winner again! Reg Parnell during the National Trophy Race at Turnberry, August 23, 1952.

then – failure." Taruffi was penalised for jumping the start, but González, unaware of this, set off at a great pace before his car limped back to the pits with a stake impaled through its radiator! He immediately bundled Wharton out of his car and repeatedly broke the lap record before retiring due to gearbox trouble. The race was won by Taruffi's Thin Wall Special with

the Ferraris of Villoresi and Landi coming second and third. Ron Flockhart was fifth in the ex-Mays' 2-litre ERA.

International Race at Boreham: August 2, 1952

The BRMs, driven by Froilán González and Ken Wharton, were painted dark green for the first time at Boreham, the object being to conceal any oil stains. *The Daily Mail* wrote of the final practice before the race: "As the green BRM hurtled round the three mile circuit with its supercharger screaming defiance at the red-painted Ferrari, the prospect of a terrific battle between these two 200mph racers today developed into an exciting certainty."

During the race González crashed his BRM on a bend in the rain while chasing Luigi Villoresi's works Ferrari at high speed, and Wharton's car retired with gearbox and brake problems on lap 59 while in ninth position.

National Trophy Race at Turnberry: August 23, 1952

50,000 people turned out to see the BRM in Scotland, and I ordered a copy of *The Scotsman* to obtain a report for the scrapbook. Ken Wharton retired due to broken steering while leading the race, and Reg Parnell won with the other BRM in spite of having to cope with an injured hand, and a car suffering from a blocked fuel system and broken gearlever. Mike Hawthorn retired during the race in the Thin Wall Special due to gearbox trouble.

BRM UP FOR SALE

After this it was revealed that BRM was up for sale, and the *Sunday Express* published the cartoon by Giles, reproduced overleaf. A major article by Raymond Mays also appeared in the *Sunday Express* with the heading:

"Raymond Mays tells the inside story of his BRM."

It began: "For a long time I have wanted to tell the

BRITISH RACING MOTORS LIMITED

DIRECTORS:
PETER BERTHON
RAYMOND MAYS
A. G. B. OWEN
B. F. W. SCOTT

Designers & Constructors of B.R.M. Racing Cars
UNDER THE COMPLETE CONTROL OF THE BRITISH RACING MOTOR RESEARCH TRUST

TELEPHONE:
BOURNE 327-328

RM/SI/BP

B O U R N E
LINCOLNSHIRE

8th September
1952

Bryan Apps,
43 Fair Oak Road.
Bishopstoke.
Eastleigh.

Dear Bryan,

Thank you for your letter. It is very kind of you to write and I do appreciate all that you say.

I think that if the present Formula 1 had run to the end of its scheduled time, and thus given us one more season of racing, we should have been able to prove that we had accomplished what we set out to do. It is a bitter disappointment that we have to give up now, but I do sincerely hope that some arrangement may be made by which the knowledge we have gained may be used for the production of a car for the new Formula. Such a car, I hope, could achieve all that we had hoped the present B.R.M. would do.

If we have done nothing else we have, as you say, stimulated interest in motor racing more than ever before in this country, and if I have gained nothing else, I have found many loyal friends such as yourself, whose enthusiasm and loyalty have been the greatest encouragement to me.

With many thanks to you, and all good wishes,

Yours sincerely,

Raymond Mays

"If only ..." Raymond Mays' letter prior to the sale of BRM.

"What do you mean—you *bought* it?"

Sunday Express, Sept. 7th, 1952

Giles' comment on the sale of the BRM in the *Sunday Express*, September 7, 1952.
(Courtesy Express Newspapers and the Cartoon Library)

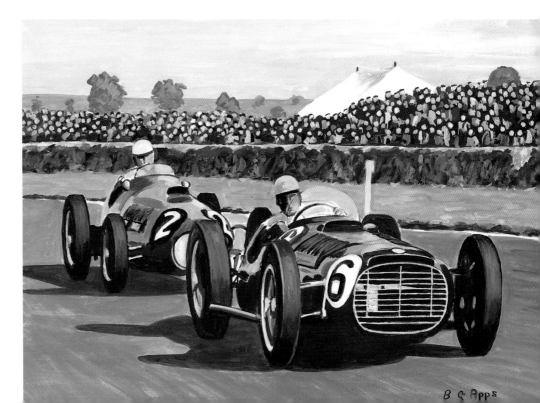

Reg Parnell's BRM, hounded by Giuseppe Farina's Thin Wall Special Ferrari during the Woodcote Cup Race at Goodwood, September 1952.

story of the BRM. Now the green-painted car, which meant so much to Britain, has a 'for sale' notice on it, I can talk." He went on to say that it had become the victim of intrigue, jealousy and backbiting. He admitted that they had tried too many ideas without having the facility to perfect them. He praised Alfred Owen, who had cheered him and urged him on, and ended with the words: "I have sacrificed everything to my ambition to see the green-painted cars of Britain rule the racing circuits. One day it will happen. I hope I will have some part in it. Then perhaps the memory of the BRM will be forgotten by everyone save Peter Berthon and myself. To us those initials will always stand for the time when we so nearly clothed our hopes with reality."

I wrote to Raymond Mays soon afterwards and received the reply on the opposite page.

Goodwood Race Meeting: September 27 1952
"It was a BRM 1, BRM 2, BRM 3 finish – rest nowhere."

After the sale of BRM had been announced, the team had a field day at the September Goodwood meeting, with Froilán González winning the five lap Woodcote Trophy Race at 87.64mph from Giuseppe Farina's Thin Wall Special and Reg Parnell in the second BRM. The BRMs of González, Parnell and Ken Wharton took the first three places in the 15 lap Goodwood Trophy, González winning at 88.13mph. Parnell broke the lap record at 90.38mph.

Autosport explained that Wharton's car failed to start before the Woodcote Cup race because the driver had inadvertently turned the fuel supply off. It also described how González "... sawing at the wheel, playing tunes on the BRM gearbox and thoroughly enjoying himself, was well in front." *Motor Sport* commented that all regretted it couldn't have happened three years before in Grand Prix racing.

International Trophy Race, Charterhall: October 11 1952
In the last race before the sale, Reg Parnell's BRM retired with back axle trouble, but Ken Wharton overtook the Thin Wall Special of Giuseppe Farina and the ERA of Bob Gerard to lead the race until being relegated to third after a spin. He closed the gap to finish second behind the ERA.

2.2

Alfred Owen rescues BRM

Offers were received for BRM from Leslie Johnson, Newman Industries Ltd, Oliver Hart, NFC Smith, Rob Walker, Vandervell Products and Alfred Owen. To the immense relief of Raymond Mays, Alfred Owen's offer, being the largest, was duly accepted.

To be more precise, BRM was bought by the brothers Alfred and Ernest Owen and their sister Jean Stanley on behalf of Rubery Owen. The amount paid was purely nominal, but they accepted responsibility for all its debts, and the great thing was that they intended to continue to race the cars. I wrote to Raymond Mays in January 1953 and received the reply shown overleaf.

THE 1953 EASTER MONDAY GOODWOOD MEETING

I see the BRM for myself!
The BRMs were warmed up in the Paddock during the Second Easter Handicap Race and their unmistakable sound could be heard above that of the cars that raced past me at Madgwick Corner.

The heavy rain which trickled down the back of my neck also blighted the chances of the BRMs of Reg Parnell and Ken Wharton in the Chichester Cup Race, the nimbler 2-litre Maserati of Baron de Graffenried being able to sprint into a lead which it held until the end. Ken Wharton closed on the Maserati as the track began to dry, but he had

Alfred Owen.

TELEPHONE: BOURNE 17

Raymond Mays

EASTGATE HOUSE
BOURNE
LINCOLNSHIRE

Bryan G. Apps,
43 Fair Oak Road.
Bishopstoke,
Eastleigh.

28th January, 1953

Dear Bryan,

Thank you very much for your letter.
I was pleased to hear from you again, and
thank you for your good wishes and interest.

We are hoping that Mr Owen is going
to enter the present B.R.M. cars in races this
season, although they may not appear very
often. It is possible that we may be at the
Easter meeting at Goodwood, if all goes
according to plan. It is not very likely that
we shall have more than two cars out at once,
although that is not yet certain, so we are
not likely to be short of drivers.

We are going ahead with our plans
etc. for an engine for the new Formula, and
it is still not quite certain how our plans
will develop as regards cars.

I hope you will be able to
come to Goodwood this year, and if you
have a chance do come and have a word
with me. I have not forgotten the very
fine book of drawings etc. which you
allowed me to see.

Yours sincerely,

Raymond Mays

A letter from Raymond
Mays, dated January
28, 1953, about Alfred
Owen's plans for the
existing cars, and the
prospect of a new engine
for the new Formula.

Raymond Mays

EASTGATE HOUSE
BOURNE
LINCOLNSHIRE

TELEPHONE: BOURNE 17

Bryan Apps,
43 Fair Oak Road.
Bishopstoke.
Eastleigh.
Hants.

19th March,1953

Dear Bryan,

Thank you for your letter. I am
glad to know that you hope to be at Goodwood,
and I think if you ask someone to fetch me
to the entrance, or to allow you to come and
speak to me we ought to be able to meet.
I hope so anyway, but you can imagine
how busy I am at these events.

I hope the weather will be better
than in the past, and that we shall have
as much success as last September.

All good wishes,

Yours sincerely,

Raymond Mays

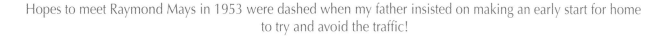

Hopes to meet Raymond Mays in 1953 were dashed when my father insisted on making an early start for home to try and avoid the traffic!

Raymond Mays, ever anxious about the BRM's progress.

to settle for second place. Ron Flockhart, driving the ex-Mays ERA finished third. Reg Parnell had never been in the picture, and the fastest lap of the race was Wharton's at 81.36mph. Both BRMs could clearly be heard all around the circuit throughout the race.

In drier conditions, Wharton led the Richmond Trophy Race from start to finish, breaking the lap record at 92.21mph. Piero Taruffi came second in the Thin Wall Special and de Graffenried third. Parnell retired on the fourth lap because of a faulty supercharger.

The weather couldn't dampen my enjoyment of seeing the BRMs in action and hearing the scream of their engines. I even managed to catch their blurred images through the lens of my Brownie camera! Sadly, I wasn't able to meet Raymond Mays, as my father, being anxious to avoid the traffic, left before the end.

After the meeting I received the following letter from Mays, in which he mentioned the plans for an entirely new car for the new 2½-litre Formula:

A letter from Raymond Mays, dated April 22, 1953, in which he looks back to Goodwood, and forwards to Albi and beyond.

Raymond Mays
EASTGATE HOUSE
BOURNE
LINCOLNSHIRE

TELEPHONE: BOURNE 17

Brian Apps,
43 Fair Oak Road,
Bishopstoke,
Eastleigh.

22nd April,1953

Dear Brian,

Thank you very much for your letter and for your good wishes. I am sorry that you were not able to get to speak to me at Goodwood, but perhaps better luck another time.

Ken Wharton drove a magnificent race and gave us a splendid start to the season, I hope we shall be able to keep it up this year. We are now working very hard for Albi, and we have promised one car, with Ken Wharton driving, for Charterhall on May 23rd. At Albi we hope to have either Fangio or Gonzalez but our plans are not quite settled as yet.

We are also hoping that there will be a race for which the B.R.M. cars are eligible at Silverstone in July, and we also hope to run at the August Charterhall, and the September Goodwood.

I wish that we could have the race against the Ferraris as you suggest, but it seems that there is no hope of any Grand Prix, other than Albi, this year for which we can enter.

We are going ahead with the engine for the new Formula, but I cannot give you any really definite news of our plans as yet.

You B.R.M. books will be of the greatest interest in the future, I think you must have one of the most complete records there is.

With all good wishes, and many thanks,

Yours sincerely,

Raymond Mays.

My first scrapbook was now full, and the time had come to embark upon a second, which, appropriately, would begin with the ownership of BRM by the Owen Organisation. I asked Alfred Owen if he would write a foreword for this second edition, and he very kindly sent the following:

RUBERY, OWEN & CO LTD

DARLASTON, SOUTH STAFFS, ENGLAND

Chairman's Office

TELEPHONE: DARLASTON 130 P.B.X.

OUR REF. O/R/OJ.

YOUR REF.

11th August, 1954.

Mr. Bryan G. Apps,
43 Fair Oak Road,
Bishopstoke,
Eastleigh,
Hants.

Dear Bryan,

     Thank you for your letter which I received here on the 28th May, and I must apologise for the delay in replying to it.

     I am very interested to read all that you say, and I shall be very happy to write a Foreword for you, although I am not quite sure on what lines you would like this to be. However, I am attaching one herewith which you might care to use for the purpose.

     Yours sincerely,

A.G.B. Owen

Enc.

Alfred Owen's reply to my letter asking him to write a foreword for my second scrapbook, and, overleaf, his foreword, in which he writes of his plans for an entirely new BRM for the new Formula.

The OWEN ORGANISATION

RUBERY OWEN & CO LTD DARLASTON SOUTH STAFFS ENGLAND.

OUR REF:

YOUR REF:

Chairman's Office.

TELEPHONE: DARLASTON 130 P.B.X.

FOREWORD

I am very pleased to have this opportunity of saying a few brief words about the B.R.M.

From its earliest days I have taken a personal interest in its development, and when so many problems forced a decision to be taken to wind up the B.R.M. Trust, I was all the more determined to try and make a success of the venture and the car.

Having found a solution for most of our technical problems in 1953, we entered all the worth while races we could, and proved that the car was both fast and dependable and equal to any car put on the road by any of our competitors.

With the new Formula, it is now our determination to produce a successor from the same stable to meet, on behalf of Britain, the world challenge for supremacy. With time now on our side, I have faith that we shall succeed, whilst racing the old B.R.M. cars as long as we can in Formula Libre events.

A.G.B. Owen

David Brown

I also wrote to David Brown, the head of Aston Martin and Lagonda, as he had been a member of the British Motor Racing Research Trust in 1947, and asked him to write a piece for my second scrapbook. I enclosed a small picture I had painted of the Aston Martin DB3S, which he told me he'd had framed and placed on the wall of his office. He enclosed the following for my book:

DIRECTORS
DAVID BROWN (Chairman and Managing)
THE RT HON LORD BRABAZON OF TARA, G.B.E.,M.C.,P.C.
SIR ALEXANDER DUNBAR
EDWIN BRYCE FULTON
ARTHUR MAXWELL RAMSDEN, C.B.,O.B.E.
JAMES WHITEHEAD

THE
DAVID BROWN
CORPORATION LIMITED
96/97 PICCADILLY
LONDON W.1

Telephone
GROSVENOR 7747

Please reply to
HANWORTH PARK WORKS
FELTHAM MIDDLESEX
Telephone: FELtham 2291

OFFICE OF THE CHAIRMAN AND MANAGING DIRECTOR

Tuesday,
31st August, 1954.

Mr. Bryan Apps,
43, Fair Oak Road,
Bishopstoke,
Hants.

Dear Mr. Apps,

Thank you for your letter and painting which I am having framed and placed upon the wall of my office.

Naturally, I would be delighted to do anything I can to help you, but before writing any words in your book it would perhaps be as well if I could see it , to give me some guidance on the subject matter.

As a matter of fact, I was only on the B.R.M. Committee for a very short time and if the book deals solely with the B.R.M. (without wishing in any way to be awkward), it may perhaps be more appropriate if you got some other Member of the Committee to write in it, although if you still so desire I will be pleased to oblige.

Yours truly,

David Brown
Chairman & Man. Director.

ASSOCIATED COMPANIES
THE DAVID BROWN CORPORATION (SALES) LIMITED
DAVID BROWN & SONS (HUDDERSFIELD) LTD   DAVID BROWN TRACTORS (ENGINEERING) LTD   THE DAVID BROWN FOUNDRIES COMPANY   ASTON MARTIN LTD   LAGONDA LTD
DAVID BROWN-JACKSON LTD   DAVID BROWN MACHINE TOOLS LTD   DAVID BROWN GEARS (LONDON) LTD   THE COVENTRY GEAR COMPANY   THE KEIGHLEY GEAR COMPANY
THE DAVID BROWN TOOL COMPANY   DAVID BROWN & SONS S A (PTY) LTD   DAVID BROWN PRECISION EQUIPMENT (PTY) LTD   DAVID BROWN (CANADA) LTD
DAVID BROWN TRACTORS (EIRE) LTD   DAVID BROWN (AUSTRALASIA) PTY LTD

David Brown's reply to my letter asking him to write some words for my scrapbook, and, overleaf, his foreword, in which he makes a frank assessment of the V16 BRM and the prospects of the new project.

THE
DAVID BROWN
CORPORATION LIMITED
96/97 PICCADILLY
LONDON W.1

Telephone
GROSVENOR 7747

Please reply to
HANWORTH PARK WORKS
FELTHAM MIDDLESEX
Telephone FELtham 2291

OFFICE OF THE CHAIRMAN AND MANAGING DIRECTOR

Monday
13th September, 1954.

      I came on to the B.R.M.
Committee very late in its history, although
of course, I was aware of its development from
the very beginning.   The re-organisation which
eventually resulted in it being taken over by
Alfred Owen was, I think, a very desirable and
necessary thing.

      Like most advanced technical
projects the car took longer to complete than was
anticipated, the result being that it was by no means
developed to fruition by the time the new formula came
into operation, thus precluding it from Grand Prix
racing.

      Of the possibilities of the design,
given time and resources for full development, there can
be no doubt, although on some circuits the advantages of
a simpler machine must, I think, prevail.   No doubt the
B.R.M. technicians in the course of its history have
acquired a great deal of experience, which I hope will
show to full advantage in the new project sponsored
by the Owen Organisation.

David Brown
Chairman & Managing Director.

Rivers Fletcher wrote a series of bulletins on behalf of the Owen Organisation for all the members of the BRMA, and Bulletin No 1 began with these words:

"This BRM project, which has become such a controversial subject, not only amongst motor racing enthusiasts but even with the general public, was started by Raymond Mays in a gallant endeavour to produce a British Grand Prix racing car to enhance this country's prestige internationally. So much has been written on this subject, and so many criticisms and different viewpoints have been expressed, that it becomes increasingly difficult to sort out the relevant details of the enterprise."

Froilán González

In 1990 I sent one of my paintings to Froilán González, and in his reply he described his experiences with the V16 BRM:

Buenos Aires,10 de mayo de 1990.

Dear Reverend Bryan Apps,

I was very glad to receive the paint of myself from the old days of motor racing. It was kind from You to send it to me after it was done,and it is obvious that this paint was done with special dedication and care,since it is detailed in every aspect.

Another thing that brought great memories to me about the old racing days was the copy from the day I broke the record on the B.R.M. at the "Goodwood Daily Graphic Trophy".

Last year I climbed again on the B.R.M. at Donnington for a short film that took place on that day,and it was about the old racing B.R.M.s This car belonged to Mister Tom Wheatcroft,and we were both very happy to be that day at Donnington hearing the wonderful noise of those sixteen cylinders together roaring at speed.I did a few laps and then I visited Mister Wheatcroft's museum,which my son Julio and I enjoyed a lot.

Once again I thank You for the nice paint and for the letter.

Sincerely,
José Froilán Gónzalez

A letter from Froilán González.

The two Argentinian aces: Juan Fangio and Froilán González.

Tony Rudd

I received the following letter from Tony Rudd after sending him a painting of the Reg Parnell's BRM at Silverstone in 1950:

Tony Rudd, under whose watch BRM would eventually win a World Championship.

A letter from Tony Rudd.

MANOR HOUSE
LITTLE MELTON
NORWICH, NR9 3AE
TEL. NORWICH 810527

Dear Fred Apps

3rd Aug 87

Thank you so very much for the painting of Reg Parnell & the old V16. It brings back so many memories. I have spent some time with Tony Merrick and the Montague Motor Museum V16, and I have been over to Donington to help sort out Tom Wheatcroft's one !!

I am also involved in a plan to make a film about Raymond Mays (who was my brother in laws cousin) and the V16, and with Doug Nye have written, or at least dictated 36 tapes on the whole BRM history, when it will be published I don't know. I am also working with Geoffrey Wilde of Rolls Royce who designed the old V16 blower. Motor racing seems very different now to 1951. we paid Reg Parnell £200 advance and £2000 a year retainer, which compares with $3 000 000 per driver today, I suppose it compares though, we once costed a V16 at £15,000 each; which compares with £35,000 for a DFY and £80,000 for a Renault. I have a L.P of the V16, I don't know whether you have heard it, one of my son's in law is in the recording business, I could get him to tape it if you would like it.

Thank you once again

Yours sincerely

Tony Rudd

Rivers Fletcher

Rivers Fletcher wrote the following in response to the gift of another of my paintings:

December 18, 1987

Dear Mr Apps,
You know that I was closely involved with the BRM project from its inception, but you may not know that I have a very good 16mm film of the Spanish Grand Prix of 1950 – unfortunately I did not make this film myself because at that time I had only just joined the company, but subsequently I made all the BRM films myself. Your painting means a great deal to me and I must say I much preferred the original light green livery to the rather dull dark green used later. I never drove the Mark I but had some exciting drives in the Mark II culminating in my drive at Shelsley Walsh for Tom Wheatcroft.

Both Raymond Mays and Sir Alfred Owen have been wonderful friends to me and I still see David and John Owen nowadays; David continues to have a great enthusiasm for the BRM and we are delighted that three V16's are now running with Tom, Wheatcroft, Lord Montagu and Nick Mason. I am very close to all three of them.
I hope we may meet one day.
Yours sincerely,
Rivers Fletcher

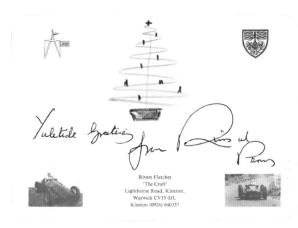

A Christmas card sent by Rivers Fletcher to the author in 1987.

Rivers Fletcher at the wheel of a P25 BRM.

1953

The Albi Grand Prix: May 30, 1953

Three BRMs, to be driven by Juan Fangio, Froilán González and Ken Wharton, arrived in France for the Albi Grand Prix in May – their last opportunity to win a major race on a fast Continental circuit. Significantly, González crashed at 180mph in practice when one of his tyres threw its tread with a report like gunfire. The order at the front of the grid after practice was Fangio (2min 52.5sec, or 115.43mph), Wharton, Alberto Ascari in a works 4½-litre Ferrari, González, and Giuseppe Farina in Vandervell's Thin Wall Special.

The BRM at Silverstone, after being driven on public roads by Raymond in order to get it there in time.

And then there were two: Ken Wharton at speed at Albi before his Mark I BRM was destroyed.

Heat two was for the Formula 1 cars, and Fangio led from Ascari at the end of the first lap. On lap three Ascari retired due to a blown engine, and the order was Fangio, González and Wharton. Then González' BRM threw a tread on lap four, and two laps later Farina retired with another blown Ferrari engine. At the end of the heat the order was Fangio, Wharton, Louis Rosier in a privately-entered Ferrari, Maurice Trintignant in a 2½-litre Gordini, and González.

Rosier jumped the start of the final, but he was overtaken on the first lap by Fangio. At six laps it was Fangio ahead of Wharton, Rosier and González. Then on lap nine Wharton's BRM threw its left hand rear tread and lost 45 seconds in the pits. On lap ten Fangio came in to change a rear wheel after its tyre had lost its tread. González was then leading the race, until on lap 12 he too suffered a thrown tread and lost 35 seconds in the pits. Then Wharton's car crashed at 130mph as it approached the village, throwing its driver out and cutting itself in half. Mercifully, Wharton escaped serious injury and later said that he had been trying too hard to match Fangio's speed. Rosier won the race and González finished in second place. A cutting from *Autosport* gives a graphic account of the race:

"Today Grand Prix racing in the grand manner returned for a short time to one of the fastest European circuits and it must go on record that the centre of interest was the team of three British cars – the BRMs driven by Fangio, González and Wharton who, in practice, showed that they are the fastest 1½-litre supercharged cars ever designed. During the racing on a day unusual at Albi, for it was not only cool but actually during the first heat rained, these cars screamed round the circuit at tremendous speeds, out-distancing both Ascari and Farina on the Formula 1 twelve-cylinder Ferraris."

The problem at Albi was that the BRMs' power was too great for their narrow tyres to transmit to the road, and this caused their treads to unwrap.

Juan Fangio crossing the line in the V16/01 to win heat two of the 1953 Albi Grand Prix.

They were now both fast and reliable but, apart from Albi, only minor British events were open to the BRM. Raymond Mays and Peter Berthon considered plans to build a car to break the world land speed record, and went as far as approaching Colonel Goldie Gardner, until Alfred Owen insisted on everyone being focused on the car for the new Formula. Two BRMs were entered for a 50 mile race at Silverstone on July 18, and mechanics worked through the night in a garage in Brackley to get Fangio's car ready for the race. Mays drove it to Silverstone on the public roads the next morning – breaking countless regulations – in order to get it to the starting line on time. In the race Juan Fangio and Ken Wharton came second and third to Giuseppe Farina in the Thin Wall Special. Then, on July 25, Ken Wharton won two races at Snetterton, breaking the lap record at 90.05mph.

Formula Libre Race at Charterhall: August 15, 1953
A single car driven by Ken Wharton shared the front row of the starting grid with the ERAs of Ron Flockhart and Bob Gerard for this 40 lap race on a small circuit, quite unsuited to the powerful BRM. Eventually, Wharton passed the ERA to lead the race but he was relegated to second place after a spin.

Goodwood: September 26, 1953
Juan Fangio and Ken Wharton took on Mike

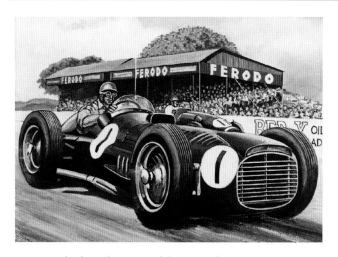

Fangio before the start of the Woodcote Cup Race at Goodwood.

Juan Fangio accelerating the Mark I BRM out of Madgwick bend at Goodwood in September 1953.

Hawthorn in the Thin Wall Special for the five lap Woodcote Cup Race. Hawthorn arrived late on the starting line with the Thin Wall, and inadvertently parked it just ahead of his line. Fangio waved to him not to worry about having it pushed back, and so they were off. The order after the start was Hawthorn, Wharton, Rolt in Rob Walker's Connaught and Fangio. Wharton spun at the chicane and Rolt went wide to avoid him, allowing Fangio to pass them both. It was a runaway win for Hawthorn from Fangio, who was 23 seconds behind, with Wharton coming home in third place. Wharton came second to Hawthorn in the Goodwood Trophy Race after Fangio had retired due to gearbox trouble. One race was left in 1953, at Castle Combe on October 3, and it provided Ken Wharton with a further win in the Mark I P15.

The P30 Mark II Sprint cars

A brief newspaper cutting announced that a short-chassis edition of the V16 BRM was being built for Formula Libre events in 1954. In *BRM,* by Raymond Mays and Peter Roberts, Mays wrote that the two cars had smaller wheels and tyres, modified de Dion layouts at the rear and magneto ignition. Tony Rudd was largely responsible for the cars, and he built the chassis, which were six inches shorter than the Mark I cars, with some Accles and Pollock tubes he had originally bought to build an Aston

Martin Special. They were 400lb lighter than the earlier cars, and were designed for minor races on the small British circuits. Rudd changed the supercharger drive gear so that the blower turned a little faster.

An extended article by Laurence Pomeroy appeared in *The Motor* entitled 'An Engineering Exercise,' which he described as "Some notes on the BRM Formula 1 Grand Prix engine, an original project which has exceeded all previous standards of brake horse-power per litre of swept volume."

1954

Ken Wharton was dispatched with two mechanics

The shorter, lighter Mark II P15 Sprint car.

and a Mark I car at the beginning of 1954 and he finished fifth in the New Zealand Grand Prix on January 9 after his front brakes failed. He managed third place in the Lady Wigram Trophy Race after having to pit for his engine to receive some attention.

Goodwood: 19 April, 1954

Ron Flockhart joined Ken Wharton at BRM for 1954, and I was at Goodwood to watch in dismay as, after spinning his Mark I car in front of me at Madgwick bend on the first lap of the Chichester Cup Race, Flockhart had to wait for the entire field to stream past him before he could get going again. The race was won by Ken Wharton driving the new Mark II car while Flockhart recovered to finish in fourth place.

Flockhart drove the Mark II BRM in the Glover Trophy and Wharton the earlier model. The Scotsman led the race until slowed by problems related to his magneto and then it was Wharton who led, chased by Roy Salvadori's 250F Maserati. A coming together on the last lap resulted in the BRM limping across the line, terminally crippled, but winning the race.

Only one Mark I car now remained until, many years later, the other two were painstakingly restored.

The Aintree 200 Miles Race: May 29, 1954

Ron Flockhart won a Formula Libre race at Snetterton on April 24th with the Mark II car while staunching the flow of fuel from a split tank with his finger! He also went on to win a short race at Ibsley, in the New Forest, on May 8th with the same car.

Then came Aintree, which offered the Mark II BRMs of Ron Flockhart and Ken Wharton a more severe challenge, as they had to compete against

Ron Flockhart driving the new Mark II BRM during the Glover Trophy Race at Goodwood in 1954.

And then there was only one: Ken Wharton winning the Glover Trophy Race with a Mark I car at Goodwood. It would be terminally damaged before the end of the race.

Peter Collins in the Thin Wall Special, Reg Parnell in a new 2½ litre Ferrari, and Stirling Moss in his 250F Maserati. The first heat was won by Parnell while Wharton finished in fourth place. Flockhart won the second heat. In the final, Flockhart finished in third place behind Moss and Parnell, while Wharton retired on lap 22 due to engine trouble.

The Goodwood Whitsun Trophy Race: June 5, 1954

A 15 lap 36 mile race saw a return of the BRM/Thin Wall Special duel, and it resulted in a win for Tony Vandervell's car. Ron Flockhart was second to Peter Collins in the Thin Wall Special, Roy Salvadori's Maserati was third and Ken Wharton fourth in the

Ron Flockhart on his way to second place in the 1954 Whitsun Trophy Race.

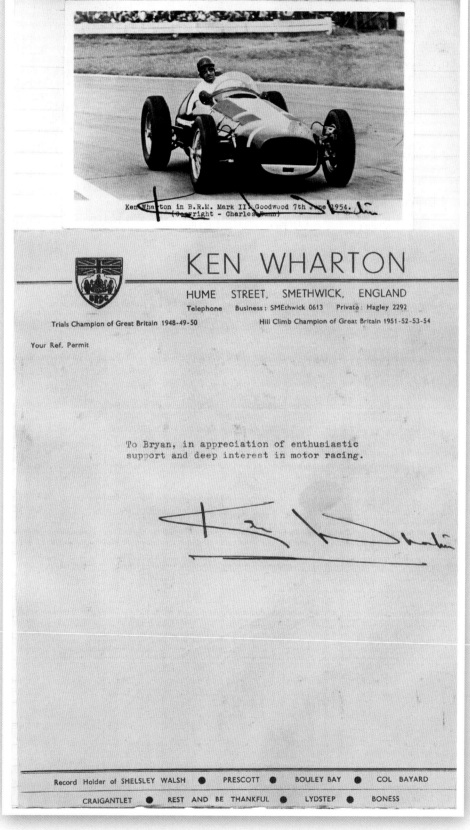

A signed photograph of Ken Wharton, with a brief message.

second Mark II BRM. Tony Vandervell, having left BRM to race his own car, at least provided the V16s with worthwhile competition in their last years.

Brief sprints

On August 14 at Snetterton, Ron Flockhart could only watch as Peter Collins drew ever further away from him in the Thin Wall Special. After a brief spin and a pause at his pit to have his bonnet strap fastened, Flockhart was lapped before finishing in second place.

On 27 August at Castle Combe, Flockhart had once more to settle for second place when, with failing brakes and a faulty magneto, he was beaten to the line by Bob Gerard's ERA. Back at Charterhall on September 4, Flockhart had gone only 200 yards from the line when a stone blocked his car's fuel system. The honours went again to Gerard's ERA.

Formula Libre Race at Aintree: October 2, 1954

The front row of the grid was composed of Stirling Moss (Maserati), Ken Wharton (Mark II BRM), Peter Collins (Thin Wall Special) and Ron Flockhart (Mark II BRM). Collins led, until retiring due to engine trouble on lap ten. Wharton's race was over when his car and Harry Schell's 250F Maserati touched, and Flockhart finished third behind the Maseratis of Moss and Sergio Mantovani.

1955

The Chichester Cup Race at Goodwood: April 11, 1955

Raymond Mays now had his eyes set on the development of the 2½-litre car for the new Formula, and, in the meantime, the Owen Maserati was fielded in Formula 1 events. However, I was thrilled to watch Peter Collins, now driving for BRM (Ken Wharton had left BRM for Tony Vandervell's stable), lead throughout to win the Chichester Cup in the Mark II Sprint car. The 250F Maseratis of Roy Salvadori and Stirling Moss were second and third. Later in the day

Collins finished in fifth place in a five lap Handicap Race after starting the BRM from scratch.

Snetterton

At Snetterton on May 28 Peter Collins' BRM was in mixed company – including an 8CM Maserati and a C Type Jaguar. He rocketed off in the lead, setting a new lap record, but was stopped by a puncture after colliding with Noel Cunningham Reid's Lister-Bristol sports car.

Back at Snetterton on August 13, Collins' race lasted only half a lap when his Mark II BRM's half shaft broke. The race was won by Peter Walker driving Rob Walker's Connaught.

The Formula Libre Race at Aintree: September 3, 1955

At Aintree for a 51 mile Formula Libre race, Peter Collins led from start to finish against Cooper-Bristols and 250F Maseratis. The crowd applauded the sight and sound of the V16 BRM, knowing that this was almost the last chance to experience it. *The Autocar* remarked that "... the sight of the BRM racing towards the end of the longest straight compensates for much of the history of the car."

Castle Combe: October 1, 1955

This 38.8 mile race was the last before the V16 cars entered retirement. If only it could have been a runaway win – but this was not to be the case. The old Owen vs Vandervell duel was renewed with Ron Flockhart driving the Mark II BRM and Harry Schell the Formula 1 Vanwall. Flockhart led briefly, but Schell overtook him to pull out a lead of 20 seconds before the end of the short race.

Postscript on the P15 by Rivers Fletcher

Rivers Fletcher wrote to me in 1994 about the original BRM: "The V16 was much the fastest and most exciting car I ever drove: a fabulous achievement, but impractical, and ahead of its time in technology and materials. Mays and Berthon are remembered as people who attempted too much, but nevertheless achieved a brilliant and memorable racing car."

Peter Collins in the V16 Mark II BRM in the paddock at Snetterton on May 28, 1955.
At far right are Peter Berthon and Alfred Owen.

An e-mail from Sir Stirling Moss

Stirling Moss sent me the following comments on the V16 BRM: "Believe me, neither Ferrari, Alfa, or any realistic race car designer would have considered such a design. A very poorly designed chassis, and an undriveable power curve, a good gearbox and brakes, and that was it! One needs torque and not peak power. You had to use over 9000rpm to get away, and 12,000 was the max!"

The Owen Maserati

In October 1953 Ken Wharton persuaded Alfred Owen to buy a 250F Maserati to enable him and the BRM team to gain experience in World Championship events before the launch of the new 2½-litre BRM. Wharton contributed £1000 to the project himself, and the car arrived from Modena in June 1954. Its performance was disappointing at Rheims for the French Grand Prix, and Mays

The V 16 was much the fastest and most exciting car I ever
drove, a fabulous achievement but impracticle and ahead of
it's time in technology and materials.   Mays and Berthon
are remembered as people who attempted too much but nevertheless
achieved a brilliant and memorable racing car.

The 16 cylinder B.R.M was probably the
best sounding worst car I ever drove.
The 4 cylinder was great

To Bryan Apps — a
fervent long standing BRM supporter
with best wishes, especially for
your fantays

Tony Rudd

15th October 1944

Postscripts on the P15 by Rivers Fletcher, Sir Stirling Moss and Tony Rudd. From the
inside front cover of *The Saga of BRM: Volume 1* ...

Peter Collins notching up a win for the Owen Maserati in the International Trophy Race at Silverstone in 1955.

insisted that a Maserati mechanic and spare parts be despatched to Bourne to bring it up to the required standard.

Alfred Owen persuaded Prince Bira to allow Ron Flockhart to drive his 250F in the 1954 British Grand Prix to enable the young Scot to benefit from the experience, but Flockhart rolled Bira's car during the race, causing extensive damage. Owen appeased Bira by swapping the Owen Maserati for Bira's car, but Ken Wharton was unaware of this until Bira innocently commented on the fact that his Owen Maserati had a shorter chassis than the original car.

Wharton left BRM abruptly, and his place was taken by Peter Collins, who went on to win the International Trophy race at Silverstone, and the London Trophy Race at the Crystal Palace. Sadly, Ken Wharton was killed in 1957 during a sports car race in New Zealand.

Raymond Mays deep in conversation with Peter Berthon.

2.3

The 4-cylinder BRMs

THE INTRODUCTION OF THE P25 AND P48 2½-LITRE CARS

1955

The P25 represented a fresh start for BRM, and a chance to silence its critics. Its unsupercharged 2½-litre 4-cylinder engine was designed by Stuart Tresilian in 1952, when 4-cylinder Ferraris were winning all the races, but Peter Berthon insisted that it should have two valves per cylinder instead of the intended four. It was initially developed by Tresilian with Alec Stokes and Aubrey Woods, but

The shapely and diminutive P25 4-cylinder BRM when it was first unveiled.

in 1955, when Tresilian left to work on aero engines, and Berthon was injured in a road accident, it fell to Tony Rudd to develop the new car.

It had a multi-tubular space frame, which was riveted to beaten panels to form a semi-monocoque. Dunlop disc brakes were chosen for the front wheels, and a single inboard disc brake at the rear. Weber carburettors would later be replaced by fuel-injection. The car's front suspension consisted of double wishbones and oleo-pneumatic struts, and the rear a De Dion with transverse leaf springs and shock absorbers.

The car was remarkably small. Peter Collins said that it had better acceleration than the V16 – it could go from 0-120mph in less time – and that, unlike the earlier car, the power came in right through the range, and claimed to develop 248bhp at 9000rpm. It was first shown to an enthusiastic press on August 29, 1955.

The debut of the new car was to have been at the International Meeting at Aintree on September 3, but Peter Collins spun the car during practice, when oil from a broken seal sprayed on to a rear wheel. Some damage was caused to its stressed skin construction, so it was withdrawn from the race.

The Oulton Park Gold Cup: September 24, 1955

The new BRM was beset with problems during practice – clutch trouble; a broken oil pipe; a broken propeller shaft, and a broken engine – so it had to start at the back of the grid. Ahead of Peter Collins were the works Lancia-Ferraris, Maseratis, Vanwalls and Connaughts, but he proceeded to charge through the field so that he lay fifth at the end of the first lap. On lap four he was challenging Luigi Musso for second place.

On lap ten, however, Collins came into the pit, his instruments indicating a dramatic loss of oil pressure. It was later found to be merely due to a faulty gauge. *Autosport* commented that "... for those ten laps the little green car thrilled everyone, matching the speed of Italy's latest F1 machines."

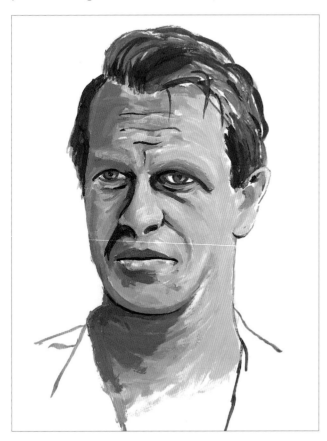

Peter Collins: one of the all-time greats.

Peter Collins frightening the opposition with his spectacular performance at Oulton Park in the new 2½-litre BRM.

The exciting Lancia D50 – later to become the Lancia-Ferrari – as it first appeared in 1954.

Winter testing

Over the winter the new car was tested at Oulton Park by Stirling Moss, but it was Mike Hawthorn who was signed as BRM's number one driver for 1956, with Tony Brooks as his team-mate. In response, Alfred Owen contributed a further £200,000 to the effort. During a demonstration to ORMA members Hawthorn had a narrow escape when the bonnet flew off his car at speed, hitting him in the face and smashing his visor.

1956

The Glover Trophy, Goodwood: April 11, 1956

I saw the new P25 BRMs in action at Goodwood

Mike Hawthorn leading Archie Scott Brown and Stirling Moss during opening laps of the 1956 Glover Trophy Race at Goodwood.

on Easter Monday, driven by Mike Hawthorn and Tony Brooks. Stirling Moss had a works 250F Maserati, Archie Scott Brown a B Type Connaught, and Robert Manzon the new eight-cylinder Gordini. It was an impressive line-up, and Hawthorn led the field around the first lap of the race. Brooks, having missed practice, charged through from the back of the grid to fifth place before retiring on lap nine because of falling oil pressure. Then, as Hawthorn was running second to Moss with nine laps to go, he crashed at top speed at Fordwater and his car overturned – fortunately without serious injury to the driver. The cause was a split oil gaiter, which resulted in the seizure of a suspension joint. The race was won by Stirling Moss after Scott Brown retired with a broken piston.

The International Aintree 200: April 21, 1956

Mike Hawthorn and Tony Brooks were at Aintree, competing with the 250F Maseratis and B Type Connaughts. Initially, Archie Scott Brown led the BRMs in his Connaught, but Hawthorn overtook him on lap three. On the following lap, Hawthorn discovered that his brake pedal was missing. Searching for it with his foot, he only succeeded in finding

The deceptively fast Tony Brooks.

the accelerator, sending the car off the circuit at great speed, but eventually stopping without mishap.

Brooks then took up the chase and then the lead when Scott Brown retired because of another broken piston.

At 30 laps Brooks was 27 seconds ahead, but his brakes began to fade through overheating, and he finished second behind Moss. The Maseratis of Jack Brabham and Louis Rosier came third and fourth.

Tony Brooks leading the Aintree 200 Race in the P25 BRM.

International Trophy Race at Silverstone: May 5, 1956

Mike Hawthorn was on the front row of the grid at Silverstone, his lone BRM having equalled Fangio's time in the Lancia-Ferrari. It was the first race of the Frank Costin-designed Vanwalls of Stirling Moss and Harry Schell, who were in first and second positions.

Hawthorn overtook Fangio to lead the race at Stowe Corner, and he extended his advantage over the next 12 laps. Then a timing gear broke,

Mike Hawthorn taking the BRM out in front during the *Daily Express* International Trophy Race at Silverstone on May 5, 1956.

Mike Hawthorn.

and the BRM coasted to a stop. The race was won by Stirling Moss, but Hawthorn hadn't yet lost faith in the BRM, declaring that he had held his revs down to 8000 and was still able to outpace the other cars.

John Bolster wrote in *Autosport*: "I watched the cars cornering, and there was absolutely no doubt in my mind that the BRM was the steadiest machine in the race. Now, some of that may have been due to the impeccable artistry of Mike Hawthorn, but the way the wheels seemed glued to the road made a deep impression on many spectators ... Furthermore, Mike was clearly able to leave Fangio on the straight, proving that the 4-cylinder BRM engine has a better power curve than the V8 Lancia. Yet Raymond Mays assured me that this was a 'cooking' engine; the two best units being saved for Monaco! The BRM is not perfect, but it is becoming steadily more formidable. In the hands of Hawthorn, it is a hot candidate for a Grand Prix victory before long."

The Monaco Grand Prix: May 13, 1956

It was just after the wedding of Prince Rainier and Grace Kelly and, for the first time since 1951, two BRMs were set to compete in a World Championship race with two top flight drivers. However, during practice the large inlet valves of the engines became distorted and the cars had to be withdrawn. Tony Brooks, writing in *Tony Brooks: Poetry in Motion*, records that the BRMs were so over-geared that it was impossible to get them into top, and that the cars had insufficient steering locks to get them round the Gasworks and Station hairpins.

The BRMs of Mike Hawthorn and Tony Brooks leading the field during the opening laps of the 1956 British Grand Prix.

The British Grand Prix: July 14, 1956

Three cars for Mike Hawthorn, Tony Brooks and Ron Flockhart were at Silverstone for the British Grand Prix, all now with modified valves. Hawthorn was on the front row of the grid, having been third fastest in practice. Brooks was ninth and in the third row, and Flockhart 17th in row five.

Hawthorn shot away from the start to lead the race, and Brooks, making a sensational start, was soon behind him in second place, while Flockhart's race was over on lap two due to stripped timing gears. On lap five, Fangio overtook Brooks at Copse Corner, but Brooks was past him again when the Argentinian spun at Becketts on lap seven. On lap 15 it was Stirling Moss who went past Hawthorn to lead the race, and nine laps later Hawthorn retired with oil leaking from a driveshaft. On lap 40, it was Brooks' turn to stop with a broken throttle control. Resuming the race after an improvised repair, Brooks spun off violently at Abbey Curve with his car's throttle stuck open. Fortunately, he was thrown out before his car turned over and caught fire. It was totally destroyed, but mercifully Brooks survived – albeit with a broken jaw.

The race was won by Fangio's Lancia-Ferrari at 98.65mph. The BRMs were the fastest cars in the race, but Alfred Owen was furious and demanded higher standards from all who were responsible for the preparation of the cars. He also insisted that the cars should be driven hard for 300 miles without breaking down before racing again.

Brooks and Flockhart tested longer chassis cars at Monza, covering 2000 miles and, as a result, Alec Issigonis (of Mini fame) offered suggestions as to how the cars' suspension could be improved.

1956 BRM memories, the 'if only' car with so much potential lacking only a focused development programme.

To Bryan with very best wishes — Tony Brooks

Memories of Tony Brooks, circa 1956. From the inside front cover of *The Saga of BRM, Volume 1.*

1957

The Glover Trophy, Goodwood: April 22, 1957

The cars were fast, but had proved both dangerous and unreliable, and at the end of 1956 Mike Hawthorn and Tony Brooks decided to leave BRM. I was disappointed, but still came to Goodwood to watch Roy Salvadori and Ron Flockhart drive the cars in 1957. The brakes of Salvadori's car seized on its warm-up lap, and on the first lap of the race they seized again, causing him to spin out. Flockhart also spun twice, but managing to continue, finishing in third place behind the Connaughts of Stuart Lewis-Evans and Jack Fairman.

The Monaco Grand Prix: May 19, 1957

Locking brakes plagued the practice sessions at Monaco, so Ron Flockhart and Roy Salvadori could only achieve 11th and 16th places in practice. Salvadori failed to qualify, and decided to leave BRM and move to Cooper instead.

Stirling Moss, Peter Collins and Mike Hawthorn (Lancia-Ferrari) were all eliminated by a succession of incidents in the first lap, and Flockhart ran in sixth place until retiring on lap 60 due to a broken timing gear. The race was won by Juan Fangio (Maserati) at 64.722mph from Tony Brooks (Vanwall).

After Monaco, and on the advice of Colin Chapman, coil springs with telescopic dampers were introduced at the rear of the cars in place of transverse leaf springs, and coils also took the place of the oleo-pneumatic struts in the front. Raised cockpit sides provided greater rigidity with less weight.

The French Grand Prix: July 7, 1957

Herbert MacKay-Fraser, a young American driver, took Roy Salvadori's place in the team for the French Grand Prix and came 12th in practice, just one tenth of a second slower than Ron Flockhart.

He made a magnificent start and was in sixth place before the end of the first lap. Flockhart spun on some oil from Salvadori's Vanwall and his car

Herbert Mackay-Fraser's high-sided P25, pursued by Mike Hawthorn's Ferrari, during the 1957 French Grand Prix at Rouen.

Stirling Moss, after taking over Tony Brook's Vanwall, gains the first World Championship win for a British car in the British Grand Prix.

was too badly damaged to continue, but MacKay-Fraser continued to battle with the Lancia-Ferraris, and was still in seventh place on lap 26, when he came in to the pits due to an oil leak and had to retire. The race was won by Juan Fangio's Maserati at 100.016mph, ahead of the Lancia-Ferraris of Luigi Musso and Peter Collins.

Sadly, MacKay-Fraser was killed driving a Lotus in a sports car race the following week.

The British Grand Prix: July 20, 1957

With Ron Flockhart still injured after Rouen, BRM was without drivers for the British Grand Prix at Aintree, so Jack Fairman and Les Leston agreed to drive the two cars. All the early promise of the P25 seemed to have evaporated, as Leston was only 12th and Fairman 16th in practice, while at the front of the grid were Stirling Moss (Vanwall), Jean Behra (Maserati) and Tony Brooks (Vanwall). The two BRMs stayed around 14th and 15th, until Leston retired with stripped auxiliary drive gears on lap 45 and Fairman went out due to a cracked cylinder head on lap 48. The race produced a famous win for the Vanwall of Brooks/Moss at 86.79mph from the Lancia-Ferraris of Musso and Hawthorn.

The Caen Grand Prix: July 27, 1957

"FRENCH ACE BEATS BRM JINX: JEERED-AT BRM IS NOW NO 1"

Sensational newspaper headlines demonstrated that BRM was still capable of stirring strong emotions. As the Maserati team would not be racing at Caen, Jean Behra asked Raymond Mays if he could drive a BRM, and two cars were dispatched from Southampton on a Silver City transport plane.

Behra had his car's seat strengthened so that it no longer flexed. He found that this transformed its handling, and broke the lap record in practice. Harry Schell, whose Maserati had failed during practice, jumped at the opportunity to drive the second, spare BRM.

Behra led the race from the start, and Schell was soon in second immediately behind him. The two exchanged the lead more than once until Schell's engine blew up with a broken piston rod. In spite of gear selection difficulties, Behra won with ease from Roy Salvadori's Cooper-Climax, his speed over whole race exceeding the previous lap record. After the race, Behra raised a

The French ace, Jean Behra.

number of concerns about the car's handling to Tony Rudd, all of which he found helpful.

International Trophy, Silverstone: September 14, 1957

"CAR THEY LAUGHED AT WINS 100,000 CHEERS: 1–2–3 BRMS TRIUMPH AT SILVERSTONE"

In the absence of the main works teams, Jean Behra and Harry Schell were again available to drive the BRMs and they were joined by Ron Flockhart. Behra won the first heat, creating a new lap record of 103.3mph, and Flockhart came second. Schell won heat two, and so all three BRMs were on the front row of the grid for the 102 mile final.

The three led from start to finish in the order of Behra, Schell and Flockhart. Their most formidable rival would have been Tony Brooks in Rob Walker's 2-litre Cooper-Climax, but his car failed on the starting line of the first heat.

BRM had proved that its cars were fast, and that they could finish races, but also that they would need top quality drivers if they were going to be able to win World Championship events against the works teams.

A win at last! Jean Behra would lead Harry Schell and Ron Flockhart across the line to win the 1957 International *Daily Express* Trophy Race at Silverstone.

Modena Grand Prix: September 21, 1957

"ITALIAN CARS SWEEP THE BOARD – AND BRMs GO PHUT"

Stuart Lewis-Evans was to have driven a BRM at Modena, but Tony Vandervell, for whom he usually drove, stopped this, so Ron Flockhart's team-mate was Joakim Bonnier. Run over two 118 mile heats, the race offered BRM the opportunity to compete against two V6 Dino Ferraris with 2-litre engines and the works 250F Maserati team. Unfortunately, both BRMs had to retire during the course of the race, Flockhart's with a fuel pump failure and Bonnier's with a broken rear hub.

Moroccan Grand Prix, October 27, 1957

Ron Flockhart was in Casablanca for the Moroccan Grand Prix, with Maurice Trintignant in the second BRM. Flockhart's car made contact with a bird, and as a result his throttle linkage was damaged, and his race ended. Juan Fangio lost time after his works Maserati was mistakenly black flagged, and Trintignant's BRM finished the race in third place behind Jean Behra's Maserati and Stuart Lewis-Evans' Vanwall.

1958

Alfred Owen made it clear to Raymond Mays and Peter Berthon that 1958 had to be a more successful year for BRM, as he was anxious to sell the 2½-litre BRM engine to other British teams and private owners. The cars had new tubular front ends, designed by Tony Rudd, to accommodate Colin Chapman's revised suspension. A new five-bearing crankshaft offered greater reliability, and the performance of the engine was improved. Jean Behra and Harry Schell were to drive the BRMs throughout 1958.

The Glover Trophy, Goodwood: April 7, 1958

Two 1957 BRMs were driven in the 100 mile Glover Trophy Race by Jean Behra and Harry Schell,

Raymond Mays

EASTGATE HOUSE
BOURNE
LINCOLNSHIRE

TELEPHONE: BOURNE 17

Bryan G.Apps,Esq.,
St.David's College,
Lampeter,
Cardiganshire   5th November,1957

Dear Bryan,

        On my return from Casablanca I received
your letter of 20th October. It is most kind of
you to invite me to come and speak at the Union
Debate, and I should have very much liked to come,
but unfortunately Bourne is such a long way from
Lampeter that I cannot fit in the journey.
As you can imagine I have a great deal to do,
and many appointments to keep, even out of the
actual racing season. I hope you will have a
very successful debate, the subject sounds most
interesting.

        I am delighted to hear that you still
have the scrap book, and have kept it up to date,
it must be a marvellous record, and sometime I should
like to see it again.

        My good wishes to you, and I hope we meet
sometime,

            Yours sincerely,

                    Raymond Mays

A letter from Raymond Mays after his return from Casablanca in 1957.

The legendary Colin Chapman.

Jean Behra crashing into the Goodwood chicane.

and Behra led from the start, followed by Mike Hawthorn's Ferrari.

I had positioned myself just before the chicane, anticipating that this would afford me a good view of all the cars. But I watched in horror as Behra shot past where I stood, and into the brick chicane head-on and without brakes. The front left quarter of the BRM disintegrated as a result of the violent impact, but fortunately Behra escaped with only minor injuries. Mays accompanied him to Chichester Hospital for him to be checked out.

Schell continued, until a fire broke out at the rear of his car due to an overheating disc brake. The reason behind both incidents turned out to be the servo pistons, which had stuck off in Behra's car, and stuck on in Schell's. It was decided after the race to adopt a non-servo braking system.

The Aintree 200: April 19, 1958

After his crash at Goodwood, Jean Behra came to Aintree to drive a BRM wearing protective straps across his rib cage. He was fastest in practice.

At the end of the first lap, Stirling Moss led Behra in Rob Walker's Cooper and he steadily increased his lead until Behra had to give up the chase when his brakes failed again through lack of fluid. On this occasion, he was able to drive slowly to the pit to retire!

International Trophy Race, Silverstone: May 3, 1958

Jean Behra had the 1958 car for Silverstone while Ron Flockhart had a 1957 model. They were on the second row of the grid, and it was Peter Collin's Ferrari that led the race for the first three laps. Behra then passed Collins after setting a new lap record at 105.37mph, and led until lap ten when his goggles were smashed by a stone thrown up by another

Opposite: Jean Behra's P25 BRM leading the 1958 Monaco Grand Prix.

car. Tony Rudd offered first aid and a spare pair of goggles, and then Behra set off again in 11th place to eventually finish fourth. Flockhart moved up to second place after Behra's pit stop, but took to the grass after making contact with Bruce Halford's Maserati, and was forced to ram into an earthen bank to avoid spectators. His car was wrecked.

The Monaco Grand Prix: May 18, 1958

There were two 1958 cars in Monaco for Jean Behra and Harry Schell, with space frames and detachable bodies. Behra was second in practice to Tony Brooks' Vanwall, while Schell was back in 11th place as he was still finding his way around the new car.

Behra overtook Roy Salvadori's Cooper-Climax on the first lap to lead the race from Brooks, while Schell was held up by the works Ferraris some way back. Behra broke the lap record while protecting a comfortable lead, and Hawthorn's Ferrari took up the chase from Brooks. Then, on lap 28, Behra was out of the race due to a failed rear brake. Schell finished fifth, nine laps behind Maurice Trintignant (Cooper-Climax), who led the Ferraris of Luigi Musso and Peter Collins across the line.

The Dutch Grand Prix: May 26, 1958

Three Vanwalls filled the front row of the starting grid at Zandvoort, but Jean Behra was fifth and Harry

Harry Schell at Zandvoort.

Schell eighth, both cars having had new engines fitted, which had been flown over from Bourne.

The Vanwalls of Stirling Moss and Stuart Lewis-Evans led from Schell's BRM at the start, with Behra back in fifth. On lap 12, Schell passed Lewis-Evans to finish second behind Moss, while Behra came third.

The Belgian Grand Prix: June 15, 1958
During practice, Jean Behra spun at 160mph when his engine overheated and hot oil from the breather pipe sprayed onto a rear wheel, but he managed to control it without injury to himself or damage to the car. After this considerable fright, he was still ninth fastest, while Harry Schell was seventh.

Both BRMs made good starts in the race, and Behra took the lead from Moss (Vanwall) before the end of the first lap. He then slowed, and was forced to retire on lap five due to low oil pressure. The race was won by Tony Brooks' Vanwall, with Schell finishing fifth.

The French Grand Prix: July 6, 1958
Harry Schell's BRM was on the front row of the grid of the very fast Rheims circuit alongside the Ferraris of Mike Hawthorn and Luigi Musso. Jean Behra was in the fourth row behind Maurice Trintignant who was placed seventh in a third BRM.

Initially Schell took the lead, but it was Hawthorn who stayed in front to the finish. Behra battled with Stirling Moss (Vanwall) and Juan Fangio (Maserati) for second place, but none of the BRMs finished the race: Trintignant went out on lap 24 with a broken camshaft, Behra on lap 40, also because of a broken camshaft, and Schell on the same lap with an overheated engine.

The British Grand Prix: July 19, 1958
Stirling Moss' Vanwall was fastest in practice, and Harry Schell's BRM was alongside him on the grid. Jean Behra was in the third row having made the eighth fastest time.

The order during the race swiftly became Peter Collins (Ferrari), Stirling Moss (Vanwall), Mike Hawthorn (Ferrari), and Schell (BRM). Behra was trailing, lacking confidence in his car, and he retired on lap 20, believing the front suspension to have been damaged when he ran into a hare, but it was later discovered that a rear tyre had been punctured. Schell was lapped by Collins, but stayed with him to finish in fifth place with Collins, Hawthorn, Roy Salvadori (Cooper-Climax) and Stuart Lewis-Evans (Vanwall) ahead of him.

The Caen Grand Prix: July 20, 1958
Burning the midnight oil in order to prepare the cars for Caen, the BRM mechanics must have recalled the early days of the P15. Harry Schell was given the latest car, which upset Behra.

Harry Schell in the P25 BRM during the 1958
British Grand Prix.

Yet it was Behra who led the race, while Schell took third behind Moss, who was driving Rob Walker's Cooper. At half distance Behra retired due to broken timing gear, and Schell stopped after a problem with his gearbox scavenging pump. The race was won by Moss.

The German Grand Prix: August 3, 1958
Vanwalls and Ferraris filled the front row of the grid at the Nürburgring. Harry Schell and Jean Behra were on the third row, having only come eighth and ninth in practice, being unused to the challenging circuit.

It was a tragic race, costing the life of Peter Collins, whose car flipped as he attempted to overtake. Disillusioned with his car, Behra had retired on lap four, only to discover that he might have finished in second or third place had he continued. Schell was forced to retire because of failing front brakes on lap nine, and the race was won by Tony Brooks' Vanwall.

Harry Schell at the Nürburgring.

The Portuguese Grand Prix: August 24, 1958
Stirling Moss (Vanwall) was on pole position while the BRMs of Jean Behra and Harry Schell were fourth and seventh on the starting grid. In the early stages of the race, Behra lay third behind Mike Hawthorn (Ferrari) and Moss, but he moved up when Hawthorn pitted after 40 laps for adjustments to his brakes. Behra's engine then started to sound rough due to a failed sparkplug, which caused him to drop behind Hawthorn and Stuart Lewis-Evans.

He retained fourth position until the end of the race, and Schell came sixth, the two BRMs being separated by Wolfgang von Trips' Ferrari.

The Italian Grand Prix, September 7, 1958
Jean Behra and Harry Schell were joined by Joakim Bonnier at Monza, and the three were eighth, ninth and tenth in practice. Schell was eliminated on the first lap after his car and Wolfgang von Trips' Ferrari touched at high speed, luckily without serious injury to either driver, and Bonnier retired on lap 15 because of a transmission failure. Behra kept close company with the leading pack, but retired on lap 43 due to defective brakes. The race was won by Tony Brooks' Vanwall, followed by the Ferraris of Mike Hawthorn and Phil Hill.

Raymond Mays recalls that Behra's puppy was stolen during the race and was only returned to its distraught owner after an appeal on television.

The Moroccan Grand Prix: October 19, 1958
No less than four BRMs arrived in Casablanca to be driven by Jean Behra, Joakim Bonnier, Harry Schell and Ron Flockhart, who proceeded to come fourth, eighth, 19th and 15th in practice.

Stirling Moss led at the start with his Vanwall, and Bonnier ran in fourth position behind him, Phil Hill (Ferrari) and Mike Hawthorn (Ferrari). Tragically, Stuart Lewis-Evans' car crashed and caught fire when its engine seized, and he died later from his burns.

In the end the order was Moss, Hawthorn, Hill, Bonnier and Schell. Flockhart and Behra retired on laps 16 and 27.

After the race, Behra announced that he would drive for Ferrari in 1959, and Vanwall withdrew from racing. That month, it was also announced that from 1961 the new Formula 1 would be for unsupercharged cars of 1½ litres, or supercharged cars of 750cc.

1959

Down Under
A BRM was sent to New Zealand for Ron Flockhart to drive, but after winning the first heat of the New

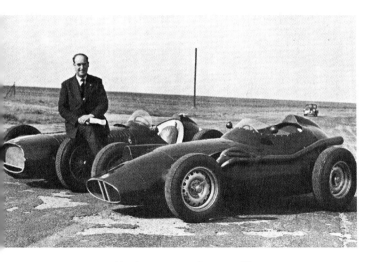

Alfred Owen with two of his BRMs.
(Courtesy Rivers Fletcher)

Zealand Grand Prix on January 10, he retired with a broken engine breather in the final. He went on to win the Lady Wigram Trophy Race on January 24 from Jack Brabham's Cooper-Climax, and, after a poor start, came third in the Teretonga Trophy Race on February 7 behind the Coopers of Merv Neil and Jack Brabham.

The Goodwood International 100: March 30, 1959
Harry Schell's BRM was fastest in practice for the Glover Trophy Race, and he led the race from Stirling Moss (Rob Walker Cooper-Climax) and Joakim Bonnier's BRM. First Moss and then Jack Brabham (Cooper-Climax) went ahead, however, and the BRMs of Schell and Bonnier finished third and fourth.

The International Aintree 200: April 18, 1959
Harry Schell had a new P25 for Aintree, and Stirling Moss drove a Cooper with a 2½-litre BRM engine. At the start, Masten Gregory (Cooper-Climax) led from the BRMs of Harry Schell and Joakim Bonnier. Moss went in front of the BRMs on lap two, while Bonnier retired because of a broken connecting rod. After Gregory retired on lap 19, Moss led in the Cooper-BRM until vibration from the 4-cylinder engine loosened a nut on the car's Colotti gearbox, and he was forced to retire. Schell also retired with a sick engine.

The International Trophy Race, Silverstone: May 2, 1959
Stirling Moss drove a works BRM and, after breaking the lap record in practice at 106.87mph, asked for his engine to be put into another chassis for the race.

Overtaking Jack Brabham's Cooper on lap two, Moss led the race while Ron Flockhart held onto fifth place in the second BRM. Moss then found that his brakes had become inoperable, and skilfully spun the car before bringing it safely to a stop. Flockhart finished in third place behind Brabham's Cooper and Salvadori's Aston Martin.

The BRP BRM
Stirling Moss wanted to drive BRMs, but had more faith in his own mechanics. After Silverstone it was agreed with Alfred Owen that the British Racing Partnership should be formed, and that a BRM, painted light green and prepared by Ken Gregory, would be driven by Moss. Raymond Mays would have much preferred him to have driven for the works team, but was pleased that Moss would be driving a BRM again.

The Monaco Grand Prix: May 10, 1959
The BRMs of Joakim Bonnier, Ron Flockhart and Harry Schell were seventh, ninth, and tenth in practice. Stirling Moss was fastest after choosing to drive Rob Walker's Cooper-Climax.

Jean Behra (Maserati) led initially, but he was overtaken by Moss and Jack Brabham (Cooper-Climax) while Schell was nose-to-tail with Tony Brooks' Ferrari. Bonnier retired with brake trouble on lap 46, and Schell followed suit after spinning on lap 49, as did Flockhart on lap 65, also after spinning with brake trouble when in sixth place. Moss continued to lead the race by a wide margin until his rear axle failed on lap 82, and it was Brabham who finally won.

The Dutch Grand Prix: May 31, 1959 – A Grand Prix victory for BRM at last!
Joakim Bonnier put his BRM on pole at Zandvoort with Jack Brabham (Cooper-Climax) and Stirling

Moss (Cooper-Climax) joining him on the front row of the starting grid. Harry Schell was sixth in the second BRM.

Bonnier led from the fall of the flag, but he was overtaken by Masten Gregory's Cooper on lap two. Bonnier was ahead again on lap 12 as the Cooper fell back due to gear selection difficulties. Moss started to make progress after a poor start, but, after overtaking Bonnier, had to retire on lap 63 due to a broken gearbox, while Schell had retired on lap 47 because of gearbox trouble.

Bonnier went on to mark up BRM's first World Championship race victory. Raymond Mays records that, after the race, he burst into tears of joy while the BRM mechanics danced a jig around him. Louis and Jean Stanley gave a party at the Bouwes Hotel in Zandvoort so that they could all celebrate the occasion in style.

The French Grand Prix: July 5, 1959

Stirling Moss drove the light green BRP BRM at Rheims, while Joakim Bonnier, Harry Schell and Ron Flockhart had the three dark green works cars. Moss was fourth in practice while the others were sixth, ninth and thirteenth on the starting grid.

Moss had only Tony Brooks (Ferrari) ahead of him at the start of the race, but he was then overtaken by Trintignant (Cooper-Climax) and Jack Brabham (Cooper-Climax). After dropping further back, Moss sped up and closed on Phil Hill's Ferrari in second place, setting a new lap record in the process. However, his clutch had failed and, spinning on melted tar on lap 43, he was unable to push-start his car in the hot sun.

The race was won by Tony Brooks with Flockhart sixth and Schell seventh. Bonnier retired with engine trouble on lap seven.

The first World Championship Grand Prix victory for a BRM: Joakim Bonnier at Zandvoort in 1959.

 **OWEN RACING ORGANISATION**

PHONE: BOURNE 327/328

BOURNE
LINCOLNSHIRE

B.G.Apps,Esq.,
 University College of St.David.
Lampeter,
<u>Cardiganshire</u>   3rd June,1959

Dear Bryan,

      Thank you so much for your very kind
letter of 2nd which I greatly appreciate. We were
all delighted with the fine race which Bonnier drove,
and our victory was immensely popular with everyone
at Zandvoort.

      I note all your news, and I hope that
you will be successful in your finals. Many thanks for
your good wishes for the future.

          Yours sincerely,

          Raymond Mays

Raymond Mays' letter of June 3, 1959, in which he expresses his delight at Bonnier's victory in Holland.

The British Grand Prix: July 18, 1959

Jack Brabham (Cooper-Climax) was fastest in practice with Roy Salvadori (Aston Martin) second and Harry Schell (BRM) third. Stirling Moss was sixth in the BRP BRM, Joakim Bonnier (BRM) ninth and Flockhart (BRM) eleventh.

Brabham established an immediate lead from the BRMs of Moss and Schell. Bruce McLaren (Cooper) succeeded in overtaking Schell, and Moss gained on Brabham, until he stopped to replace a tyre on lap 50, and again for fuel on lap 66. He still recorded the fastest lap of the race in the process of beating McLaren, to finish second to Brabham,

thus achieving BRM's best British Grand Prix result. Schell was fourth, while Bonnier had retired on lap 38 because of a broken throttle linkage and Flockhart on lap 54 after a spin.

The German Grand Prix: August 2, 1959

Stirling Moss drove Rob Walker's Cooper-Climax at Avus, while Joakim Bonnier and Harry Schell

Stirling's British Racing Partnership (BRP) BRM being pursued by Bruce McLaren at Aintree.

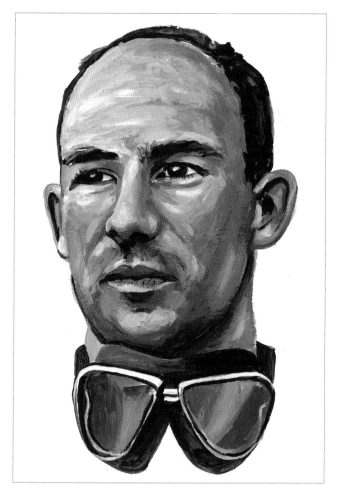

The champion without a crown: Stirling Moss.

Stirling Moss in the pale green BRM at Aintree.

were joined by Hans Herrmann in the BRM team. Bonnier was seventh, Schell eighth and Herrmann 11th in practice. Tragically, Jean Behra was killed while driving a Porsche RSK in a sports car race before the start of the Grand Prix.

Tony Brooks won the first heat for Ferrari, while Schell, Bonnier and Herrmann finished fifth, seventh and eighth. Brooks won again in the second heat, and Bonnier and Schell came fifth and seventh. Herrmann crashed spectacularly in his BRM on lap seven, the car disintegrating after leaping into the air while, amazingly, the driver was thrown clear without serious injury.

The final classification was Brooks first, Dan Gurney (Ferrari) second and Phil Hill (Ferrari) third. Bonnier was again fifth and Schell seventh.

The Portuguese Grand Prix: August 23, 1959
Stirling Moss was fastest in practice driving Ron Walker's Cooper-Climax. The BRMs of Joakim Bonnier, Harry Schell and Ron Flockhart were fifth, ninth and 11th. From halfway around the first lap Moss led by an increasing margin to the end of the race. Schell finished in fifth place, and Flockhart was seventh. Bonnier retired on lap 11 with fuel starvation.

The Italian Grand Prix: September 13, 1959
The prototype rear-engined 2½-litre P48 BRM caused excitement at Monza when it was tested during practice, but it wasn't ready to be raced. Stirling Moss was on pole position in Walker's Cooper-Climax while the P25 BRMs of Harry Schell, Joakim Bonnier and Ron Flockhart were seventh, 11th and 15th in practice.

Moss led from Phil Hill (Ferrari) Jack Brabham (Cooper-Climax), Dan Gurney (Ferrari) and Schell (BRM) on the first lap, but was then overtaken by Phil Hill's Ferrari. On lap 33 Hill stopped for tyres and Moss was left to win the race by 47 seconds from the American, with Jack Brabham (Cooper-Climax) in third place. The three BRMs of Schell, Bonnier and Flockhart were seventh, eighth, and 13th.

BRM stayed away from the United States Grand Prix at Sebring to save costs.

The Silver City Trophy Race, Snetterton: October 10, 1959
Ron Flockhart and Bruce Halford drove the BRMs at Snetterton, with Flockhart taking pole position for the 25 lap race. He led for most of the race, but was challenged by Graham Hill's Lotus-Climax, which briefly passed him. After Hill retired due to mechanical problems Flockhart had a comfortable win from Brabham's Cooper and Halford's BRM.

Over the winter Graham Hill and Dan Gurney were signed to drive for BRM in 1960, joining Bonnier, who stayed with the team.

1960

The rear-engined P48 BRM
In 1960 BRM brought the P48 to the starting grid. The car consisted of the front half of a P25, with a new, tubular structure welded to it to carry the engine, with double wishbone suspension at the rear. The added weight of the engine at the back of the car meant that a single rear disc brake was insufficient. At the end of the year, 'Wilkie' Wilkinson of Ecurie Ecosse became the racing manager, leaving Rudd more time to develop the new car.

Argentine Grand Prix: February 7, 1960
Two P25 BRMs were sent to Argentina for Joakim Bonnier and new driver Graham Hill, and both were on the front row of the starting grid in third and fourth places. Stirling Moss was on pole with Rob Walker's Cooper-Climax and Innes Ireland second with a works rear-engined Lotus 18. Three works Ferraris filled the second row.

Ireland led at the start but, after a spin, the order became Bonnier and Hill in the BRMs, followed by Moss, Jack Brabham (Cooper-Climax) and Ireland. Moss overtook Hill on lap 11 and Bonnier on lap 14. The day was extremely hot, and Graham Hill retired on lap 38 due to an overheating engine. Moss stopped because of a collapsed suspension, and Bonnier then led by a wide margin until he lost time in his pit, his car also overheating. The race was won by Bruce McLaren's Cooper-Climax and Bonnier finished in seventh place.

Formula Libre Race, Cordoba: February 14 ,1960

Graham Hill was back in England testing the new P48, so the P25s were driven by Joakim Bonnier and Dan Gurney, who came third and fourth fastest in practice for the race.

The Coopers of Jack Brabham, Bruce McLaren and Maurice Trintignant led at the start, followed by the two BRMs. Brabham retired due to fuel starvation and Gurney led from Trintignant. Bonnier stopped with his brakes overheating, and on lap 50 Gurney's gearlever broke, enabling Trintignant to pass him. Stuck in fourth gear, Gurney finished second to Trintignant, and Bonnier was fifth with only four other cars left in the race.

Goodwood International 100: April 18, 1960

This race saw two new rear-engined P48s for Graham Hill and Dan Gurney, while Joakim Bonnier elected to give the P25 its last race.

Innes Ireland (Lotus-Climax) led throughout from Stirling Moss (Rob Walker's Cooper-Climax). Graham Hill was fifth, and Joakim Bonnier sixth. Dan Gurney crashed on the Lavant Straight without injury to himself, and afterwards Hill suggested that modifications would have to be made to the suspension to enable the P48 to leave the racing line in overtaking other cars.

International Trophy Race, Silverstone: 14 May 1960

Stirling Moss (Cooper-Climax) was fastest in practice and he had alongside him Joakim Bonnier (BRM), Dan Gurney (BRM) and Phil Hill (Ferrari). Graham Hill was in the third row with the third P48 BRM. Sadly, Harry Schell was killed in practice when he was thrown out of his Cooper at Abbey Curve.

Initially the order at the start of the race was Bonnier, Gurney, Graham Hill, then Moss, but Moss led by the end of the first lap and until lap 33, when his suspension broke under the strain

of high speed cornering. Gurney dropped back to retire and Bonnier was also eliminated by failing brakes. The race went to Ireland, followed by Jack Brabham's Cooper and Graham Hill's BRM.

Monaco Grand Prix, May 29, 1960

Stirling Moss was fastest in practice driving Rob Walker's Lotus 18. The P48 BRMs of Joakim Bonnier, Graham Hill and Dan Gurney were fifth, sixth and 14th.

Bonnier led initially from Jack Brabham (Cooper-Climax), and he remained in front until Moss passed him on Lap 17, only to be delayed by a loose plug, and so Bonnier took the lead once again. Gurney retired on lap 45 when a rear hub carrier buckled, and Graham Hill had already spun off the circuit. After losing the lead again to Moss, Bonnier had to withdraw due to another buckled rear hub carrier. The race was a win for Moss, and modified hubs were fitted to the BRMs before the Dutch Grand Prix.

Dutch Grand Prix: June 6, 1960

Stirling Moss was fastest in practice with the Lotus-Climax while the BRMs of Joakim Bonnier, Graham Hill and Dan Gurney were fourth, fifth and sixth.

Jack Brabham led the race, pursued by Moss. On lap 12, Gurney's brakes failed and his car somersaulted, tragically killing an 18-year-old spectator who was in a prohibited area. Gurney was uninjured, but understandably in shock.

On lap 17 Brabham's car dislodged some concrete, which burst Moss' tyre and damaged his hub, costing him several laps. The result was a win for Brabham, followed by Ireland, Hill and Moss, the last named having fought his way back after a lengthy pit stop. Bonnier retired in lap 55 due to engine trouble.

Belgian Grand Prix: June 19, 1960

Jack Brabham (Cooper), Tony Brooks (Cooper) and Phil Hill (Ferrari) were on the front row of the grid at Spa while the BRMs of Graham Hill, Joakim Bonnier and Dan Gurney were fifth, sixth and 11th.

Brabham led from the start of the race from

Innes Ireland (Lotus), while Bonnier and Graham Hill took fourth and sixth positions. Graham Hill was third on lap 22 and second by lap 35, but he then retired due to a blown engine. Gurney retired on lap five, and Bonnier on lap 15, both with engine failures. Sadly, Chris Bristow and Alan Stacey were killed in separate accidents. The race was won by Jack Brabham.

Back at Bourne the cars were lengthened at the front as a result of wind tunnel tests during the previous winter, and they had smaller radiators installed.

French Grand Prix: July 3, 1960

Graham Hill was third fastest in practice at Rheims, and shared the front row of the grid with Jack Brabham (Cooper-Climax) and Phil Hill (Ferrari). Dan Gurney and Joakim Bonnier stood seventh and tenth.

Graham Hill's race ended when he was shunted from behind while finding a gear at the start, and the BRMs of Gurney and Bonnier retired on laps 18 and 23, both due to engine trouble. The race went again to Brabham, with the Cooper-Climax cars of Gendebien, McLaren and Taylor occupying the next three places.

Graham Hill's BRM at Spa in 1960.

British Grand Prix: July 16, 1960 – An epic charge by Graham Hill

Jack Brabham was on pole at Silverstone, with Graham Hill beside him in second place. Bruce McLaren came next, and Joakim Bonnier completed the front row in fourth place. Just behind them on the second row was Dan Gurney in sixth.

After stalling, Graham Hill eventually got away at the back of the field and then proceeded to pass car after car in a truly epic drive. Breaking the lap record at 111.6mph, he eventually overtook Brabham to take the lead on lap 55. Sadly on lap 72, while he was being pressed hard by Brabham, Hill slid off the circuit at Copse Corner and his race was run. Gurney finished in tenth place; Bonnier had retired on lap 60 with a collapsed rear suspension. The race was won by Jack Brabham, but all the applause of the crowd was for Graham Hill's memorable performance in the BRM.

Silver City Trophy, Brands Hatch: August 2, 1960

Jim Clark drove a works Lotus 18 from pole position and lay second to Jack Brabham's Cooper for much of the race, followed by Graham Hill's P48. The race ended with Hill coming second to Brabham, the young Scottish driver having retired.

Portuguese Grand Prix: August 14, 1960

Of the three BRM drivers at Oporto, it was Dan Gurney who shone brightest, coming second in practice, and sandwiched between John Surtees (Lotus-Climax) and Jack Brabham (Cooper-Climax) on the front row of the grid. Graham Hill was fourth and Joakim Bonnier 13th.

Hill, anticipating the start, caused a general creeping forward of cars, but it was Gurney who led from Brabham. Brabham passed Gurney on the first lap, only for Gurney to recover his lead immediately, and after five laps the order of cars was Gurney, Surtees, Moss, then Brabham, with Bonnier's car already slowing with engine trouble. On lap 11, Gurney spun with oil spraying onto his rear wheel, and he stopped briefly at his pit on lap 24 before retiring on the next lap. Bonnier had

Joakim Bonnier driving the P48 BRM in the 1960 British Grand Prix.

Graham Hill, after starting off in last place, coming closer than anyone else to winning the British Grand Prix in a BRM.

Graham Hill, whose name was to become synonymous with BRM.

Graham Hill leading Jack Brabham during the
Portuguese Grand Prix.

retired on lap seven, and Graham Hill had followed on lap nine because of a defective gearbox. The race went to Brabham who was followed across the line by Bruce McLaren's Cooper-Climax.

The Mark II P48

Back at Bourne a new Mark II P48 BRM had been produced under the direction of Tony Rudd. It was lower, with a half-inch longer wheelbase, four brakes, and a wishbone rear suspension. The driver reclined to a greater degree than was the case in the Mark I model, and it had a lower centre of gravity. The Mark II was designed to take a 3-litre engine and sufficient fuel to last a race, in case that was chosen for the new Formula. Because of this, it was the heaviest of the cars on 1961 starting grids.

Lombard Trophy, Snetterton: September 17, 1960

The new Mark II P48 was brought to Snetteron but, after making pole position with Graham Hill at the wheel, flat batteries prevented it from actually being raced.

Racing instead with the Mark I P48, Hill ran in fourth position behind the Lotus team, with Bonnier two places behind him. Hill had to retire on lap 23, and Bonnier finished in third, his Mark I car down on power through a broken valve spring.

Gold Cup, Oulton Park: September 24, 1960

Graham Hill was only fourth in practice in the Mark II car and fell to sixth as the race began. Dan Gurney and Joakim Bonnier were back in mid-field with earlier cars. The race went to Stirling Moss in Rob Walker's Lotus 18, then came Jack Brabham's Cooper-Climax and Hill's BRM. Bonnier and Gurney finished in fifth and sixth.

United States Grand Prix: November 20, 1960

Three Mark I P48s were flown to Riverside. Dan Gurney was on the front row of the starting grid, despite having been beaten in practice by Stirling Moss (Lotus-Climax) and Jack Brabham (Cooper-Climax). Joakim Bonnier was fourth and Graham Hill 11th.

Moss led, followed by Gurney and Bonnier, in the opening stages of the race, with Graham Hill lying in sixth. Gurney retired on lap 19 due to his car overheating, and Graham Hill on lap 35 with gearbox trouble. The race was won by Moss from Innes Ireland (Lotus-Climax), Bruce McLaren (Cooper-Climax), Brabham (Cooper-Climax), and Bonnier (BRM).

The 1960 World Championship

Jack Brabham won the World Championship again, but BRM was still to make any real impact, with Graham Hill and Joakim Bonnier tying for 16th place with four points each. In fact, BRM's best placing through the 1960 season had been Hill's third in Zandvoort. Joakim Bonnier left BRM for Porsche at the end of the year.

1961

The BRM-Climax

At the beginning of 1961, the new Formula 1 for 1.5-litre unsupercharged cars came into force. The Mark II P48 was retained for the Inter-Continental races Down Under, and, as an interim measure until the V8 engine was ready, BRM introduced the P57, with a 4-cylinder Coventry-Climax engine.

'Wilkie' Wilkinson of Ecurie Ecosse had joined BRM late the previous year, which gave Tony Rudd more time to devote to the new car. Rudd designed the chassis, while Peter Berthon and Aubrey Woods were responsible for the V8 engine which embraced a number of features from the old V16.

Down Under in 1961
Two Mark I P48s with modified valve springs were sent to New Zealand for Dan Gurney and Graham Hill to race in the Grand Prix on January 7. Hill and Gurney came joint third in the heats, but while Hill also finished third in the final, Gurney was forced to retire through engine trouble.

After sharing the front row of the grid for a Formula Libre race at Sydney on January 29, both BRMs retired during the race, Hill due to a ruptured fuel tank and Gurney because of a leaking fuel pipe.

Graham Hill and Dan Gurney both won their heats at Ballarat on February 12th, and they finished first and second in the final – Gurney being first to cross the line.

Goodwood: April 3, 1961 – The Lavant Cup
Tony Brooks returned to BRM in 1961 to partner Graham Hill, and they drove the 2½-litre Mark II P48s in the 21-lap Lavant Cup Race for Inter-Continental cars. Hill was third fastest in practice and Brooks fourth.

The race went to Stirling Moss (Lotus-Climax) from Bruce McLaren (Cooper.Climax) and Graham Hill. Tony Brooks finished sixth in the second BRM.

The Glover Trophy Race
John Surtees (Yeoman Credit Cooper-Climax) led the 100 mile race for Formula 1 cars, closely challenged by Stirling Moss (Lotus-Climax.) Moss eventually retired through engine trouble, and Graham Hill inherited second place with the P57 BRM-Climax.

The Aintree 200: April 22, 1961
Graham Hill was fastest in practice with the BRM-

Climax, and the rest of the front row was composed of Jack Brabham, Bruce McLaren and John Surtees, all in Cooper-Climax cars. Tony Brooks was tenth on the starting grid.

In extremely wet conditions, Brabham led on the first lap from Jim Clark (Lotus-Climax), McLaren and Hill. Surtees advanced while Clark fell back, so Hill retained fourth place before passing Surtees. The race went to the two Coopers, followed by Hill, while Brooks retired on the 44th of 50 laps.

The Syracuse Grand Prix: April 25, 1961
Dan Gurney (4-cylinder Porsche) was on pole, with Giancarlo Baghetti (V6 Ferrari), John Surtees (Cooper-Climax) and Graham Hill (BRM-Climax) alongside him. Tony Brooks was 14th on the grid.

Surtees led the race initially, while Graham Hill ran in fourth position, before retiring on lap 53 due to a blown engine. Brooks had retired on lap 15 and Giancarlo Baghetti won the race in the shark-nosed Ferrari.

The International Trophy, Silverstone, May 6, 1961
Bruce McLaren was fastest in practice in a low-line Cooper-McLaren, and Stirling Moss was next to him in Rob Walker's Cooper. Graham Hill was fourth, with Tony Brooks back in the third row.

Jack Brabham's Cooper led the race in the rain and John Surtees, driving a rear-engined Vanwall, was fourth behind Moss and McLaren. Brooks and Hill both spun in the wet conditions. Brooks eventually finished in sixth place, beating an American Scarab to the line, while Hill was classified as 11th, having completed only 64 of the 80 laps.

The Monaco Grand Prix: May 14 , 1961
I watched the Monaco Grand Prix in the Oxford Union, and was impressed by the striking appearance of the new Ferraris. At BRM, Graham Hill had the latest version of the 4-cylinder Coventry-Climax engine installed in his car. He came fourth in practice, and Tony Brooks fifth. Ahead of them both were Stirling Moss (Lotus-Climax), Richie Ginther (Ferrari), and Jim Clark (Lotus-Climax).

Tony Brooks, back with BRM at Monaco.

Ginther established an early lead, followed by Clark and Moss, but Joakim Bonnier (Porsche) soon moved up into third place. On lap 14 both Moss and Bonnier overtook Ginther, who had his two Ferrari team-mates in his mirrors. The Ferraris of Phil Hill and Ginther overtook Bonnier, but for a while, made little impression on Moss. As the distance between Moss and his pursuers began to diminish, Wolfgang von Trips overtook Bonnier. Despite the presence of the Ferraris, Moss held his lead until the end, and was followed across the line by Ginther, Hill and von Trips. Hill retired on lap 12 due to a defective fuel pump, and Brooks was classified thirteenth, having stopped just before half distance after running into Bonnier's Porsche.

The Dutch Grand Prix: May 22, 1961
The three Ferraris of Phil Hill, Wolfgang von Trips and Richie Ginther filled the front row of the grid at Zandvoort. Graham Hill was fifth fastest in practice, with Tony Brooks in eighth place.

At first Hill ran third to von Trips and Phil Hill, until he was overtaken by Stirling Moss in Rob Walker's Lotus-Climax. He continued to slip back through the field, ultimately finishing in eighth place.

The race went to von Trips, followed by Phil Hill, Clark and Moss. Brooks was ninth in his Climax-engined BRM.

The Silver City Trophy, Brands Hatch: June 3, 1961
Stirling Moss was fastest in practice with a UDT Laystall Lotus 18/21. John Surtees (Cooper-Climax) was second, Jim Clark (Lotus-Climax) third, Graham Hill fourth and Tony Brooks fifth.

Hill retired because of a faulty magneto on the 57th lap, and the race was won by Moss, with Surtees second and Brooks third.

The Belgian Grand Prix: June 18, 1961
Ferrari's occupied the front row again with Phil Hill, Wolfgang von Trips and the Belgian Olivier

Gendebien, while Graham Hill and Tony Brooks were in the third row with Stirling Moss (Lotus-Climax).

Graham Hill leapt into an early lead, but was soon overtaken by the entire Ferrari team before retiring on lap 24 due to an oil leak. Tony Brooks finished 13th – six laps behind the four Ferraris.

The French Grand Prix: July 2, 1961

The Ferraris of Phil Hill, Wolfgang von Trips and Richie Ginther filled the front of the grid again at Rheims, while Stirling Moss was fourth and Jim Clark fifth. The BRMs of Graham Hill and Tony Brooks were sixth and 11th.

The Ferraris led from the start, as expected, while Giancarlo Baghetti, in a fourth Ferrari, climbed through the field from 12th place. Then the leading Ferraris faded one by one: von Trips and Ginther with blown engines and Phil Hill finishing ninth, two laps behind the winner. It was Baghetti who won the race from Gurney's Porsche and Clark's Lotus. Brooks retired his BRM on lap four due to overheating, while Graham Hill finished in sixth place.

The British Empire Trophy, Silverstone: July 8, 1961

Tony Brooks and Graham Hill came sixth and eighth in practice, and it was Stirling Moss who led the race in a Cooper, followed by John Surtees and Bruce McLaren, also in Coopers. Graham Hill's BRM was in fifth place.

After ten laps, Graham Hill was challenging McLaren for third, and Brooks was lying fifth. Then Brooks retired with a broken valve spring and Hill passed McLaren. The result was a win for Moss, followed by Surtees, Hill and McLaren. Moss also established the fastest lap of the race at 109.31mph.

The British Grand Prix: July 15, 1961

There were three cars on the front row at Aintree with identical times: Joakim Bonnier's Porsche,

and the Ferraris of Phil Hill and Richie Ginther. Tony Brooks was sixth fastest and Graham Hill 11th.

The BRMs failed to feature prominently in the race, which was dominated by the Ferraris, although Brooks established the fastest lap at 91.68mph. He finished ninth, two laps behind the Ferraris of Wolfgang von Trips, Phil Hill and Ginther. Graham Hill retired due to a broken valve spring on lap 44.

The German Grand Prix: August 6, 1961

Phil Hill's Ferrari was on pole position at the Nürburgring, followed by Jack Brabham (Cooper-Climax), Stirling Moss (Lotus-Climax) and Joakim Bonnier (Porsche). Graham Hill was sixth and Tony Brooks ninth.

Moss led the race from Phil Hill, Bonnier, Dan Gurney (Porsche) and Graham Hill in heavy rain. Then on lap two Hill's BRM-Climax touched Gurney's Porsche, and was out of the race. Stirling Moss went on to win, followed by the two Ferraris of von Trips and Phil Hill. Tony Brooks retired on lap seven when a detached valve head wrecked his engine.

The Guards Trophy, Brands Hatch: August 7, 1961

John Surtees led from the start of this Intercontinental formula race for 2½-litre cars with his Yeoman

Tony Brooks driving a BRM-Climax during the 1961 German Grand Prix.

Credit Cooper, followed by Stirling Moss, Graham Hill (Mark II P48 BRM) and Jack Brabham's Cooper-Climax. Hill dropped back, while Tony Brooks advanced to second place, before retiring due to a broken throttle linkage, and Jim Clark overtook Hill with his Lotus-Climax. The result was a win for Brabham, who was followed by Clark and Hill.

Shelsley Walsh: August 27, 1961
Tony Marsh entered his Mark II P48, with the support of three BRM mechanics and Wilkie Wilkinson, for the Shelsley Walsh August Meeting. He made the fastest time of the day and established a new course record of 34.41 seconds.

The Modena Grand Prix: September 3, 1961
In the absence of the works Ferraris, this was a race between the British teams and the German Porsches. Graham Hill and Tony Brooks were running in fourth and seventh for much of the race, until Hill suffered a puncture, caused by the debris from one of the other cars, and lost time having a new wheel fitted. Brooks and Hill finished the race in sixth and seventh, and the race was won by Stirling Moss in the UDT Laystall Lotus 18/21.

The Italian Grand Prix: September 10, 1961
Wolfgang von Trips' Ferrari was fastest in practice with the Ricardo Rodriguez' Ferrari sharing the front row. Only Graham Hill's BRM-Climax in fifth place prevented Ferraris from filling the first three rows exclusively! Tony Brooks was in 13th place. Hill also gave a prototype P57, powered by the new BRM V8 engine, a brief outing during practice to see how it drove, and was fifth fastest.

At the start of the race Hill, Jim Clark and Jack Brabham challenged the Ferraris for the lead. Tragically, Wolfgang von Trips' Ferrari and Clark's Lotus-Climax touched at the Parabolica. Von Trips was thrown out of his car and died, as did eleven spectators when the Ferrari literally flew off the course.

As a result of this sad race, Phil Hill won the World Championship for Ferrari. Brooks finished fifth, while Graham Hill retired on lap 11.

The Austrian Grand Prix: September 17, 1961
Tony Marsh had his own P48 BRM-Climax at Zeltweg for the Austrian Grand Prix, painted in a bright green with a white radiator cowl. He was seventh in practice, and ran in third position until his engine failed at lap 50 of 80.

The Oulton Park Gold Cup race: 23 September, 1961
The four-wheel drive front-engined Ferguson-Climax was the star at Oulton Park, finished in Rob Walker's colours and driven by Stirling Moss. Jim Clark led initially in his Lotus-Climax, but he was overtaken by Graham Hill's BRM-Climax on lap three. Then Moss, able to out-brake the other cars, came through to lead from lap six. Jack Brabham (Cooper-Climax) overtook Hill before the BRM's race was abruptly ended by a broken piston. Bruce McLaren was then promoted to third place and Tony Brooks brought the second works BRM home in fourth. Tony Marsh finished in seventh place with his P48 BRM-Climax.

The Lewis-Evans Trophy, Brands Hatch: October 1, 1961
Tony Marsh gained pole position for this 30 lap race in a BRM-Climax. He led throughout from Mike Spence (Emeryson-Climax) and Tim Parnell's Lotus 18.

The United States Grand Prix: October 8, 1961
Jack Brabham, his Cooper now powered by the long-awaited V8 Coventry-Climax engine, was fastest in practice at Watkins Glen, 1.1 seconds faster than Graham Hill's BRM-Climax. Then came Stirling Moss (Lotus-Climax), Bruce McLaren (Cooper-Climax), Jim Clark (Lotus-Climax), and Tony Brooks (BRM-Climax) – the Ferrari team was absent following the tragic death of Wolfgang von Trips.

Brabham leapt into the lead, but was immediately overtaken by Moss, followed by Innes Ireland (Lotus-Climax) and Graham Hill, with Tony Brooks in eighth place. On lap three Hill dropped to fifth, and Brabham was back in front on lap six, he and Moss drawing away from the rest. Then on laps 58 and 59 Brabham and Moss retired with engine trouble, and Ireland now led from Graham Hill, but the BRM driver was delayed on lap 74 because of magneto trouble. Roy Salvadori (Cooper-Climax) was gaining on Ireland when his engine blew on lap 97. The final result was a win for Innes Ireland's Lotus. Tony Brooks was third, and Graham Hill fifth. It was Tony Brooks' last World Championship race and BRM's best result in 1961.

1961 World Championship

Tony Brooks came tenth in the World Championship with six points, and Graham Hill thirteenth with three points. BRM came fifth in the Constructors' Championship with seven points. Alfred Owen demanded greater success in 1962, and warned that the survival of BRM depended upon it ...

Tony Brooks

Tony Brooks sent me a letter (below) in 2003. He believed that Graham Hill was given preference within the team, contrary to a verbal agreement.

> 12/6/03
>
> To Bryan
>
> I started and ended my F1 World Championship career with BRM (1956 & 1961). The first year nearly killed me and the last disillusioned me to the point of retiring from the sport!! They meant well.
>
> Very best wishes for a long and happy retirement.
>
> Tony Brooks

Tony Brooks' BRM memories after the last race in 1961, from the front cover of the author's copy of *The Saga of BRM Vol 1*.

2.4

The V8 BRM & the 1962 World Championship

The design of the new engine was completed in 1960. The team had opted for a V8, to provide, as Raymond Mays said, "... maximum potential for minimum bulk." Amherst Villiers joined BRM as a consultant at the beginning of 1961.

The new car, designated the P578, was lower, narrower and sleeker than its Coventry-Climax-engined predecessor. Its two vertical bars were merely to strengthen the air intake, and not to direct air to the fuel-injection system, as was originally the case with the P25.

Two of these new cars had been taken to Monza in 1961, where they were tested and found to be fast during practice for the Italian Grand Prix.

Nevertheless, Alfred Owen was of the opinion that, having spent £100,000 with nothing to show for it, BRM should be closed down. It was thanks to the pleading of Jean Stanley that he relented, but he insisted that the cars win at least two World Championship races in 1962. He made Tony Rudd the Chief Engineer at Bourne as well as Team Manager, while Peter Berthon became Chief Consultant at Rubery Owen. Tony Rudd later said that he never seriously considered the possibility that a BRM would win the World Championship in 1962 until it had actually been achieved!

The new fuel-injected V8 engine developed 190bhp at 10,500rpm. The vertical exhaust pipes were soon replaced, as they had a tendency to drop off. The car's main opposition would come from Jim Clark in the new Lotus 25 which had a revolutionary monocoque chassis in place of the multi-tubular space frame.

Richie Ginther replaced Tony Brooks, and on March 17 he tested the new car. Unfortunately, it caught fire and was completely destroyed. This loss represented a major setback for BRM, immediately before the beginning of the season ...

PHONE: BOURNE 327/328

OWEN RACING ORGANISATION
Spalding Road
BOURNE
LINCOLNSHIRE

The Rev.B.G.Apps,
13 Parkville Road,
Swaythling,
Southampton.

26th February, 1962

Dear Bryan,

      I was so very pleased to hear of you again, and to know that you still keep your interest in the B.R.M. Your letter did not reach me until today, so I sent the telegram, which I hope arrived in time for you to read it out at the meeting.

      The new V-8 B.R.M. promises well, and the engine gives great hopes for a good showing this year. We expect to run two cars, with Graham Hill and Richie Ginther as our team drivers. We shall probably appear at Snetterton on 14th April, and Goodwood at Easter, before the full Grand Prix season starts on May 20th at Zandvoort.

      My very kind regards to you, and best wishes for encouraging results in the work you are undertaking in Southampton.

      Yours sincerely,

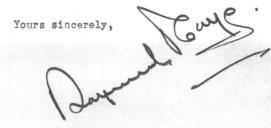

Raymond Mays
Director of Racing.

Raymond Mays letter of February 26 ,1962 containing encouraging news of the new V8 BRM.

The Brussels Grand Prix: April 1, 1962

Only one works BRM was available for the Brussels Grand Prix, and it was driven by Graham Hill. Tony Marsh drove his own car – a 1961 P57 with a new BRM V8 engine. Jim Clark and Stirling Moss had V8 Coventry-Climax engines in their Lotus cars and at the end of practice the order was Clark, Moss, Hill, Marsh and Willy Mairesse (V6 Ferrari).

Moss led at the start of heat one, but took to the escape road when his brakes locked up. Then it was Hill who led in the new BRM, followed by Marsh. Mairesse overtook Marsh on lap four and Moss came up through the field to take second place on lap 15. The result was a win for Hill who was followed by Moss, Mairesse and Marsh.

Both BRMs stalled at the start of the second heat, and both were disqualified for being push-started.

The Lombard Trophy, Snetterton: April 14, 1962

Stirling Moss was fastest in practice in his UDT Laystall V8 Lotus-Climax, Graham Hill was second in his P578 BRM, and Jim Clark third in the works Lotus-V8 Climax.

Hill went straight into the lead, followed by Moss and Clark, but Moss overtook Hill on lap six. On lap 16 Clark also passed Hill and two laps later also passed Moss to lead the race. Moss was pitted with throttle linkage problems, letting Hill up to second place, but the BRM's engine began to sound less crisp – one of the plugs had oiled up and the engine

Graham Hill with Tony Rudd at Goodwood.

was running only on seven cylinders. Clark held his lead to the end of the race followed by Hill and Joakim Bonnier's 4-cylinder Porsche.

Graham Hill winning the new V8 BRM's first race at Goodwood on Easter Monday.

The Goodwood 100: April 23, 1962

Graham Hill led the race from lap three to win at 102.65mph from Bruce McLaren's Cooper-Climax and Innes Ireland's Lotus. Richie Ginther had difficulty getting his BRM off the line at the start, but the whole race was clouded by Stirling Moss' crash in the Rob Walker V8 Lotus-Climax, which was on-loan to UDT Laystall. Moss had stopped at his pit to have gear selector problems sorted, costing him three laps before he set off at great speed in a race that was already lost. At St Marys he was approaching Hill's BRM when, unaccountably, his car left the circuit at high speed. Seriously injured, the accident brought his professional career to an end, but mercifully he eventually made an excellent recovery. I missed the race, which Graham Hill went on to win, as my wedding took place the same day in St Peter's Church, Carmarthen. Kath and I woke to the sad news of the crash the next day.

The Pau Grand Prix: April 23, 1962

Jack Lewis and Anthony Marsh privately-entered two 1961 P57 BRMs for this race. Jim Clark was fastest in practice in his V8 Lotus-Climax, Lewis seventh and Marsh eighth on the grid.

Maurice Trintignant led for most of the race in a Lotus-Climax, and Bonnier's Porsche held second place until it was beset with gearbox troubles. It was Ricardo Rodriguez (Ferrari) who followed Trintignant's Lotus across the finishing line, and the two BRMs of Lewis and Marsh were third and fourth.

The Aintree 200: April 28, 1962

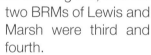

The front row of the starting grid consisted of Jim Clark (V8 Lotus-Climax), Graham Hill (V8 BRM), and John Surtees (V8 Lola-Climax). Richie Ginther came from behind to lead at the start, followed by

Jim Clark.

Hill, Clark and Bruce McLaren (4-cylinder Cooper-Climax). On lap two Clark displaced the two BRMs, and when Ginther retired due to a broken gearbox, Surtees inherited third place. Graham Hill retired on lap 44 due to a blown engine, and the result was an emphatic win for Clark.

The International Trophy: Silverstone, May 12, 1962

The BRMs of Graham Hill and Richie Ginther were first and fourth on the starting grid, separated by Jim Clark's Lotus-Climax and John Surtees, Lola-Climax. The privately-entered BRMs of Jack Lewis and Anthony Marsh were fifth and 11th. Innes Ireland drove a Ferrari, painted red with a green stripe, in recognition of the agreement that Stirling Moss would have driven a Ferrari throughout the season, had it not been for his accident.

It was Clark who led from Ginther and Ireland on lap one, but Hill was soon in second place. Ginther crashed heavily at Club Corner on lap three without injury, and Hill began to slow as he lost his vertical exhaust pipes. Surtees took up the chase from Ireland ahead of Hill, but the BRM began to pick up speed once more, and Hill overtook first Ireland, and then Surtees. In the end, Clark won the race by inches from Hill. Anthony Marsh was seventh and Jack Lewis ninth.

The Dutch Grand Prix: May 10, 1962

"BRM BEATS HOODOO AT LAST"

The result of the Dutch Grand Prix demonstrated that BRM could still make the headlines! In this first round of the World Championship series, Jim Clark set the fastest time in practice, Graham Hill (BRM) came second, John Surtees (Lola-Climax) third, and Richie Ginther seventh. The Ferraris of Phil Hill and Giancarlo Baghetti were tenth and 12th.

The order after the start of the race was Clark, Hill, Dan Gurney (Porsche). Hill led on lap nine after Clark

Overleaf: Front page headlines in the *Daily Sketch* from the scrapbook.

DAILY SKETCH

BRM BEATS HOODOO AT LAST

GRAHAM HILL WINS IN B.R.M.

DUTCH
GRAND
PRIX

1ST

Roaring to victory . . . Graham Hill in the B.R.M. yesterday

stopped with clutch trouble, and Bruce McLaren (Cooper-Climax) lay second when Gurney retired, minus his gearlever. Surtees crashed on the same lap when his front suspension collapsed, McLaren was out on lap 22. Graham Hill now led from Phil Hill by 25 seconds.

Trevor Taylor overhauled the Ferrari to finish in second place behind Graham Hill, who won the race at an average speed of 95.439mph. Ginther had retired on lap 72 when his car touched Taylor's then second-place Lotus while being lapped. Clark finished in ninth place.

This was only the second World Championship win for BRM, the first being at Zandvoort in 1959. In the closing stages of the race, the BRM's lead was such that Graham Hill had been given the 'slow down' signal, but Raymond Mays, in intense anxiety, crept away to a corner of the pits to avoid company regardless. Afterwards, he was delighted to receive the congratulations of everyone in the pit lane.

All eyes on Graham Hill's V8 BRM at Zandvoort.

The winning BRM amidst the woods at Zandvoort.

The Monaco Grand Prix: June 3, 1962

Graham Hill was second in practice to Jim Clark's Lotus-Climax, and Richie Ginther was back in 13th place.

During the race, Willy Mairesse shot ahead of the pack in his Ferrari, but spun at the hairpin. A multiple pile-up ensued when Ginther's throttle jammed. He crashed into Maurice Trintignant's Lotus-Climax, and a wheel from Ginther's BRM flew off, tragically killing a photographer.

The order after the crash was McLaren, Graham Hill, Phil Hill (Ferrari) and Joakim Bonnier (Porsche). On lap seven Graham Hill took the lead, followed by McLaren's Cooper. Jim Clark's Lotus-Climax moved up to third place on lap 22 and had closed on Graham Hill by lap 45. However, on lap 56, Clark fell back due to clutch trouble and retired, and the BRM proceeded to build up a substantial lead until, on lap 93 of 100, its engine broke.

McLaren (Cooper-Climax) won at 70.461mph, and Graham Hill was classified sixth, gaining a point that would be valuable to him as the season progressed.

Graham Hill at Monaco in the P578 BRM.

The Belgian Grand Prix: June 17, 1962

Graham Hill was fastest in practice at Spa, with Bruce McLaren (Cooper-Climax) and Trevor Taylor (Lotus-Climax) completing the front row of the grid. Richie Ginther was in the fourth row in ninth place, and Jim Clark was 12th, after experiencing engine problems in practice.

Hill's BRM led at the start from Taylor, McLaren, Clark and Mairesse (Ferrari), until Clark finally overtook Hill and proceeded to pull away. Richie Ginther retired on lap 23 due to transmission trouble, and Taylor and Mairesse collided while competing for second place. The Ferrari overturned in flames, and Taylor hit a telegraph pole which split and descended upon his car. Taylor escaped with bruises, but Mairesse was more seriously injured. Clark (Lotus-Climax) won the race at 131.895mph from Graham Hill, the BRM having been slowed by a problem with its fuel feed.

The Rheims Grand Prix: July 1, 1962

Jim Clark's Lotus was on pole position at Rheims, with Graham Hill's BRM and John Surtees' Lola also sharing the front row of the grid. Richie Ginther's BRM was in ninth place.

Surtees surged ahead at the start, followed by Bruce McLaren (Cooper), Clark (Lotus), Jack Brabham (Cooper), and Hill, with Ginther's BRM in eighth position. Clark was up to second place on lap two, but stopped three laps later due to a split water tank. He overtook Peter Arundell's Lotus to resume the chase after a visit to the pit. Hill overtook McLaren so that he only had Brabham and a distant Surtees in front of him. Then the Lola slowed and relinquished its substantial lead with a loss of power, and retired. Ginther retired due to gearbox trouble, and the race was ultimately won by McLaren (Cooper-Climax) from Graham Hill's BRM.

The French Grand Prix: July 8, 1962

The BRMs of Graham Hill and Richie Ginther were second and tenth in practice, and Hill had Jim Clark's Lotus and Bruce McLaren's Cooper on either side.

Graham Hill winning the 1962 German Grand Prix.

Hill led from the fall of the flag, while Ginther's BRM failed to start because of a loose plug lead. At 30 laps the leading BRM was 22 seconds in front of Clark's Lotus, but spun when rammed by the Cooper of Jack Lewis. This allowed Clark to take the lead, but the Scotsman had problems with his front suspension and retired on lap 34. Graham Hill led again, now from Dan Gurney's Porsche, but a problem with his fuel-injection seriously reduced his pace, and he only finished in ninth place, ten laps behind Gurney, who won at 103.225mph. After his delayed start, Richie Ginther came third.

The British Grand Prix: July 21, 1962

It was Jim Clark's race at Silverstone. He was fastest in practice, with Surtees in a Lola-Climax second, Innes Ireland's Lotus-Climax third, Graham Hill's BRM fourth and Richie Ginther eighth.

Clark led away followed by Surtees, Dan Gurney (Porsche), Bruce McLaren (Cooper-Climax), Jack Brabham (Cooper-Climax) and Hill. Gurney dropped back two laps behind the leader with clutch trouble and Graham Hill improved his position to claim fourth place. Clark won at 92.25mph from Surtees,

McLaren, Hill and Brabham, with Ginther finishing in 13th place – five laps behind Clark.

The German Grand Prix: August 5, 1962 – A fine win by Graham Hill

Dan Gurney was on pole position at the Nürburgring in his Porsche with Graham Hill's BRM, Jim Clark's Lotus and John Surtees Lola alongside him. Richie Ginther was seventh in practice and found himself on the second row. Graham Hill had a narrow escape during practice, when a camera fell off de Beaufort's Porsche into his path, causing oil to spill and the BRM to spin off the circuit at high speed.

The start of the race was delayed through heavy rain, and Clark's Lotus failed to get away when the flag finally fell. Gurney led narrowly from Graham Hill, who was followed first by Phil Hill, and then by Surtees. On the third lap the BRM took the lead with Gurney and Surtees close behind. They remained in touch throughout the race, Graham Hill winning at 80.351mph, with Surtees and Gurney second and third. Clark recovered to finish in fourth place. Ginther was eighth.

Motoring News said that this was one of Graham Hill's finest races and commented: "That

BRM have won on the really gruelling Nürburgring demonstrates to a once scoffing Continent that the Bourne firm have really emerged from their 'bad days.'"

The Oulton Park Gold Cup Race: September 1, 1962

The front row of the grid consisted of Richie Ginther (BRM), Jim Clark (Lotus-Climax), Graham Hill (BRM) and Bruce McLaren (Cooper-Climax). The South African Bruce Johnstone drove a third works BRM. Clark led from start to finish, followed initially by Hill and Ginther. Then Ginther retired due to engine trouble, and at the end only Hill could remain on the same lap as Clark. Johnson finished in fourth place.

The Italian Grand Prix: September 16, 1962 – a win for BRM at Monza

Jim Clark was fastest in practice at Monza in his Lotus-Climax, with Graham Hill and Richie Ginther second and third in their BRMs.

Clark led at the fall of the flag but was overtaken by Graham Hill on the first lap. Clark was then delayed with a pit stop, and later retired on lap 13 with transmission trouble. As the leading BRM drew away from the flock, Ginther challenged John Surtees (Lola-Climax) for second place. Surtees was out on lap 43 because of engine trouble and the two BRMs were unchallenged to the end, Hill winning at 123.616mph, the fastest lap being set by him at 125.732mph.

It was a field-day for BRM, and Raymond Mays said that he could now live with the memory of Monza in 1951. He added that there was just enough fuel left in the winning car to fill a cigarette lighter!

The United States Grand Prix: October 7, 1962

Jim Clark's Lotus was again fastest in practice at Watkins Glen with the BRMs of Richie Ginther and Graham Hill second and third.

It was Clark who led at the start of the race, followed closely by Hill and Ginther, who was challenged in turn by Gurney's Porsche. Hill took the lead on lap 12, but seven laps later lost it to Clark, who then held it to the end of the race. Ginther retired because of engine trouble on lap 35. Clark won the race at 108.476mph and recorded the fastest lap at 110.4mph.

Graham Hill winning the 1962 at Monza.

The South African Grand Prix: December 29, 1962

The kind of headline I had craved for my scrapbooks since 1950!

GRAHAM JOINS THE WORLD CHAMPIONS

In East London the last World Championship race of the year would decide the new World Champion. Jim Clark gained the advantage, being fastest in practice in his Lotus 25, but Graham Hill was just 0.3 seconds slower. Richie Ginther was back in seventh place.

Clark gained a narrow lead from Hill at the start as the BRM was slowed by wheel spin, and the Lotus-Climax maintained its position to the end of the first lap before steadily drawing away from the BRM, setting the fastest lap of the race on lap three. Then, when the Lotus driver seemed to have the race and the World Championship in his pocket, he drew into his pit on lap 62 of 82 due to falling oil pressure and had to retire. It was discovered that a bolt had dropped out of his crankcase.

Hill's Championship was now secure, whatever the result of the race, but he continued to lead until the end when he was 50 seconds ahead of McLaren's Cooper-Climax. Ginther finished seventh, four laps behind.

1962 World Championship

Graham Hill won the Drivers' championship with 42 points against Jim Clark's 30. Richie Ginther was eighth with ten points. The Constructors' Championship was won by BRM with 42 points as against the 36 points of Lotus-Climax.

Graham Hill

World Champion Graham Hill with plenty to smile about!

Motor Sport

In its issue of February 1963 the Editor of *Motor Sport* wrote: "We congratulate Graham Hill on clinching the 1962 Drivers' World Championship, and BRM on winning the Manufacturers' Championship. It is splendid that Sir Alfred Owen's faith in the BRM has at last been justified, after former failures and vicissitudes, especially as this all-British car has its own engine, not a proprietary unit, which is in the true tradition of Grand Prix motor racing down the years."

He went on to congratulate "Chief Engineer Tony Rudd and all the BRM mechanics – not forgetting Raymond Mays, who kindled the first sparks of enthusiasm for a British Racing Motor."

Two winners from the Rubery Owen stable.

PART THREE

British Racing Motors 1963-1976

3.1

From 'Old Faithful' to the H16

The CSI ruled that the 1½-litre Formula would continue until 1966, and Tony Rudd introduced the P61: a slimmer, lighter version of the P578, which would eventually replace it. The P61 had a 6-speed gearbox, a monocoque centre section with space frames front and back, and its V8 engine had single-plane crankshafts, coupled exhausts, cast iron oil pumps and integral oil filters.

Lotus, Cooper and Lola had improved versions of the V8 Coventry-Climax engine with fuel-injection.

The Monaco Grand Prix: May 26, 1963 – BRMs first and second

Graham Hill drove the 1963 P578, and was second to Jim Clark's Lotus-Climax in practice, while Richie Ginther shared the second row with John Surtees' Ferrari.

Monaco would become 'Graham Hill's circuit,' and both BRMs led Clark after the start. Clark overtook Hill on lap 19, and Surtees also displaced him at about half distance. Hill, with his engine recovering its crispness, re-passed Surtees and gained on Clark, while Ginther also passed Surtees. It was Clark's turn to have his engine go off-tune, before his gearbox failed on lap 78, at which point he retired. The BRMs of Hill and Ginther reeled off the remaining 58 laps to take the first two places, while Bruce McLaren

Richie Ginther's 1963 P578 at Monaco.

The first of many: Graham Hill winning the 1963 Monaco Grand Prix.

(Cooper-Climax) and Surtees took third and fourth.

The Belgian Grand Prix: June 9, 1963

Graham Hill was fastest in practice at Spa, and he had Dan Gurney's Brabham-Climax and Willie Mairesse's Ferrari alongside him on the grid, while Richie Ginther was fourth. Both BRM drivers had experienced problems with the cars' 6-speed gearboxes during practice.

Jim Clark led from the start in his Lotus after coming up from the third row, followed by Hill. The two drew away from the field with the interval between them and the other drivers increasing, until Hill's gearbox failed on lap 18. Clark went on to win; Ginther was fourth.

The Dutch Grand Prix: June 23, 1963

The new P61 BRM appeared in practice at Zandvoort but Graham Hill, who found it to be unstable on the straights, elected to drive the earlier

Richie Ginther leading Dan Gurney's Brabham during the 1963 Dutch Grand Prix.

P578, and took second place in practice to Jim Clark's Lotus.

With Clark out in front, Hill was passed briefly by Jack Brabham (Brabham-Climax) on lap five. Clark continued to extend his lead while Hill, after charging through the field to recover his position after a pit stop, was forced to retire due to a seized engine on lap 70. Clark won the race, and Ginther finished fifth behind Innes Ireland's BRP-BRM.

The French Grand Prix: June 30, 1963

Driving the P61, Graham Hill was second to Jim Clark in practice at Rheims, with Richie Ginther back in 12th place in a P578. Lorenzo Bandini was last of all with the Centro-Sud BRM, which, being Graham Hill's championship-winning car, had become known as 'Old Faithful,' and was now painted red. Nine of the cars on the grid had BRM engines!

Hill was given a one-minute penalty for being push-started, and Clark led from Ginther, who was disputing second place with several cars until he retired on lap five when a stone punctured his radiator. Clark retained his lead to the end. Hill finished in third place but the CSI disallowed his four points because of his assisted start. Bandini finished tenth, eight laps behind Clark.

The British Grand Prix: July 20, 1963

Back in a P578, Graham Hill was third fastest to Jim Clark's Lotus-Climax and Dan Gurney's Brabham-Climax. Richie Ginther was on the third row of the grid.

The Brabhams of Gurney and Jack Brabham led initially, but Clark soon took control of the race. Brabham retired due to engine trouble on lap 28 and Gurney on lap 60. After this, Hill and Surtees competed for second place until Hill, having firmly secured an advantage, ran out of fuel on the last lap. Surtees snatched second place as he coasted towards the line. Ginther was fourth.

The German Grand Prix: August 4, 1963

The Centro-Sud BRM of Lorenzo Bandini and the works P578 of Graham Hill were third and fourth in practice at the Nürburgring, sharing the front row of the grid with Jim Clark's Lotus-Climax and John Surtees' Ferrari. Richie Ginther was in sixth place.

Surtees took the lead from Clark, whose engine was down on power, and Bandini crashed on lap one. Hill retired on lap three because of gearbox trouble and Surtees won the race from Clark – with Ginther finishing third.

The Italian Grand Prix: September 8, 1963

The order after practice at Monza was John Surtees (Ferrari), Graham Hill (BRM), Jim Clark (Lotus-Climax) and Richie Ginther (BRM), but Hill led at the start of the race, followed by Surtees and Clark. Hill dropped back with clutch trouble, stopping at the pit on lap 50. Ginther eventually finished second to Clark; Hill was classified 16th after eventually retiring on lap 59.

The United States Grand Prix: October 6, 1963 – another clean sweep

Graham Hill's BRM was fastest in practice at Watkins Glen, followed by Jim Clark (Lotus-Climax), John Surtees (Ferrari) and Richie Ginther (BRM).

Graham Hill on his way to third place in the 1963 British Grand Prix.

Richie Ginther's BRM being passed by Ireland's BRP BRM and Bandini's Ferrari at Monza

Graham Hill's BRM during the 1963 South African Grand Prix.

Clark was left on the line because of a flat battery, and the two BRMs led the race, until Surtees squeezed past them both.

After having led for most of the race, Surtees retired on lap 83 due to a broken engine, and, despite Hill's anti-roll bar giving way, he managed to claim first. Ginther came home second, followed by Clark and Jack Brabham (Brabham-Climax).

The Mexican Grand Prix: October 27, 1963

Jim Clark (Lotus-Climax) and John Surtees (Ferrari) monopolised the front row in Mexico City, and Graham Hill and Richie Ginther came third and fifth in practice.

It was Clark's race throughout, while Hill lost time selecting a gear at the start. Dan Gurney (Brabham-Climax) followed Clark until he was slowed by fuel starvation, and the finishing order was Clark, Jack Brabham, Ginther and Hill.

The South African Grand Prix: December 28, 1963

Jim Clark was again fastest in East London, and he had the Brabhams of Jack Brabham and Dan Gurney with him at the front of the grid. Graham Hill and Richie Ginther were back on the third row with Trevor Taylor's Lotus-Climax.

Clark won the race followed by Gurney, and Hill came third after John Surtees' Ferrari pulled out

with engine trouble. Ginther retired on lap 44 due to a broken driveshaft.

1963 World Championship

Jim Clark won the Drivers' World Championship with 55 points. Graham Hill came second with 29, and Richie Ginther third with 22. The Constructors' Championship was won by Lotus-Climax with 44 points and BRM came second with 36.

The Rover BRM in 1963

A Rover BRM gas turbine car appeared at Le Mans in 1963 based on the Formula 1 car that Richie Ginther crashed at Monaco in 1962. Driven by Graham Hill and Richie Ginther, the object was to become the first gas turbine car to cover 2237 miles at an average speed of 93mph. Bearing the number 00, it was the last car to be flagged off and, in the course of the 24 hours, it completed 2582 miles at an average speed of 107.84mph and was timed at 140mph on the Mulsanne Straight.

1964

The P261

In 1964 the BRM P61 was replaced by the P261, which had a central monocoque attached to full-

The Rover-BRM silently reeling off the laps at Le Mans.

length stressed skins. In addition, the four-wheel drive P67, developed by Mike Pilbeam, made a number of appearances but wasn't raced.

The Monaco Grand Prix: May 10, 1964 – a BRM one-two

The front row of the grid consisted of Jim Clark's Lotus-Climax and Jack Brabham's Brabham-Climax. The P261 BRMs of Graham Hill and Richie Ginther were third and eighth.

Clark led from Brabham and Hill, with Ginther in sixth place. Gurney overtook Hill on lap 12, and then Clark lost his position when he pitted with a trailing anti-roll bar. Gurney then led from Hill, until the BRM overtook him – establishing a new lap record on lap 53 of 74.922mph. At the end it was Hill first, Ginther second, and Peter Arundell (Lotus-Climax) third.

Graham Hill winning the 1964 Monaco Grand Prix.

Palais de Monaco

March 10th, 1986

Dear Reverend

      I should like to thank you
personally for your kind letter of March 4th, and
for the enclosed painting you performed of the late
Graham Hill winning the Monaco Grand Prix in 1964.

      I am deeply touched by your
thoughtful gesture especially since Mr. Graham Hill
was a man for whom I have always held a great deal
of admiration for his courage and determination.

      Enclosed please find a 1986
Grand Prix poster numbered 00010 and two stickers of
the 44th Monaco Grand Prix.

      With all best wishes,

The Revd. Bryan G. Apps, M.A., B.A.,
All Saints' Vicarage
14 Stourwood Road
Southbourne
Bournemouth BH6 3QP
England

Prince Rainier's letter.

The Dutch Grand Prix: May 24, 1964

Dan Gurney (Brabham-Climax), Jim Clark (Lotus-Climax) and Graham Hill (BRM) shared the front row of the grid and Clark led away from the BRM at the start of the race. John Surtees (Ferrari) passed Hill on lap 22 and Hill was also overtaken by Peter Arundell's Lotus-Climax on lap 47, slowed due to a defective fuel pump. The order at the end remained Clark, Surtees, Arundell and Hill, with Ginther in 11th place.

The Belgian Grand Prix: June 14, 1964

Graham Hill was second fastest in practice for the Belgian Grand Prix with Dan Gurney's Brabham-Climax on pole. Richie Ginther was on the third row.

Peter Arundell (Lotus-Climax) led initially, but on lap two the order was Gurney, John Surtees (Ferrari), Clark (Lotus-Climax) and Hill. Surtees dropped out due to engine trouble on lap four, and Bruce McLaren's Cooper overtook Hill's BRM. In the later stages of the race, Hill moved up to second place behind Gurney and in front of Clark. Then, when the Brabham stopped for fuel, it was the BRM's turn to lead until Hill was forced to stop with an empty tank on the penultimate lap. Clark won the race from McLaren and Brabham. Ginther came fourth, and Hill was classified as fifth.

The French Grand Prix: June 28, 1964

On the front row of the starting grid at Rouen were Jim Clark's Lotus-Climax, Dan Gurney's Brabham-

Graham Hill at Zandvoort before he was slowed due to fuel pump problems.

Graham Hill on his way to second place in the Belgian Grand Prix.

Graham Hill holding on to Jim Clark during the British Grand Prix.

Climax and John Surtees' Ferrari. Unusually, Graham Hill was back on the third row and Richie Ginther on the fourth.

Clark led from Gurney and Surtees at the start, and Hill spun on lap three. Surtees retired on lap seven and Clark on lap 32, both with engine trouble, and in the end it was Gurney who won, followed by Hill (who had steadily moved up the field) and Jack Brabham (Brabham-Climax). Ginther finished in fifth place.

The British Grand Prix: July 11, 1964

At the front of the grid, Graham Hill's BRM was sandwiched between Jim Clark's Lotus-Climax and Dan Gurney's Brabham-Climax, with Richie Ginther only 14th fastest in practice. The four-wheel drive P67 appeared at the practice session for testing, but wasn't raced.

Clark led from Gurney and Hill at the start, but after passing Gurney, Hill remained hard on the heels of the Lotus for the 40 remaining laps. Clark won by less than three seconds from Hill. John Surtees (Ferrari) was third and Ginther eighth. Giancarlo Baghetti finished twelfth in 'Old Faithful,' and Anthony Maggs retired on lap 38 due to gearbox trouble in a fourth BRM.

The German Grand Prix: 2 August 1964

John Surtees' Ferrari was fastest in practice with the BRMs of Graham Hill and Richie Ginther fifth and 11th. Ronnie Bucknum was last on the grid in the new Honda. Sadly, during practice, Carel Godin de Beaufort crashed his Porsche, and died the next day from his injuries.

Jim Clark's Lotus led from the start, ahead of Dan Gurney (Brabham), Surtees and Hill. However, Clark slowed to retire on lap eight due to engine trouble and, after Gurney also dropped back, Surtees finally won from Hill. Behind them Lorenzo Bandini (Ferrari) finished third, and the three BRMs of Maurice Trintignant (with 'Old Faithful' now finished in blue), Anthony Maggs and Richie Ginther filled the next three places.

The Austrian Grand Prix: August 23, 1964

Graham Hill's BRM was fastest in practice at the Österreich and Richie Ginther's car was fifth.

Jim Clark (Lotus-Climax) made a poor start when he had difficulty finding a gear, and Hill was also slow to get away. Dan Gurney (Brabham-Climax) led, followed by the Ferraris of John Surtees and Lorenzo Bandini, and Ginther's BRM. Hill retired on lap five due to mechanical problems. Surtees retired because of a broken suspension on lap nine, and the order became Gurney, Bandini and Clark. Clark passed Bandini and set about catching Gurney's Brabham until retiring due to a broken driveshaft. Bandini's Ferrari then led Ginther's BRM across the line. Bonnier's Brabham-Climax slowed with a failing engine, so that it was Robert Anderson who finished in third place in his Brabham-Climax.

The Italian Grand Prix: September 6, 1964
John Surtees' Ferrari was fastest in practice, and he shared the front row of the starting grid with Dan Gurney's Brabham and Graham Hill's BRM. Richie Ginther was on the third row with the Ronnie Bucknum's Honda.

Hill was left at the start because of a failed clutch, and Bruce McLaren's Cooper-Climax led until overtaken by Gurney, Surtees and Clark. Surtees then took the lead and the four cars drew away from the rest of the field. Clark retired because of a broken piston on lap 28, and the result was another Ferrari victory for Surtees, with McLaren second, Lorenzo Bandini (Ferrari) third, and Richie Ginther fourth.

The United States Grand Prix: October 4, 1964 – Another win for Graham Hill
Jim Clark (Lotus) and Surtees (Ferrari) were on the front row of the grid at Watkins Glen. Graham Hill was fourth, and Richie Ginther 13th.

Mike Spence (Lotus-Climax) made a magnificent start from the third row to run in second place behind Surtees. Hill passed Spence, but was overtaken in turn by Clark, who went on to overtake Surtees as well. On lap 40 Clark slowed due to fuel starvation, and was passed by Surtees, Hill and Dan Gurney (Brabham). However, it was Hill who battled through to take the lead, which he held by an increasing margin to the end. He was followed across the line by Surtees, Jo Siffert (Brabham-BRM), and Ginther in the second BRM.

The Mexican Grand Prix: 25 October 1964
The front row consisted of Jim Clark (Lotus) and Dan Gurney (Brabham), while Graham Hill and Richie Ginther were sixth and 11th.

Clark led the race while Hill lost time at the start when the strap of his goggles broke. The order on the second lap was Clark, Gurney and Lorenzo Bandini (Ferrari), with the BRMs of Ginther and Hill only ninth and tenth. Hill drove heroically to catch

up to third place, ahead of Surtees' Ferrari. If he had kept this position until the end of the race the World Championship would have gone to Hill, but Bandini's Ferrari nudged the BRM on entry to the hairpin bend, resulting in Hill having to stop twice at the pits. Clark's engine seized on the penultimate lap, so Gurney won the race, followed by the Ferraris of Surtees and Bandini. Ginther was eighth, and Hill only 11th.

1964 World Championship
John Surtees won the World Championship with 40 points, becoming the first person to be World Champion on both two wheels and four. Graham Hill was second with 39, Jim Clark third with 32, and Richie Ginther and Lorenzo Bandini shared fourth place with 23 points.

Ferrari won the Constructors' Championship with 45 points while BRM came second with 42.

1965 and another year with the P261s.
At the end of 1964, Raymond Mays invited Jackie Stewart to join Graham Hill at BRM in 1965. It was to be the last year for the 1½-litre P261 BRMs, and the cars were largely unchanged as Bourne focused on preparations for the 3-litre Formula.

Coventry-Climax produced a 32-valve V8 engine, while Ferrari used a flat-12 engine in addition to its V8.

The South African Grand Prix: January 1, 1965
Jim Clark was fastest in practice with his Lotus-Climax 33, John Surtees (Ferrari) was second, and Jack Brabham (Brabham) third. Graham Hill was fifth alongside Mike Spence (Lotus-Climax), and Jackie Stewart was 11th in his first World Championship race.

Clark led, followed by Spence, until lap 43, when Spence spun and was overtaken by Surtees and Hill. They finished in that order behind Clark, with Jackie Stewart in sixth place, thus picking up his first World Championship point.

The Monaco Grand Prix: May 30, 1965 – Graham Hill and BRM yet again
Graham Hill's BRM was fastest in practice with Jack Brabham's Brabham next to him on the front

row. Jackie Stewart was third alongside Lorenzo Bandini's Ferrari.

The two BRMs led the race, followed by Bandini, John Surtees (Ferrari) and Brabham. Hill lost half a minute avoiding the crippled Brabham-Climax of Anderson, but eventually regained his lead, breaking the lap record in the process at 76.719mph. The Monaco Grand Prix went again to Hill, with Bandini coming second and Stewart, who had periodically taken the lead from Hill before spinning, finished in third.

The Belgian Grand Prix: June 13, 1965
The BRMs of Graham Hill and Jackie Stewart were both on the front row of the grid at Spa, sandwiching

Jim Clark's Lotus. Clark overtook Hill to take the lead on lap one, and Stewart took second place from Hill, driving with quite exceptional skill in very heavy rain. Clark won the race with only Stewart remaining on the same lap, 15 seconds behind him. Hill was fifth.

The French Grand Prix: June 27, 1965
Jackie Stewart was second to Jim Clark (Lotus-Climax) in practice at Clermont-Ferrand with Lorenzo Bandini (Ferrari) third. Graham Hill was back in 11th place after crashing at speed when his throttle stuck open.

Stewart's throttle was troublesome again at the start of the race, and it was Clark who led from Bandini. Regardless, Stewart moved up behind Clark, and this was how they finished, with Hill in fifth place.

The British Grand Prix: July 10, 1965
Graham Hill and Jackie Stewart were second and fourth in practice with Jim Clark's Lotus on pole position and Richie Ginther (Honda) third.

The Honda led briefly from Clark but was soon overtaken by Clark, Hill and John Surtees (Ferrari). There followed a race-long duel between Clark and Hill, both far ahead of the rest, and the finishing order was Clark, Hill, Surtees, Spence (Lotus-Climax) and Stewart.

The Dutch Grand Prix: July 18, 1965
Graham Hill made the fastest time in practice at Zandvoort, followed by Jim Clark's Lotus and Richie Ginther's Honda. Jackie Stewart was sixth.

Once again, Ginther's Honda took the lead, but he had to give way to Hill and Clark. By the end of the first lap the leaders were being followed by Dan Gurney (Brabham-Climax) and Stewart. Hill dropped back, while Stewart advanced to second place. Clark won from Stewart with Gurney third and Hill fourth. Ginther's Honda finished sixth.

Graham Hill preparing to overtake the Ferraris of Lorenzo Bandini and John Surtees to win the 1965 Monaco Grand Prix.

Jim Clark and Graham Hill during the 1965 British Grand Prix at Silverstone.

The brilliant Jackie Stewart.

The German Grand Prix: August 1, 1965

The BRMs of Jackie Stewart and Graham Hill were second and third on the grid at the Nürburgring, with Jim Clark (Lotus-Climax) and John Surtees (Ferrari) on either side of them.

The order on lap one was Clark, Hill, Stewart and Dan Gurney (Brabham-Climax). Stewart retired after damaging his suspension on lap three, and the race went to Clark – with Hill finishing 16 seconds behind him. Gurney was third, and Jochen Rindt came fourth in a Cooper-Climax.

The Italian Grand Prix: September 12, 1965 – Jackie Stewart's first Grand Prix win

The 1965 Italian Grand Prix was a memorable one for BRM. In practice, Jackie Stewart was third and Graham Hill fourth, while Jim Clark's Lotus and John Surtees' Ferrari were first and second. The privately-entered BRMs of Roberto Bussinello, Giorgio Bassi and Masten Gregory filled the very last row of the starting grid.

Clark was first away, followed by Stewart, Hill and Lorenzo Bandini (Ferrari). The Lotus and the BRMs took turns to lead at high speed, with Stewart seeming to have a marginal advantage over the other two. Clark stopped due to a faulty fuel pump on lap 63, enabling Stewart and Hill to complete the

race unchallenged, in that order. Gurney (Brabham) was third, and Bandini fourth.

The United States Grand Prix: October 3, 1965 – a further win for Hill

Graham Hill's BRM was fastest in practice at Watkins Glen, Clark second with the new 32-valve Coventry Climax engine, and Jackie Stewart sixth in the second car from Bourne.

It was Hill who led from Clark and Stewart at first, but Clark took the lead on lap two. Hill recovered the position three laps later, and Stewart pitted due to a broken throttle cable. Clark retired after engine trouble on lap 12, and Hill enjoyed a comfortable cushion between himself and Dan Gurney (Brabham) in second place. The BRM won the race with Gurney 12 seconds behind and Jack Brabham (Brabham) third. Stewart, after returning to the race with his car's throttle cable repaired, retired on lap 13 when its suspension collapsed.

Jackie Stewart winning his first World Championship Grand Prix at Monza in 1965 with his P261 BRM.

Graham Hill winning the 1965 United States Grand Prix.

The Mexican Grand Prix: October 24, 1965

The last race of the year found Graham Hill and Jackie Stewart back in fifth and seventh places on the starting grid, with Jim Clark's Lotus and Dan Gurney's Brabham on the front row.

Richie Ginther led away in his Honda, while Stewart, making a magnificent start, came through to second place. Stewart fell back, eventually to retire due to a slipping clutch, and Clark dropped out because of engine trouble. Ginther continued to lead to the end, followed by Gurney, but Hill was forced to retire due to engine trouble on lap 57. Mike Spence (Lotus-Climax) finished in third place.

1965 World Championship

Jim Clark won the World Championship with 54 points. Graham Hill was second with 40 points, and Stewart third with 33. Lotus-Climax won the Constructors' Championship with 54 points, while BRM came second with 45.

Sir Jackie Stewart

In his first year, Jackie Stewart had already firmly established himself in Formula 1. He wrote to me in 2008 about his time with BRM (overleaf).

Le Mans in 1965

A coupé version of the Rover BRM gas turbine car was brought to Le Mans in 1965 to be driven by Graham Hill and Jackie Stewart. It was numbered 31, and was the first British car to finish the race. A turbine blade was damaged by sand when Hill ran wide on a bend, but in spite of this, the car covered 2370.7 miles at an average speed of 98.88mph.

1966

The H16 P83

Both Graham Hill and Jackie Stewart remained with BRM in 1966 when the new

A letter from Sir Jackie Stewart at the end of 1967, regarding his years with BRM.

Sir JACKIE STEWART, O.B.E.

CLAY DA HOUSE GUTLEUS CROSS
HILLSBOROUGH HOUSE HR77 OQR

Telephone   +44 (0) 1892 8u0513
Facsimile   +44 (0) 1392 820049
Email   jackyb@bexx.bexx.com

6 May 2008

The Revd. Bryan Apps MA
14 Garfield Drive
Castledean Park
Bournemouth
BH7 7JU

Dear Bryan

Thank you for your letter of 11 March and I apologise for the very late response, but I note that my Secretary Karen has acknowledged your letter in my absence. In fact, I arrived back home and then shot straight off on another trip, so please excuse the extra delay.

Regarding the BRMs; when I joined BRM in 1965, it was my entry into Formula One as a works driver; a very big moment in my life and my career. The Team Manager was Tony Rudd, a very able man, Graham Hill was to be my teammate, Raymond Mays was still around and at that time, although perhaps not as fast as the Lotus, the BRM was the most robust. I was lucky enough to win a non-Championship Formula One race at the Daily Express International Trophy race at Silverstone, followed by the Italian Grand Prix later in the season, while finishing second three times to Jim Clark at the Belgian, French and Dutch Grands Prix. I finished third in the World Championship that year, driving a very strong, robust and reliable BRM.

I stayed on with BRM until the end of 1967, when frankly the H16 BRM was simply uncompetitive and career wise I had to make a move. They were happy years and I received great counsel and advice from Graham Hill and was able to be a #2 driver, stepping up when Graham left to join Lotus in 1967 to be the #1 driver; all very good experience. I hope these words might be helpful as requested.

I do remember the painting that you gave to me in 1985 and as you say, Ken and Norah were two great people.

Thank you for sending me a copy of the Tyrrell in Monte Carlo. Much appreciated.

All best wishes.

Yours sincerely

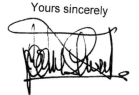

The Rover-BRM in the hands of Hill and Stewart at Le Mans in 1965.

3-litre Formula was introduced, but the 3-litre P83 was far from ready. Its H16 engine consisted of two flat-8 units mounted one on top of the other with their crankshafts coupled to a single outlet. The engine had many components in common with the successful V8, and formed a structural part of the P83 by bearing its rear suspension behind the monocoque.

Tony Rudd later said that the H16 was his biggest mistake because, in playing safe with its design and the materials used, he had made it too heavy and complicated. It was also prone to oil leaks. In the meantime, the V8 BRM engine, which had been enlarged to two litres in order to compete in the Tasman Series, and could run for 1000 miles before being overhauled, continued to be used. With Reg Parnell's son Tim in charge of the Tasman series, it won nine of its ten races, and Jackie Stewart the Championship.

For 1966, Reg Parnell Racing had two 2-litre BRM-engined Lotus 25s, which were driven by Mike Spence and Richard Attwood. Coventry-Climax

pulled out of racing that year, and so Brabham produced the Australian V8 Repco engine while Lotus, turning to BRM in the short term, gave the H16 engine its only win. Colin Chapman persuaded Ford to back Cosworth and produce Keith Duckworth's Ford DVF, which would ultimately cause the demise of BRM; Ferrari modified its V12 sports car engine; Honda produced a new V12; Cooper adopted a V12 Maserati engine, and Dan Gurney built a V12 Weslake engine for the Eagle.

The Monaco Grand Prix: May 22, 1966 – Jackie Stewart's turn again

BRM arrived at Monaco with two 2-litre V8 cars. The drivers, Jackie Stewart and Graham Hill, were behind Jim Clark (Lotus) and John Surtees (Ferrari), and on the second row of the grid.

Surtees led from the start, but Stewart passed him on lap 14 when the Ferrari slowed and retired. Hill ran in third place for much of the race behind Jochen Rindt's Cooper-Maserati, but he was eventually overtaken by Bandini's Ferrari. Clark, recovering from a disastrous start, sped past Hill, only to retire because of a broken suspension. Rindt retired with engine trouble, and Stewart won by over 20 seconds from Bandini and Hill.

The Belgian Grand Prix: June 12, 1966 – Jackie Stewart's narrow escape

A Lotus 43 with an H16 BRM engine was at Spa for Peter Arundell to drive, but Jim Clark chose to drive a Lotus 33 with a 2-litre Coventry-Climax engine. BRM used the V8 cars again, and Jackie Stewart was third fastest in practice. Graham Hill was back in tenth place, his car down on power, and alongside Clark's Lotus-Climax. On the front row with Stewart were John Surtees (Ferrari) and Jochen Rindt (Cooper-Maserati).

Surtees took the lead, followed by Joakim Bonnier's Cooper-Maserati and Mike Spence's V8 Lotus-BRM. A sudden downpour caused a number of cars to spin off on the first lap, and a multiple-car accident took out the three BRMs of Bob Bondurant, Jackie Stewart and Graham Hill. Stewart was trapped in his car, injured and

Jackie Stewart emerging from the tunnel
at Monaco in 1966.

Surtees leading Stewart at Monaco.

soaked in fuel. He was rescued by his fellow BRM drivers – with the help of a spanner borrowed from a spectator – and eventually taken to hospital, determined to do all he could to make Formula 1 less dangerous in the future. There were only five finishers – Surtees winning the race from Rindt and Bandini, followed by Brabham in fourth and Ginther (Cooper-Masterati) in fifth.

The French Grand Prix: July 3, 1966

Mike Parkes drove a Formula 1 Ferrari at Spa and was on the front row of the grid with team-mate Lorenzo Bandini. Separating them was John Surtees, now driving a monocoque Cooper-Maserati. There were two H16 BRMs and a V8 car, all of which were for Graham Hill, as Jackie Stewart was still recovering from his accident at Spa. Hill achieved eighth place with the V8-engined car.

Surtees dropped out of the lead with a broken fuel pump, and Bandini led from Jack Brabham (Brabham-Repco) and Parkes, who was harried by Hill as the race progressed. Then Hill retired because of engine trouble on lap 14. Bandini dropped out due to a broken throttle cable and it was Brabham who won, followed by Parkes and Hulme (Brabham-Repco).

The British Grand Prix: July 16, 1966

Still with the 2-litre V8 cars, Graham Hill and Jackie Stewart were fourth and seventh in practice at Brands Hatch. The front row of the grid consisted of Jack Brabham and Denny Hulme (Brabham-Repco's) and Dan Gurney (Eagle-Climax).

Brabham led away from Gurney at the start with Hill in sixth place. Stewart made good progress after a poor start, but retired due to a broken engine on lap 17. Gurney's Eagle-Climax retired on lap nine, and Hill took second place from Jochen Rindt, only to lose it to Denny Hulme. The Brabham-Repcos took the first two places at the end of the race, with Hill's BRM finishing third.

The Dutch Grand Prix: July 24, 1966

The BRMs of Graham Hill and Jackie Stewart were on the third row of the grid at Zandvoort, behind Jack Brabham and Denny Hulme (Repco-Brabhams), Jim Clark (Lotus–Climax) Dan Gurney (Eagle-Climax) and Mike Parkes (Ferrari).

Brabham led from Clark and Hulme while Hill lay fourth. Hulme dropped back and Hill moved up to second behind Brabham after Clark stopped to take on more water. Eventually, Hill and Stewart finished second and fourth, Brabham having led the race throughout.

Graham Hill at Zandvoort in 1966 with his 2-litre P261 'Tasman' BRM.

The German Grand Prix: August 7, 1966

Jim Clark (Lotus-Climax), John Surtees (Ferrari), Jackie Stewart and Ludovico Scarfiotti (Ferrari) were at the front at the Nürgburgring, while Graham Hill was back in tenth place. V8s were chosen in preference to the H16s.

The order on the first lap was Surtees, Jack Brabham (Brabham-Repco), Lorenzo Bandini and Jochen Rindt. Scarfiotti was overtaken by Stewart, Hill and Clark, before Hill went on to pass Stewart, too. Dan Gurney's Eagle-Climax then passed Clark, Stewart and Hill on lap three. Clark crashed on the last lap and Gurney slowed when his condenser bracket broke. Brabham won, followed by Surtees, Rindt, Hill, Stewart, Bandini and Gurney.

The Italian Grand Prix: September 4, 1966

Three H16 engines were involved in practice for the Italian Grand Prix: two in the P83 BRMs of Graham Hill and Jackie Stewart, and one in the Lotus 43 of Jim Clark. The Ferraris of Mike Parkes and Ludovico Scarfiotti were first and second in practice, while Clark was third, Stewart ninth and Hill 11th.

Three Ferraris led at the start of the race, Lorenzo Bandini joining his two team-mates, while Hill retired due to engine trouble on the first lap. Stewart was out five laps later due to a fuel leak. Clark stopped on lap 59 with gearbox trouble and Scarfiotti won the race, followed by Parkes and Denny Hulme (Brabham-Repco).

The United States Grand Prix: October 2, 1966 – a win at last for the H16 engine

Jim Clark was on the front row of the grid in the H16 BRM-engined Lotus 43, second to Jack Brabham (Brabham-Repco) with Lorenzo Bandini (Ferrari) and John Surtees (Cooper-Maserati) third and fourth. Graham Hill and Jackie Stewart were fifth and sixth in P83 BRMs.

At the end of lap one Clark was second to Bandini, while Stewart and Hill were still fifth and sixth. Bandini's engine blew on lap 35, and Hill stopped on lap 53 because of a broken crownwheel and pinion. Stewart was out on lap 54 due to engine trouble and Brabham retired on the following lap, also with engine trouble. This left Clark a clear winner, with a lap in hand from Jochen Rindt's Cooper-Maserati. The H16 BRM engine scored what would be its only World Championship win.

The Mexican Grand Prix: October 23, 1966

Jim Clark was second fastest in the Lotus 43, although his H16 engine broke in practice. John Surtees (Cooper-Maserati) was on pole, while Graham Hill and Jackie Stewart stood only seventh and tenth in their P83 BRMs.

Richie Ginther's Honda led the race, followed by Jochen Rindt (Cooper-Maserati) and Jack Brabham (Brabham-Repco). Clark retired due to gearbox trouble on lap nine after a disappointing race, and Stewart moved up to fifth before dropping back again due to an oil leak, only to retire on lap 26, Hill already having retired on lap 18 because of engine trouble. Surtees won, with Brabham and Hulme (Brabham-Repcos) coming second and third.

The 1966 World Championship

Jack Brabham was the 1966 World Champion with 42 points, while Graham Hill came fifth with 17 and Jackie Stewart seventh with 14. Brabham-Repo won the Constructors' Championship, and BRM came fourth behind Ferrari and Cooper-Maserati.

1966 was also Graham Hill's last season with BRM. Everyone at the company regretted his departure, but Hill felt that he was in danger of being regarded as part of the furniture! He would excel at Lotus, but tragically lose his life in a plane crash on November 31, 1975.

Bette Hill wrote the following to me in 2003:

"Graham's successful seven years with BRM were phenomenal – he and Tony Rudd worked so well together and the rest of BRM were well behind them.

"Monaco, of course, was the place where BRM was put on the map. Raymond Mays' determination to have 'British' was exactly up Graham's street. His wins at Monte Carlo were the highlights, I feel, because the glamour and the grace of the people and their Royal Family really made it stand out in our lives. But every win Graham had was exciting because of his popularity. People loved him for his humbleness towards the public. He would sit on old tyres signing autographs and be the very last driver – Champion or not – to leave the circuit. The children, nanny, and I would all be crunched up in a van, waiting for him – but the fans came first."

1967 and the first appearance of the V12 engine

In 1967 the McLaren M5A made its appearance with a 3-litre V12 BRM engine, designed by Geoff Johnson, and originally intended for use in sports cars. It was modified for Formula One and eventually fitted with four valves per cylinder. It cost only £2000 to make, and Tony Rudd later said that he should have adopted it in 1966 instead of persevering with the H16.

However, BRM soldiered on with the P83, and Jackie Stewart was joined by Mike Spence. Tim Parnell, of Reg Parnell Racing, managed a second team of BRMs (with Piers Courage and Chris Irwin, in close collaboration with Bourne), and his drivers were also available for the works team.

Graham Hill had joined Jim Clark at Lotus, and the new Ford Cosworth DFV engine was introduced with the Lotus 49. There was a new Honda for John Surtees and a new Repco engine for the Brabhams.

The South African Grand Prix: January 2, 1967

The Repco-Brabhams of Jack Brabham and Denny Hulme were fastest in practice, with Clark's Lotus-BRM third. The BRMs of Jackie Stewart and Mike

Spence were back in tenth and 14th positions.

Hulme led the race, initially from Brabham and John Surtees (Honda), until Brabham dropped back after a spin. Stewart's H16 engine gave out on lap three, and Hulme lost an unassailable lead at three-quarters' distance with brake trouble. Spence, never in contention, retired on lap 39. The race was won by Pedro Rodriguez's Cooper-Maserati from John Love's Cooper-Climax, with Surtees' Honda coming third.

The Monaco Grand Prix: May 7, 1967

Jack Brabham (Brabham-Repco) and Lorenzo Bandini (Ferrari) were at the front of the grid, while the P261 BRMs of Jackie Stewart, Mike Spence and Piers Courage were sixth, 12th and 13th respectively.

Stewart was third on lap one behind Bandini and Hulme (Brabham-Repco), and then both Hulme and Stewart overtook Bandini. Stewart retired due to a broken crownwheel and pinion on lap 15, and Courage was forced to stop following a spin on lap 65. Tragically, on lap 82, Lorenzo Bandini's Ferrari caught fire when he crashed at a chicane. He later died from his burns.

Hulme won the race from Graham Hill in his Lotus-BRM V8, and Chris Amon's Ferrari came third. Spence finished in sixth place.

Mike Spence's H16 BRM being followed by Chris Amon's Ferrari at Monaco in 1967.

The Dutch Grand Prix: June 4, 1967 – a win for the Ford Cosworth DFV

Graham Hill was fastest in practice with his new Ford Cosworth-powered Lotus 49, sharing the front row of the grid with Dan Gurney (Eagle-Weslake) and Brabham (Brabham-Repco), while Jim Clark, in a second Lotus-Ford, was on the third row of the grid. Jackie Stewart and Mike Spence, in lightened versions of the P83, managed only 11th and 12th.

At the start, Hill established a lead over Brabham, but his engine broke on lap 11. Stewart retired on lap 41 with brake trouble, but Clark recovered from his relatively poor grid position to lead the race, establishing the fastest lap in the process. He won by a wide margin from Brabham and Hulme, while Spence finished in eighth place – three laps behind.

The Belgian Grand Prix: June 18, 1967

Jim Clark and Graham Hill were first and third in practice, their Lotus-Fords sandwiching Dan Gurney's Eagle-Weslake. Jackie Stewart and Mike Spence were sixth and 11th in their P83 BRMs, while Chris Irwin was 13th in his P261.

Clark led the race from Jochen Rindt (Cooper-Maserati) and Stewart, while Hill and Gurney were left behind. Irwin's engine failed on the first lap, but Stewart moved up to second place, ahead of Gurney. Eventually, Clark dropped back, and Gurney overtook Stewart, so the race went to the Eagle-Westlake, with Stewart in second place in front of Chris Amon's Ferrari, Jochen Rindt's Cooper-Maserati, and Spence's BRM.

The French Grand Prix: July 2, 1967

The French Grand Prix was held on a shortened circuit at Le Mans. Graham Hill was fastest at practice in the Lotus-Ford, with Jack Brabham (Brabham-Repco) and Dan Gurney (Eagle-Weslake) next to him. The BRMs of Chris Irwin, Jackie Stewart and Mike Spence were ninth, tenth and 12th, Stewart opting for a P261.

Hill led from Gurney, Brabham and Jim Clark (Lotus-Ford). Then the order switched, and Brabham led, with Jim Clark was third behind Hill. Soon Clark was leading from Hill, until the second

Lotus-Ford retired due to a broken crownwheel and pinion. Clark retired soon after with a similar problem, and the two Brabham-Repcos of Brabham and Hulme led to the end of the race from Stewart's BRM. Irwin slowed due to an oil leak to finish in fifth, and Spence retired because of transmission problems on lap ten.

The British Grand Prix: July 15, 1967
Jim Clark had pole position at Silverstone while the BRMs of Mike Spence, Jackie Stewart, Chris Irwin, David Hobbs and Piers Courage were 11th, 12th, 13th, 14th and 16th on the grid. For the race, however, Courage had to withdraw, as his car was required by Stewart.

It was Clark's race, and he won with ease from Denny Hulme's Brabham-Repco and Chris Amon's Ferrari. Stewart retired on lap 20 with mechanical problems and Spence on lap 44 due to ignition failure. Irwin and Hobbs finished seventh and eighth.

The German Grand Prix: August 6, 1967
Jackie Stewart managed to put the P83 BRM on the front row at the Nürburgring, bettered only by Jim Clark's Lotus and Denny Hulme's Brabham. Mike Spence and Chris Irwin were 11th and 15th.

Clark took the lead, with Hulme and Dan Gurney (Eagle-Weslake) in close attendance, until he slowed and retired due to suspension failure on lap four – Spence had already retired on lap three with a broken crownwheel and pinion. Stewart was running well in fourth place, ahead of Jack Brabham, until the same trouble stopped him on lap six. Hulme won, followed by Jack Brabham and John Surtees (Honda), while Chris Irwin finished in seventh place.

The Canadian Grand Prix: August 27, 1967 – the introduction of the McLaren-V12 BRM
The V12 engine appeared for the first time in Mosport, fitted to Bruce McLaren's McLaren M5A. It was sixth fastest in practice ahead of the

Jackie Stewart gaining a rare second place at Spa with the P83 in 1967.

works H16-engined BRMs. Jackie Stewart was ninth, Mike Spence tenth, Chris Irwin 11th, and David Hobbs 12th. Jim Clark's Lotus was on pole position with Graham Hill (Lotus) and Denny Hulme (Brabham) alongside him.

It was Clark who led the race at first, followed by Hulme, Hill and Stewart. McLaren moved up from fifth place to overtake Clark and run second to Hulme. Irwin stopped on lap 18 after a spin. Stewart slipped into third place behind McLaren, but retired on lap 65 due to a broken throttle. Clark was forced to stop due to engine trouble, and Brabham (Brabham-Repco) eventually won a hard-fought race. Spence was fifth, McLaren seventh after slowing with a failing battery, and Hobbs was ninth in his BRM.

The Italian Grand Prix: 10 September, 1967
Bruce McLaren was third fastest in practice for the Italian Grand Prix with his V12 BRM-engined McLaren. Jim Clark's Lotus-Ford was on pole position, and between them was Jack Brabham's Brabham-Repco. Jackie Stewart, Mike Spence and Chris Irwin were seventh, 12th and 16th in their P83 BRMs.

The starter gave an uncertain signal, but the field got away, and Dan Gurney (Eagle-Weslake) led from Brabham (Brabham-Repco), Graham Hill (Lotus-Ford), Jim Clark (Lotus-Ford) and Bruce McLaren (McLaren M5A). More competitive than the BRMs, the McLaren was well placed until it retired due to engine trouble on lap 47. Irwin retired on lap 17; Stewart on lap 46. Spence finished in fifth place – a lap behind the leader. The race went to John Surtees' Honda, with Brabham and Clark in second and third places.

The United States Grand Prix: October 1, 1967
The two Lotus-Fords of Graham Hill and Jim Clark filled the front row. Bruce McLaren was ninth in practice in his McLaren-BRM, and Jackie Stewart, Mike Spence and Chris Irwin were tenth, 13th and 14th in the BRMs.

Jackie Stewart's H16 BRM during the 1967 British Grand Prix.

Bruce McLaren.

Clark and Hill dominated the race and finished first and second, with Denny Hulme's Brabham-Repco in third, one lap behind. Jo Siffert (Cooper-Maserati) finished in fourth place – two laps behind the winner. Spence retired on lap 36, Irwin on lap 42 and Stewart on lap 73, all because of mechanical problems. McLaren retired on lap 17 after a spin damaged a water pipe.

The Mexican Grand Prix: October 22, 1967
The V12 BRM-engined McLaren continued to show the way to the H16 works BRMs, and while Bruce McLaren was eighth in practice in Mexico City, Mike Spence, Jackie Stewart and Chris Irwin could only manage ninth, tenth and 13th. Jim Clark was on pole with his Lotus-Ford, with Chris Amon's Ferrari next to him.

Stewart and Irwin retired from the race due to engine trouble, while Spence finished fifth – two laps behind Clark, who won in spite of being rammed at the start by Dan Gurney's Eagle. Graham Hill's Lotus-Ford retired because of a broken driveshaft on lap 18. The Brabham-Repcos of Jack Brabham and Denny Hulme finished in second and third places, but the McLaren stopped on lap 45 with falling oil pressure.

The 1967 World Championship
Denny Hulme won the World Drivers' Championship with 51 points from Jack Brabham with 46. Jackie Stewart, Mike Spence and Chris Irwin were ninth, tenth and 18th. Brabham-Repco won the Constructors' World Championship with 63 points from Lotus-Ford with 44. BRM came sixth with 17 points.

3.2

The V12 BRMs

THE 3-LITRE CARS OF LEN TERRY AND TONY SOUTHGATE

1968 and the P126

The entirely new P126 BRM, designed by Len Terry, was introduced in 1968, powered by an improved version of the V12 engine which McLaren had used the previous year. Later in 1968, the P133 appeared with a monocoque that extended to the whole length of the car. Later still, the P138 was introduced with a BRM gearbox. Pedro Rodriguez joined Mike Spence at BRM, taking the place of Jackie Stewart who left to drive for Ken Tyrrell, believing BRM to be running out of steam.

Lotus and Ken Tyrrell opted for the successful Ford Cosworth DFV engine, while Cooper adopted the BRM V12. McLaren used both Ford and BRM engines. Lotus introduced a new livery with the sponsorship of Players Gold Leaf.

Tony Rudd

Tony Rudd wrote to me on July 1, 2003 about his long association with BRM (reproduced overleaf).

The South African Grand Prix: January 1, 1968

Ford engines filled the front row at Kyalami, with Jim Clark and Graham Hill in Lotus-Fords, and Jackie Stewart in Ken Tyrrell's Matra-Ford. Pedro Rodriguez was tenth in the P126 BRM, after it had burnt out several transistor boxes during practice. Mike Spence was 13th in a P83.

Following our decision to move to an easier to manage house early in 2002 I experienced some health problems. After surgery on 3rd September, we moved here on 12th December. Doug and I exchanged drafts by fax until I left to convalesce in the Caribbean on 17-02-03. In April he told me the final version had gone to the printers. Early in June my sister in law, who lives in Bourne, sent me press cuttings of the launch of Volume 2 by the Bourne bookshop. Doug told me on 20th June that there had been some mix up at the printers in sending out copies to him and me. Whatever the problem is I still have not seen the finished product.

As I told in my book 1962 was rather a blur, very exciting. Although he had access to Rubery Owen's records Doug chose not to reproduce the budgets. These showed we built our own engines and gearboxes as well as the cars, paid the drivers and won the championship for £96,000. When I became Chairman of Team Lotus International in 1989 I tried to find their corresponding figures without much success. Their drivers were paid by Esso, with a contribution towards the Climax engines, who in any case gave them special terms once they were in the running for the Championship.

1965 was better; I felt the 261 monocoques were the better than the opposition – Italian GP at Monza and the best cars BRM had built. After that it went sour for me with the pressure to commercialise and the various third parties trying to manage Bourne. Ironically I built Lotus Engineering into the business Sir Alfred was seeking in the late 1980s when General Motors owned the company.

When I eventually get to see the book I will try and oblige.

Yours sincerely,

Tony Rudd

Tony Rudd's letter from July 1, 2003, in which he wrote of his time with BRM. Taken from the inside back cover of the author's copy of *The Saga of BRM: Vol 2*.

Stewart led from Clark and Jochen Rindt's Brabham-Repco until Clark took the lead and Stewart lost second place because of engine trouble on lap 44. Spence retired on lap eight, and Rodriguez on lap 20, both with fuel feed problems.

Clark won, with Hill and Rindt coming second and third. Denny Hulme, now with McLaren, was fifth in a McLaren-BRM.

The Spanish Grand Prix: May 12, 1968

Tragically, Jim Clark had been killed at Hockenheim in a Formula 2 race on April 7, and Mike Spence had also lost his life while practising for the Indianapolis 500 in a Lotus a month later. Both were sadly missed in Spain, where the front row of the grid consisted of Chris Amon's Ferrari, Pedro Rodriguez's BRM, and Denny Hulme's McLaren-

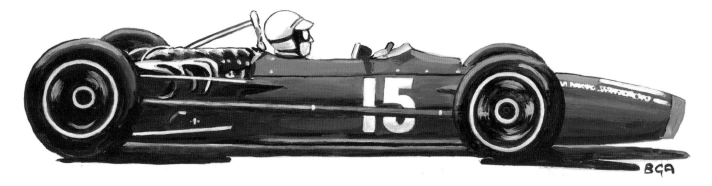

Richard Attwood in the V12 P126 at Monaco.

Ford. Piers Courage was on the last row of the grid with his BRM.

It was a promising race for BRM, and Rodriguez led the field for the first 11 laps, after which he was overtaken by Jean-Pierre Beltoise's Matra-Ford and Amon's Ferrari. He was out of the race on lap 28 after shedding two wheels during a spin. Courage retired on lap 53 due to mechanical problems, and the race was won by Graham Hill's Lotus-Ford from Hulme's McLaren-Ford and Brian Redman's Cooper-BRM.

The Monaco Grand Prix: May 26, 1968

Richard Attwood joined BRM for Monaco, and was sixth fastest in practice in a V8 P261. Pedro Rodriguez was ninth in a P133, and Piers Courage 11th. Graham Hill was on pole position in his Lotus-Ford, while Johnny Servoz-Gavin was second fastest in a Matra-Ford.

Servoz-Gavin led until a driveshaft broke on lap four, and Hill headed the field for the rest of the race. Attwood took up the chase with his BRM and remained in close company, holding second place behind Hill to the end of the race. Courage retired with handling problems on lap 12 and Rodriguez crashed on lap 17. Third and fourth places went to Lucien Bianchi and Ludovico Scarfiotti in Cooper-BRMs.

The Belgian Grand Prix: June 9, 1968

Jackie Stewart's Matra-Ford was sandwiched between the Ferraris of Chris Amon and Jacky Ickx at the front of the grid. Piers Courage, Pedro Rodriguez and Richard Attwood were seventh, eighth, and 11th in practice.

The Ferraris led at the start, with Rodriguez and Courage running sixth and seventh. Then John Surtees took the lead in the Honda, followed by Amon and Ickx, only for Ickx to be overtaken by Denny Hulme (McLaren-Ford) and Stewart as he dropped back. Attwood retired due to a fractured water pipe on lap six, Redman crashed in his Cooper-BRM without serious injury on the following lap, and Amon retired on lap eight. Surtees was the next to retire, because of suspension failure, and the two BRMs were then running behind Hulme, Stewart, and McLaren. Hulme's driveshaft broke, Courage retired due to a failed engine on lap 22, and Stewart lost time refuelling. This left Bruce McLaren to win the race from Rodriguez's BRM, with Ickx coming third in the Ferrari.

The Dutch Grand Prix: June 23, 1968

Practice did not augur well for the BRMs, with Pedro Rodriguez, Piers Courage and Richard Attwood in 11th, 14th and 15th places. Chris Amon (Ferrari) was fastest, Jochen Rindt (Brabham-Repco) second and Graham Hill (Lotus-Ford) third.

Soon after the start of a wet race, Stewart (Matra-Ford) was leading Hill and Amon and had established a comfortable lead. Jean-Pierre Beltoise (Matra) overtook Hill before dropping down to seventh place after a brief spell in the pits. Beltoise recovered second place from Hill on lap 50. Then Hill spun off at the hairpin bend and Rodriguez finished third in his BRM, one lap behind

Pedro Rodriguez leading John Surtees, Jack Brabham and Jean-Pierre Beltoise during the 1968 Dutch Grand Prix.

Stewart and Beltoise. Attwood was seventh – five laps behind the winner.

The French Grand Prix: July 7, 1968
Jochen Rindt (Brabham-Repco), Jackie Stewart (Matra-Ford) and Jacky Ickx (Ferrari) lined up on the front row of the grid at Rouen. Pedro Rodriguez, Richard Attwood, and Piers Courage were tenth, 12th and 14th in their BRMs.

It was raining at the start of the race, and Ickx led from Stewart and Rindt. Near the back Jo Schlesser crashed in his Honda and, tragically, died in the blazing wreck of his car. Ickx continued to lead, now from Surtees (Honda) and Rodriguez. The BRM took the lead after Ickx dropped back,

having spun on the wet road, but he recovered the lead again before Rodriguez stopped at the pits because of a slow puncture. Ickx was the clear winner; Surtees took second. Courage and Attwood finished sixth and seventh. It was a fine race by Rodriguez, who established the fastest lap at 111.285mph, but the day had been marred by Schlesser's death.

The British Grand Prix: July 20, 1968
The Lotus-Fords of Graham Hill and Jackie Oliver were first and second in practice, and Chris Amon's Ferrari completed the front row of the grid. The BRMs of Pedro Rodriguez, Richard Attwood and Piers Courage were 13th, 15th and 16th on the grid.

At the start of what threatened to be a wet race, Oliver led from Hill and Jo Siffert (Lotus-Ford). Hill then took the lead until he retired with suspension failure on lap 27, and Rodriguez was hampered by the decision to opt for wet tyres on a track that was drying. Eventually, the race went to Siffert's Lotus-Ford from the Ferraris of Amon and Jacky Ickx. Courage finished eighth in his BRM, eight laps behind the winner. Attwood retired on lap 18 (radiator) and Rodriguez on lap 53 (engine).

The German Grand Prix: August 4, 1968
Jacky Ickx (Ferrari), Chris Amon (Ferrari) and Jochen Rindt (Brabham-Repco) made up the front row of the grid at the Nürburgring with the BRMs of Piers Courage, Pedro Rodriguez and Richard Attwood eighth, 14th and 20th in practice.

From the third row of the starting grid Jackie Stewart (Matra-Ford) drove brilliantly in the treacherous conditions to lead from start to finish. Graham Hill (Lotus-Ford) came second and Jochen Rindt third, Amon having crashed out of third place on lap 12. Rodriguez finished in sixth place, Courage in eighth and Attwood 14th.

The Italian Grand Prix: September 8, 1968
A long way behind Chris Amon (Ferrari), Bruce McLaren (McLaren-Ford) and John Surtees (Honda) in the front row, the BRMs of Pedro Rodriguez, and Piers Courage were 14th and 16th on the starting grid at Monza.

Surtees led at first, but was overtaken by McLaren at the Curva Grande on the first lap. Chris Amon and Surtees crashed on lap nine and McLaren extended his lead over Jackie Stewart's Matra-Ford and Graham Hill's Lotus-Ford. Then Hill was out, having lost a wheel, and his place was taken by Jo Siffert (Rob Walker's Lotus-Ford). McLaren stopped, his car lacking oil, and Denny Hulme inherited the lead, followed by Stewart and Siffert. Both Stewart and Siffert retired with engine trouble, and Johnny Servoz-Gavin improved his position in his Matra-Ford to finish second to Hulme's McLaren-Ford. Courage finished in fourth place, while Rodriguez retired because of engine trouble on lap 23.

The Canadian Grand Prix: September 22, 1968
Jochen Rindt (Brabham-Repco), Chris Amon (Ferrari) and Jo Siffert (Lotus-Ford) filled the front row of the grid at St Jovite. Pedro Rodriguez and Piers Courage were 12th and 14th in their BRMs.

Amon led initially from Siffert, Rindt, Dan Gurney (McLaren-Ford) and Graham Hill (Lotus-Ford) but on lap 29 Siffert's engine failed due to an oil leak and he was out. Gurney stopped on lap 30 due to a leaky radiator, and Rindt retired on lap 40 with engine trouble. Amon's Ferrari stopped on lap 73 due to transmission failure. At the end it was Denny Hulme's Brabham that won the race, followed by McLaren and Rodriguez. Courage retired with gearbox trouble on lap 23.

The United States Grand Prix: October 6, 1968
The front row of the grid at Watkins Glen consisted of Mario Andretti's Lotus-Ford and Jackie Stewart's Matra-Ford. Pedro Rodriguez, Piers Courage and Bobby Unser were 11th, 14th and 19th in the BRMs. It was Unser's first race with a BRM, and he crashed during practice, before his engine failed.

Andretti led from Stewart and Graham Hill (Lotus-Ford), who was soon overtaken by Chris Amon's Ferrari, who took his place in third position. Amon later spun, and Andretti had to stop for repairs. Stewart then led from Hill, and they both held their positions to the end, with John Surtees coming third in the Honda. Unser had retired on lap three due to engine trouble, Rodriguez on lap 67 because of a collapsed suspension, and Courage on lap 94 with a dry fuel tank.

The Mexican Grand Prix: November 3, 1968
The front row in Mexico City featured Jo Siffert (Lotus-Ford) and Chris Amon (Ferrari). Pedro Rodriguez and Piers Courage were 12th and 19th.

Graham Hill (Lotus-Ford) led the race from John Surtees (Honda) and Jackie Stewart (Matra-Ford), with Jo Siffert's Lotus-Ford not far behind. The three exchanged places during the first quarter of the race but, while leading, Stewart's throttle cable broke, causing him to lose precious time in the pits. After this, Stewart recovered to run close behind Hill in second, while Rodriguez was lying seventh. Stewart then fell back with multiple mechanical problems, and Hill won the race from Bruce McLaren (McLaren-Ford) and Jackie Oliver (Lotus-Ford). Rodriguez finished fourth, but Courage had been forced to retire because of engine trouble on lap 26.

The 1968 World Championship

Graham Hill won the Drivers' World Championship with 48 points, and Jackie Stewart came second with 36. Of the BRM drivers, Pedro Rodriguez came sixth with 18 points, Richard Attwood 13th with six, and Piers Courage 20th with four. The Constructors' Championship was won by Lotus-Ford with 62 points. BRM came fifth with 28.

1969

Little change

The new P139 BRM was little changed from the previous year's models, as the team was awaiting the entirely new P153, designed by Tony Southgate, who had become the chief designer following the departure of Tony Rudd. Louis Stanley's role became more significant after Sir Alfred Owen suffered a stroke. Tim Parnell became the new Team Manager, and both John Surtees and Jackie Oliver joined Pedro Rodriguez in the

The 1969 V12 BRM.

BRM driver line-up. John Surtees later said that the V12's cylinder head had a tendency to overheat, resulting in a significant loss of performance after the first few laps.

The South African Grand Prix: March 1, 1969.

Ford engines filled the first four places on the starting grid at Kyalami in the order of Jack Brabham (Brabham), Jochen Rindt (Lotus), Denny Hulme (McLaren) and Jackie Stewart (Matra). The BRMs of Jackie Oliver and Pedro Rodriguez were 14th and 15th while John Surtees, having encountered problems with his car during practice, was at the back of the grid.

The order on the first lap was Brabham, Stewart and Rindt. Stewart pushed ahead, pursued by Graham Hill (Lotus-Ford), Brabham having fallen back with a broken rear wing. The two finished the race in that order, with Hulme third. The BRMs never really featured, and Oliver finished seventh, three laps behind Stewart. Rodriguez retired on lap 38 and Surtees on lap 40.

The Spanish Grand Prix: May 4, 1969

Jochen Rindt (Lotus-Ford), Chris Amon (Ferrari) and Graham Hill (Lotus-Ford) made up the order of the front row. In fact, apart from Amon's Ferrari, Ford engines occupied the first seven places. They were followed by the BRMs of John Surtees and Jackie Oliver, while Pedro Rodriguez was 14th and last.

At the start of the race Rindt led from Amon, Jo Siffert (Lotus-Ford) and Hill. Then, on lap nine, Hill hit the barriers at high speed when his car's rear wing suddenly collapsed, and on the following lap Rindt's Lotus crashed and overturned for the same reason. Fortunately, both drivers escaped serious injury.

Amon then led from Jo Siffert (Lotus-Ford), Jackie Stewart (Matra-Ford) and Jack Brabham (Brabham-Repco). First Siffert and then both Brabham and Amon retired with blown engines. The rear wing on Jacky Ickx's Brabham-Ford also failed, but he was able to stop at the pits for repairs. Stewart won the race from Bruce

McLaren (McLaren-Ford) and Jean-Pierre Beltoise (Matra-Ford). Surtees finished fifth, six laps behind. Oliver had retired on lap one, and Rodriguez on lap 73.

The Monaco Grand Prix: May 18, 1969

Jackie Stewart (Matra-Ford), Chris Amon (Ferrari), Jean-Pierre Beltoise (Matra-Ford), and Graham Hill (Lotus-Ford) were on the first row at Monaco, while John Surtees was on the third row with Jo Siffert (Lotus-Ford). The BRMs of Jackie Oliver and Pedro Rodriguez were 13th and 14th.

Stewart led Amon and Hill on lap one, while Oliver retired after hitting the barriers. Surtees' gearbox jammed in the tunnel and Jack Brabham (Brabham-Repco) crashed into him. Amon stopped because of a broken differential, and the Matras of Beltoise and Stewart retired due to broken driveshafts. Hill won the race after leading throughout from Piers Courage (Brabham-Ford) and Siffert. Rodriguez retired on lap 16 with engine trouble.

John Surtees leading Jacky Ickx at Monaco in 1969.

The Dutch Grand Prix: June 21, 1969

Fastest in practice was Jochen Rindt (Lotus-Ford), followed by Jackie Stewart (Matra-Ford) and Graham Hill (Lotus-Ford). John Surtees and Jackie Oliver were in 12th and 13th places in their BRMs.

Hill led away from Rindt and Stewart but was soon overtaken by both: Stewart taking second and Rindt the lead. Hill dropped back with handling difficulties, and third place was claimed by Jo Siffert (Lotus-Ford). Behind him came Denny Hulme (Brabham-Repco), Chris Amon (Ferrari), Jacky Ickx (Ferrari), and Jack Brabham (Braham-Repco). The race eventually produced another assured win for Stewart, followed by Siffert, Amon, Hulme and Ickx. Surtees finished in ninth place, three laps behind, while Oliver retired on lap ten due to gearbox trouble.

The French Grand Prix

The BRMs were not at Clermont-Ferrand because of changes necessitated by the regrettable departure of Tony Rudd.

The British Grand Prix: July 19, 1969

Jochen Rindt (Lotus-Ford), Jackie Stewart (Matra-Ford) and Denny Hulme (McLaren-Ford) were on the front row of the grid at Silverstone. John Surtees and Jackie Oliver were sixth and 13th.

John Surtees; the only World Champion on both two wheels and four.

Rindt and Stewart disputed the lead ahead of Surtees, but on lap two his BRM's front suspension collapsed and third place was taken by Hulme. Rindt led narrowly from Stewart until he had to pit for repairs to his aerofoil, enabling Stewart to win the race from Jacky Ickx (Brabham-Ford) and Bruce McLaren (McLaren-Ford). Oliver retired on lap 20 with transmission trouble.

German Grand Prix: August 3, 1969

Ford engines powered the first ten cars on the grid: the leaders being the Brabham of Jacky Ickx, the Matra of Jackie Stewart and the Lotus of Jochen Rindt. John Surtees and Jackie Oliver were 11th and 13th in practice, but Surtees declined to race after experiencing numerous problems with his P139 BRM.

Stewart led the race from Jo Siffert (Rob Walker Lotus-Ford) and Rindt. Two laps in, Ickx passed Rindt and caught up with Stewart to take the lead while setting a new lap record. Stewart was then slowed due to gearbox problems and settled for second place, with McLaren coming third. Oliver retired on lap 12 with a damaged sump.

The Italian Grand Prix: 7 September 1969

Apart from the BRMs of John Surtees and Jackie Oliver in tenth and 11th, and Pedro Rodriguez's Ferrari in 12th, the entire field was Ford-powered. The front row was comprised of Jochen Rindt's Lotus and Denny Hulme's McLaren.

Rindt led at first, but was overtaken by Stewart by the end of lap one. Surtees lost time having collected the broken exhaust pipe of Hill's car, and eventually finished eight laps behind the winner. The leading five cars of Stewart, Hill (Lotus), Rindt, Jean-Pierre Beltoise (Matra) and Bruce McLaren

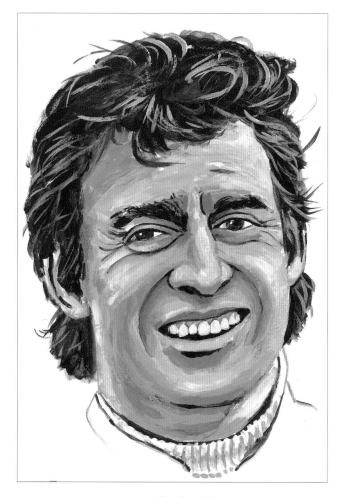

Portrait of Jackie Oliver.

Jackie Oliver in the P139 BRM during the 1969 Italian Grand Prix.

(McLaren) were only two seconds apart as the race drew towards its end. Then, with four laps to go, Hill's driveshaft broke, resulting in a further win for Stewart, followed by Rindt, Beltoise and McLaren – only 0.16 seconds separated the first four cars! Oliver retired with failing oil pressure on lap 49.

The Canadian Grand Prix: September 20, 1969
Ferrari missed the race at Mosport so that BRM alone opposed the Ford-powered cars. The drivers, Jackie Oliver, John Surtees and American Bill Brack, were 12th, 14th and 18th in practice. Jacky Ickx (Brabham) was fastest, and shared the front row with Jean-Pierre Beltoise (Matra) and Jochen Rindt (Lotus).

Rindt led initially, but was soon overtaken by Stewart and Ickx. On lap 33 Ickx attempted to overtake Stewart, and the two cars touched, resulting in Stewart's retirement, while Ickx went on to win from Jack Brabham's Brabham and Rindt. Oliver retired on lap three and Surtees on lap 16, both due to engine failures. Brack finished ten laps in arrears.

The United States Grand Prix: October 5,1969
The BRMs of John Surtees, Jackie Oliver and the American George Eaton were 11th, 14th and 18th in practice behind Jochen Rindt's Lotus and Denny Hulme's McLaren.

Rindt led initially followed by Jackie Stewart and Graham Hill. Hill remained in third place while Stewart took the lead before Rindt regained his position. Stewart retired on lap 36 due to engine trouble, and Hill was eliminated when a deflating tyre caused his car to spin and overturn, breaking both his legs. Rindt led to the end of the race, followed by Piers Courage (Brabham) and Surtees, who gained a welcome third place for BRM, two laps behind the winner. Oliver retired on lap 24 and Eaton on lap 77, both with engine failures.

The Mexican Grand Prix: October 19, 1969
The two Brabhams of Jack Brabham and Jacky Ickx were on the front row at Mexico City, with the BRMs of John Surtees, Jackie Oliver and George Eaton in tenth, 12th and 18th positions.

John Surtees in the V12 P139 BRM in 1969.

Stewart led the race followed by the Brabhams, but was overtaken by Hulme (McLaren-Ford), Ickx, and finally Jack Brabham. The four finished the race in that order, with Oliver coming sixth, two laps behind the winner. Eaton and Surtees retired on laps seven and 54 respectively due to gearbox troubles.

The 1969 World Championship
Jackie Stewart decisively won his first World Championship with 63 points from Jacky Ickx who scored 37. John Surtees was 11th with six points, and Jackie Oliver 18th with one point. The Constructors' Championship was won by Ken Tyrrell and Matra-Ford with 66 points. BRM came fifth with seven.

1970 and the P153
The eagerly awaited Tony Southgate P153 BRM appeared in 1970, sponsored by Yardley, and finished in Yardley colours, thanks to the commercial acumen of Louis Stanley. Pedro Rodriguez replaced John Surtees, but Jackie Oliver remained, joined occasionally by George Eaton.

Graham Hill left Lotus to drive for the Brooke Bond Rob Walker team. Ken Tyrrell parted company with Matra and used Ford-Cosworth-powered March 701 cars. The new Tyrrell 001, designed by Derek Gardner, appeared later in the year. The new Brabham BT33 was of monocoque construction and the flat-12 Ferrari 312B of semi monocoque construction.

Pedro Rodriguez – immensely talented and popular.

The South African Grand Prix: March 7, 1970

The March-Fords of Jackie Stewart and Chris Amon were first and second in practice at Kyalami, with Jack Brabham's Brabham-Ford completing the front row of the grid. The new P153 BRMs of Jackie Oliver, Pedro Rodriguez and George Eaton were disappointingly only 12th, 16th and 23rd.

Brabham and Amon touched at the start, and Stewart led until Brabham recovered to take over and lead on lap 20. Denny Hulme (McLaren-Ford) also overtook Stewart as the race progressed, resulting in a win for Brabham, followed by Hulme, Stewart and Jean-Pierre Beltoise (V12 Matra-Simca). Rodriguez was ninth, four laps behind Brabham, while Oliver retired on lap 22 (gear problems) and Eaton on lap 59 (engine).

Spanish Grand Prix, April 19, 1970

More promisingly, Pedro Rodriguez was on the second row of the grid at Jarama in fifth place behind Jack Brabham (Brabham-Ford), Denny Hulme (McLaren-Ford) and Jackie Stewart (March-Ford). Jackie Oliver was tenth-fastest in the second BRM.

At the start of the race Stewart took the lead from Hulme and Brabham, but Oliver's front stub axle failed on the first lap, causing him to crash into the Ferrari of Jacky Ickx. Both cars exploded in flames and were destroyed, but fortunately the drivers escaped with only minor injuries. As a precautionary measure, Rodriguez' BRM was withdrawn from the race on lap four.

On lap 16 Brabham slid on the foam left by the accident, and Jean-Pierre Beltoise passed him into second place, only to retire when his engine seized on lap 31. Brabham also retired on lap 61 because of engine trouble, and Stewart won the race from Bruce McLaren (McLaren-Ford) and Mario Andretti (March-Ford).

The Monaco Grand Prix: May 10, 1970

The March-Fords of Jackie Stewart and Chris Amon shared the front row of the grid at Monaco while Jackie Oliver and Pedro Rodriguez stood in 14th and 15th places – both BRMs had been beset with problems during practice.

After stalling just before the start, Stewart led from Chris Amon, Jack Brabham (Brabham-Ford), Jean-Pierre Beltoise (Matra-Simca) and Jacky Ickx (Ferrari). Brabham passed Amon as Stewart drew further away, but a misfire meant Stewart lost time in the pits and his lead went to Brabham. Oliver retired with engine trouble on lap 43 and Stewart followed him on lap 58, having dropped right back in the field. Amon was out due to a broken rear suspension on 61, and Jochen Rindt (Lotus-Ford) passed Brabham to win the race. Henri Pescarolo came third in his Matra-Simca. Rodriguez was

Right: Pedro Rodriguez's Yardley BRM leading Chris Amon's March Ford during the1970 Belgian Grand Prix.

delayed with throttle trouble and finished in sixth place – two laps behind the winner.

The Belgian Grand Prix: June 7, 1970 – victory for the new P153 BRM

Jackie Stewart (Matra-Ford) was on pole position at Spa with Jochen Rindt (Lotus- Ford) and Chris Amon (Ferrari) alongside him on the grid. The P153 of Pedro Rodriguez was sixth and Jackie Oliver's 14th. Sadly, Bruce McLaren had been killed testing a Can-Am car at Goodwood five days before.

Rind initially led the race, but at the end of lap one the order was Amon, Stewart and Rindt, followed by Rodriguez. Then, to the delight of BRM enthusiasts, Rodriguez passed Rindt, Stewart and Amon to take the lead on lap four. Amon remained in close company with Rodriguez, and the two drew away from the rest of the field. In the end, the

Rodriguez in the Belgian Grand Prix.

B G Apps

Pedro Rodriguez at Spa in 1970.

Jochen Rindt winning the 1970 Dutch Grand Prix
in his Lotus 72.

BRM crossed the line to win the race by just over a second from the March-Ford, at an average speed of 149.941mph. Jean-Pierre Beltoise was third in a Matra-Simca. Oliver retired on lap seven due to engine trouble.

The Dutch Grand Prix: June 21, 1970

Jochen Rindt (Lotus) was fastest at Zandvoort, Jackie Stewart (Matra) second and Jacky Ickx (Ferrari) third. Of the BRMs Jackie Oliver was fifth, Pedro Rodriguez seventh and George Eaton in 18th place, the last having paid for his seat. Rodriguez had a major accident in practice, caused by a puncture, so had to use the spare car for the race.

Oliver made a magnificent start in his BRM to run third behind Ickx and Rindt on the first lap. Then Rindt took the lead, and Oliver was passed by both Stewart and Rodriguez. He retired because of engine trouble on lap 24, and Rodriguez was delayed due to a loose nose section. Rindt won the race from Stewart, Ickx and Clay Regazzoni, who was making his Grand Prix debut in a Ferrari. Rodriguez finished in tenth place, three laps down. Eaton had retired on lap 27 with a split oil tank.

The French Grand Prix: July 5, 1970

Jacky Ickx (Ferrari) and Jean-Pierre Beltoise (Matra-Simca) were on the front row of the grid at Clermont-Ferrand. Pedro Rodriguez, Jackie Oliver and George Eaton were placed tenth, 12th and 19th in the works BRMs.

Jackie Oliver's Yardley-BRM leading Clay Regazzoni's Ferrari during the 1970 Italian Grand Prix.

Ickx led from the start, followed by Beltoise and Jackie Stewart (Matra-Ford). Stewart slowed with ignition problems and was overtaken by Chris Amon (March-Ford), Jochen Rindt (Lotus-Ford), Henri Pescarolo (Matra-Simca), and Pedro Rodriguez (BRM). Oliver retired on lap six due to an engine

TEAM BRM

British Racing Motors

Bourne
Lincolnshire
England
PE10 9LF

(Chairman)
Sir Alfred Owen CBE
(Jt. Managing Directors)
Louis T. Stanley
Jean Stanley
(Directors)
Raymond Mays
William Holmes
Peter Spear

Telephone
Bourne 2327

The Revd. Bryan Apps,
The Rectory,
125 Paynes Road,
Southampton.

8th July, 1970

Dear Bryan Apps,

     Thank you so much for your letter of 30th June, which
I received on my return from the French Grand Prix, and also
many thanks indeed for the model car, with which I am delighted.
It is extremely good of you to think of sending this.

     I am very glad to hear news of you and your family, and
when you do come this way again be sure and let me know. We
still have our troubles, as you will know, and after the really
good win in Belgium we have dropped back again, and are trying to
get out of our difficulties before the British Grand Prix next
week. I am glad to say that I am pretty well, and am never any
less busy. The book which you mention is still amongst our
records.

     With kind regards,

         Yours sincerely,

         Raymond Mays

Raymond Mays' letter following my gift of a suitably modified and detailed Crescent toy BRM.

misfire, and Rodriguez stopped on lap seven, his car stuck in fourth gear. The race went to Rindt in his Lotus-Ford from Amon and Jack Brabham (Brabham-Ford). Eaton finished in 12th place, two laps behind.

The British Grand Prix: July 18, 1970
Jackie Oliver was fourth in practice at Brands Hatch behind Jochen Rindt (Lotus-Ford), Jack Brabham (Brabham-Ford) and Jacky Ickx (Ferrari). Pedro Rodriguez and Eaton were 15th and 16th.

At the start of the race Ickx led from Brabham and Rindt, with Oliver holding a secure fourth place. Then Ickx dropped back due to transmission troubles, and Rodriguez stopped at the pits for adjustments. Eaton retired with low oil pressure on lap 11. For many laps Oliver was in a solitary third place, but he was forced to retire on lap 55 with engine trouble. Rodriguez crashed into the banking on lap 59 and so was also out of the race. The victory went to Rindt, with Brabham coming second and Denny Hulme (McLaren-Ford) third.

The German Grand Prix: August 2, 1970
Jacky Ickx gained pole position for Ferrari at Hockenheim with Jochen Rindt (Lotus-Ford) next to him. The BRMs of Pedro Rodriguez and Jackie Oliver were eighth and 18th.

Ickx took the lead at the start from Rindt, Jo Siffert (March-Ford), and Clay Regazzoni (Ferrari). Oliver retired due to engine trouble on lap six and Rodriguez on lap eight due to faulty ignition. Ickx and Rindt exchanged places while Chris Amon (March-Ford), and Jo Siffert (March-Ford) caught up, each taking turns to lead. The result was another win for Rindt from Ickx and Hulme. Oliver's BRM retired on lap six with engine trouble, and Rodriguez' on lap eight because of ignition problems.

The Austrian Grand Prix: August 16, 1970
Jochen Rindt (Lotus-Ford) was on pole with Clay Regazzoni's Ferrari next to him at the Österreichring.

The BRMs of Jackie Oliver, Pedro Rodriguez and George Eaton were 14th, 22nd and 23rd.

The Ferraris of Regazzoni and Jacky Ickx took an early lead, followed by Rindt and Ignazio Giunti (Ferrari). Jacky Ickx then led, and the two Ferraris held their positions to the end, Giunti finishing in seventh, one lap down. Rodriguez and Oliver benefitted from the retirements in front of them, and finished fourth and fifth. Eaton was 11th, and a further lap behind.

The Italian Grand Prix: September 6, 1970
The BRMs arrived at Monza with more powerful V12 engines sporting new cylinder heads. This enabled Pedro Rodriguez to qualify at the front of the starting grid alongside Jacky Ickx (Ferrari). Jackie Oliver was sixth and George Eaton 20th in the remaining BRMs. Tragically, during practice Jochen Rindt crashed into a barrier and was killed.

At the start of the race Rodriguez held second place to Ickx, with Jackie Stewart (Matra-Ford) lying third. On lap 13 Rodriguez was out with a major engine failure, but Oliver proceeded to challenge Stewart, Clay Regazzoni (Ferrari) and Ickx for the lead until his race ended because of a broken engine on lap 37. Eaton's race ended when his car overheated on lap 22. Regazzoni won his first Grand Prix from Stewart and Jean-Pierre Beltoise (Mara-Simca), but Rindt had already scored enough points to become the first posthumous World Champion.

The Canadian Grand Prix: September 20, 1970
Jackie Stewart drove spectacularly in practice, giving him the fastest time in the brand new Tyrrell-

Jackie Oliver's Yardley-BRM leading Clay Regazzoni's Ferrari during the 1970 Italian Grand Prix.

Ford. Jacky Ickx (Ferrari) was alongside him on the front row. Pedro Rodriguez, George Eaton and Jackie Oliver were seventh, ninth and tenth in the three BRMs.

Stewart took the lead at the start, followed, after a widening gap, by Ickx and Rodriguez. At quarter distance Rodriguez lost his position to Clay Regazzoni (Ferrari) and François Cevert (March-Ford). Then on lap 32 the Tyrrell's race was ended by a broken stub axle. (Years later, when Tyrrell was sold to BAR, Ken Tyrrell gave me a stub axle and wheel nut from a Tyrrell 025, as a reminder of the many years that I had enjoyed in the paddock at Silverstone with him and Norah).

The race was won by Ickx, followed by Regazzoni, Amon and Rodriguez. Eaton finished in tenth position, Oliver having retired on lap 38.

The United States Grand Prix: October 4, 1970 – a creditable second for Rodriguez

Jacky Ickx (Ferrari) and Jackie Stewart (Tyrrell-Ford) shared the front row at Watkins Glen. Having been fourth fastest, Pedro Rodriguez's BRM was on the second row, while Jackie Oliver took seventh place in the fourth row. George Eaton was 14th, while Peter Westbury failed to qualify in a fourth BRM.

At the start Stewart led from Rodriguez, who was pressed by Ickx and Chris Amon (March-Ford). On lap 16 the BRM gave way to Ickx and Clay Regazzoni (Ferrari), while Eaton and Oliver retired with engine trouble on laps 11 and 15 respectively. Regazzoni dropped out of contention after a pit stop for new tyres, Ickx pitted because of a fuel leak on lap 57, and Stewart stopped with an oil leak on lap 83, leaving Rodriguez to lead. Sadly, he had to stop for fuel, enabling Emerson Fittipaldi (Lotus-Ford) to slip past. The result was a win for Fittipaldi while Rodriguez came second. Reine Wisell was third in another Lotus-Ford.

Mexican Grand Prix, October 18, 1970

Clay Regazzoni (Ferrari) and Jackie Stewart (Tyrrell-Ford) were on the front row at Mexico City while the BRMs of Pedro Rodriguez and Jackie Oliver were seventh and 13th.

Jackie Oliver's Yardley-BRM leading Graham Hill's Lotus 72 (out of picture) and Jo Siffert's March-Ford during the United States Grand Prix.

At the start Regazzoni led from Stewart and Jacky Ickx (Ferrari), but both passed him and Ickx took over the lead. Stewart eventually slowed with steering problems and retired on lap 34. The winner was Ickx, followed by Regazzoni and Denny Hulme (McLaren-Ford). Rodriguez and Oliver finished sixth and seventh.

1970 World Championship

Jochen Rindt became a posthumous World Champion with 45 points. Rodriguez was seventh with 23 and Oliver 21st with two. Lotus-Ford won the Constructors' World Championship with 59 points, and BRM came seventh with 23.

1971

The P160

The Tony Southgate P160 Yardley BRM was a refined version of the P153 – slightly lower and wider, and with a pointed nose. It had a fully stressed 440bhp version of the 48-valve V12 engine, and a new gearbox. Jackie Oliver's place on the team was taken by Jo Siffert.

Ron Tauranac created the 'lobster claw' Brabham, and March produced the very distinctive 711, with an oval wing projecting above a blunt rounded front. The Tyrrells were essentially unchanged.

The South African Grand Prix: March 6, 1971

Jackie Stewart was fastest in his Tyrrell, and he had alongside him Chris Amon (Matra-Simca) and Clay Regazzoni (Ferrari). The P160s of Pedro Rodriguez, Jo Siffert and Howden Ganley were tenth, 16th and 24th.

Regazzoni established an early lead from Emerson Fittipaldi (Lotus-Ford) with Rodriguez

lying fifth. Denny Hume (McLaren-Ford) moved up to second place, with Rodriguez just behind him. On lap 17 Hulme took the lead, and Surtees, in his Surtees-Ford, displaced Rodriguez. Next, Mario Andretti (Ferrari) also overtook Rodriguez, who was followed by Siffert. Both he and Rodriguez retired on laps 31 and 33 respectively with overheated engines. Ganley stopped on lap 42, feeling unwell. Andretti won the race for Ferrari with Stewart second and Regazzoni third.

The Spanish Grand Prix: April 18, 1971

Pedro Rodriguez's BRM was on the second row

Jo Siffert and Pedro Rodriguez practicing for the 1971 Monaco Grand Prix in their P153s.

with Jackie Stewart's Tyrrell-Ford. Jacky Ickx (Ferrari), Clay Regazzoni (Ferrari) and Chris Amon (Matra-Simca) were in front of him. The BRMs of Jo Siffert and Howden Ganley were 11th and 17th in practice.

At the fall of the flag it was Ickx who led, followed by Regazzoni and Stewart. Stewart moved up to take the lead, which he held to the end. Ickx finished in second place, Amon third and Rodriguez fourth. Ganley was tenth; Siffert retired on lap six due to gear selection problems.

The Monaco Grand Prix: May 23, 1971

Jo Siffert was the leading BRM driver in practice, and third overall after Jackie Stewart's Tyrrell and the Ferrari of Jacky Ickx. Pedro Rodriguez was in fifth place, and Howden Ganley failed to qualify.

Siffert made an excellent start, lying second to Stewart and followed by Ickx and Rodriguez. On lap 13, Rodriguez hit a curb at the Gasworks hairpin, and dropped back. Peterson then overtook Siffert, who retired because of a fractured oil pipe on lap 59. At the end of the race the order was Stewart, Peterson and Ickx, with Rodriguez four laps behind in ninth place.

The Dutch Grand Prix: June 20, 1971

Pedro Rodriguez was on the front row of the grid with his BRM at Zandvoort, with Jacky Ickx (Ferrari) and Jackie Stewart (Tyrrell-Ford) on either side of him. Jo Siffert was sixth and Howden Ganley tenth in the other two BRMs.

Ickx and Rodriguez drew away from the rest of the field in the opening laps and Rodriguez took the lead in a closely fought dual. It was the Ferrari that won, and only Rodriguez was able to remain on the same lap. Siffert was sixth and Ganley seventh.

The French Grand Prix: July 4, 1971

Jackie Stewart (Tyrrell-Ford) had pole position at Paul Ricard, with the two Ferraris of Clay Regazzoni and Jacky Ickx sharing the front row with him. Of the BRM drivers Pedro Rodriguez was fifth, Jo Siffert sixth and Howden Ganley 16th.

Stewart made a brilliant start, and at the end

Jacky Ickx and Pedro Rodriguez in close contact during the 1971 Dutch Grand Prix.

Rodriguez finally having to settle for second place at Zandvoort in 1971.

of the first lap he was pursued by Regazzoni and Rodriguez, with Siffert lying seventh. Rodriguez first lost and then regained third place, only to retire on lap 28 due to ignition failure. The race went to Stewart, and he was followed across the line by his team-mate François Cevert. Siffert was fourth, Ganley finished in tenth place, one lap behind.

Tragically, following the French Grand Prix, Pedro Rodriguez was killed in a sports car race in Germany. It was an enormous loss to BRM.

The British Grand Prix: July 17, 1971

Jo Siffert was third fastest in practice at Silverstone, and joined Clay Regazzoni's Ferrari and Jackie Stewart's Tyrrell-Ford on the front row of the grid. Howden Ganley was 11th.

Stewart led the race and Siffert was soon lying second. Then Siffert was retaken by Regazzoni's Ferrari and slowed due to a misfire. Stewart won from Ronnie Peterson (March-Ford) and Emerson Fittipaldi (Lotus-Ford). Ganley and Siffert finished in eighth and ninth places.

The German Grand Prix: August 1, 1971

It was Jackie Stewart's Tyrrell on pole at the Nürburgring, alongside Jacky Ickx (Ferrari). Siffert's BRM was next up, while Howden Ganley was 14th. Vic Elford, in the third BRM, was 18th.

Ickx led the race initially, but Stewart was soon ahead once again while Siffert took up fifth place. When the Ferraris of Ickx and Clay Regazzoni spun on lap two, Siffert slipped through to second. Unfortunately, on lap seven his BRM misfired. He came into the pits loop to retire due to damaged suspension, but was disqualified as a result. Stewart won the race from François Cevert's Tyrrell. Regazzoni finished in third, and Elford was 11th, Ganley having retired on lap two due to engine trouble.

The Austrian Grand Prix: August 15, 1971 – a win for Jo Siffert

Peter Gethin and the Austrian Dr Helmut Marko joined Jo Siffert and Howden Ganley at BRM for the Österreichring. Siffert was fastest in practice with Jackie Stewart's Tyrrell next to him on the grid. Ganley was 14th, Gethin 16th and Marko 17th.

Siffert led from Stewart's Tyrrell from the start, and the two drew away from the field. François Cevert's Tyrrell took over the pursuit of Siffert from Stewart, who had retired on lap 36, but had to retire himself on lap 43 with gearbox problems. One of Siffert's tyres began to deflate, but he held on to his lead to win at 131.642mph, having also established the fastest lap of the race at 134.279mph. Emerson Fittipaldi (Lotus-Ford) was second, Tim Schenken

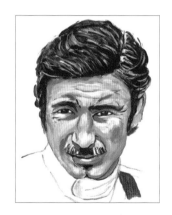

Jo Siffert had a brilliant career, tragically, cut short when he became the only driver to be killed in a BRM.

(Brabham-Ford) third while Gethin and Marko were tenth and 11th. Ganley had retired with ignition problems on lap six.

The Italian Grand Prix: September 5, 1971 – a sensational win for Peter Gethin

Jo Siffert and Howden Ganley were third and fourth in practice at Monza behind Chris Amon (Matra-Simca) and Jacky Ickx (Ferrari). The BRMs of Peter Gethin and Helmut Marko were on row six of the starting grid.

Initially, Clay Regazzoni (Ferrari) passed six cars to lead, but dropped behind Ronnie Peterson (March-Ford), Jackie Stewart (Tyrrell-Ford) and Jo Siffert before the end of lap one. The first eight cars, which included both Siffert, Ganley and Gethin, were within a second of each other in a high-speed chase for lap after lap. Stewart, Ickx and Regazzoni fell by the wayside with engine failures, and Siffert and Ganley dropped back. Gethin, however, gained ground, and caught up with Peterson, François Cevert (Tyrrell) and Mike Hailwood (Surtees-Ford). It could have been any one of them in front at the end, but it was Gethin who won by just 0.01 of a second from Peterson, and altogether it was less than a second that separated Gethin, Peterson, Cevert, Hailwood and Ganley. Siffert finished ninth, while Marko had retired due to engine trouble on lap four. After the race, Gethin said that he had raised his hand as he crossed the line in what was virtually a dead-heat, and thought that it was this that awarded him the win, at an average speed of 150.754mph.

The Canadian Grand Prix: September 19, 1971

Jo Siffert's BRM was at the front of the grid with the

Peter Gethin winning the 1971 Italian Grand Prix by just 0.01 seconds.

Tyrrell-Fords of Jackie Stewart and François Cevert on either side of him. Howden Ganley crashed in practice and his car couldn't be repaired in time for the race. Peter Gethin was 16th, Helmut Marko 19th, and George Eaton 21st in the remaining BRMs.

In driving rain, Jackie Stewart's Tyrrell went into the lead, while Jo Siffert spun on the slippery track. Ronnie Peterson's March lay second and Jean-Pierre Beltoise's Matra-Simca third. Graham Hill spun his Brabham-Ford and retired on lap three, and Clay Regazzoni crashed and escaped when his Ferrari caught fire on lap eight. All the while, Stewart continued on his way, and won the race from Peterson with nearly 40 seconds in hand. Siffert finished ninth, Marko 12th, Gethin 14th, and Eaton 15th.

The United States Grand Prix: October 3, 1971
The BRM line-up at Watkins Glen saw Jo Siffert come sixth in practice, Howden Ganley 12th, Helmut Marko 16th, Peter Gethin 21st, and John Cannon, who replaced George Eaton, 24th. Jackie Stewart (Tyrrell), Emerson Fittipaldi (Lotus) and Denny Hulme (McLaren) were on the front row.

Stewart seized the lead from Hulme, who, in turn, was chased by François Cevert's Tyrrell. Siffert was seventh and made steady progress to lie second to the flying Cevert. That was how the race ended, with Ronnie Peterson's March-Ford in third place. Ganley was fourth, Gethin ninth, Marko 13th, and Cannon 14th, all five works BRMs having completed the race.

Sadly, Jo Siffert was killed later that month when his car caught fire during the Race of Champions at Brands Hatch – making him the only driver to be killed at the wheel of a BRM. Following the death of Pedro Rodriguez, this tragic event meant that BRM had lost, in quick succession, its two star drivers.

The 1971 World Championship
Jackie Stewart won his second World Championship with 62 points. Jo Siffert was fifth with 19, while Peter Gethin and Pedro Rodriguez were joint ninth with nine each. Howden Ganley was 15th with five points. Tyrrell-Ford won the Constructors' Championship with 73 points and BRM was second with 36.

1972

Marlboro sponsorship
BRM was sponsored by Marlboro in 1972, and the cigarette manufacturer persuaded Louis Stanley to field five cars on a regular basis, even though this overstretched the team's resources. The new P180 BRM, with its rear-mounted radiators, suffered from a poor weight distribution, so for the most part P160s and P153s were used instead. Jean-Pierre Beltoise joined Peter Gethin, Howden Ganley, Helmut Marko, Alex Soler-Roig, Reine Wisell and Gijs Van Lennep in the driver line-up.

The new 005 Tyrrell appeared in the middle of the year with a lower body and enclosed engine. Lotus introduced the first of the John Player Specials, the Lotus 72D. Bernie Ecclestone bought Brabham, and Niki Lauda drove the new March 721.

The Argentine Grand Prix: January 23, 1972
Jackie Stewart's Tyrrell was fastest in practice at Buenos Aires with Carlos Reutemann's Brabham alongside him on the grid. Of the BRM drivers, Howden Ganley was 13th in a P160B, Reine Wisell 17th in a P153, Peter Gethin 18th in a P160B, Helmut Marko 19th in a P153, and Alex Soler-Roig 21st in a P160B.

Stewart led from the start, pursued by Reutemann's Brabham, until Emerson Fittipaldi's JPS Lotus, which would retire on lap 60 with a broken rear radius rod, took his place. Denny Hulme (McLaren-Ford) was lying third at that point, but he soon overtook the Lotus. It was Stewart's race, however, and he was followed across the line by Hulme and Regazzoni (Ferrari). Ganley and Marko

finished in ninth and tenth places. Soler-Roig crashed on lap one when his car's throttle stuck open, Gethin retired on lap two because of a fractured oil pipe, and Wisell on lap 59 due to a leaking water hose.

The South African Grand Prix: March 4, 1972
The front row at Kyalami consisted of Jackie Stewart (Tyrrell-Ford), Clay Regazzoni (Ferrari) and Emerson Fittipaldi (JPS Lotus-Ford). Jean-Pierre Beltoise, in his first race with BRM, was 11th, Howden Ganley 16th, Peter Gethin 18th and Helmut Marko 23rd.

Denny Hulme's McLaren-Ford led until lap two, when Jackie Stewart took command, while Beltoise, in the leading BRM, was back in eighth place. On lap 45 Stewart stopped due to an oil leak and Fittipaldi took the lead, followed by Hulme. In the end it was Hulme who won, with Fittipaldi second and Peter Revson's McLaren-Ford third. Marko finished 14th while Ganley and Gethin were unclassified several laps in arrears. Beltoise had retired due to engine trouble on lap 61.

The Spanish Grand Prix: May 1, 1972
Jacky Ickx was on pole position at Jarama in his Ferrari 312B/2, with Denny Hulme (McLaren-Ford) and Emerson Fittipaldi (JPS Lotus-Ford) completing the front row. BRM drivers Jean-Pierre Beltoise, Reine Wisell, Howden Ganley, Peter Gethin and Alex Soler-Roig were seventh, tenth, 20th, 21st and 22nd. Two new P180s were on-hand, but failed to impress.

The order on the first lap was Hulme followed by Jackie Stewart's Tyrrell, but this was reversed on lap five. Fittipaldi then passed Stewart to lead in the JPS, and Ickx took second place from Stewart. The race was won by Fittipaldi, with the Ferraris of Ickx and Clay Regazzoni second and third. All the BRMs had retired, Soler-Roig through an accident on lap seven, Beltoise with gearbox trouble on lap nine, Wisell through an accident on lap 25, Ganley with a blown engine on lap 38, and Gethin with engine trouble on lap 66.

The Monaco Grand Prix: May 14, 1972 – at last, a glorious win for BRM at Monaco
Driving P160Bs, Jean-Pierre Beltoise and Peter

Peter Gethin in the difficult P180 BRM during the 1972 Spanish Grand Prix.

Gethin were fourth and fifth on the starting grid. Emerson Fittipaldi (JPS Lotus-Ford) and Jacky Ickx (Ferrari) were in front of them, and Reine Wisell and Helmut Marko were back in 16th and 17th places in the other two BRMs.

In heavy rain, Beltoise led away, followed by Regazzoni, until the Ferrari took to the escape road after skidding on the treacherously wet track. Beltoise steadily increased his lead with a masterful display of driving in the most appalling conditions to win the race at 63.849mph after establishing the fastest lap at 70.351mph. Behind him came Ickx and Fittipaldi. Marko finished eighth, while Wisell, Gethin and Ganley had retired on laps 17, 28 and 48, the first with engine trouble and the other two due to accidents. Afterwards, Beltoise said that his Firestone tyres held the road exceptionally well in the rain and, in addition, the BRM engine was exceptionally smooth. Sadly, it proved to be BRMs last win in a major Grand Prix. In *Fifty Famous Motor*

Jean-Pierre Beltoise: the great French driver.

Jean-Pierre Beltoise notching up BRM's last Grand Prix win at a rain-drenched Monaco in 1972.

Races, Alan Henry described the race as "BRM's surfing swan song."

The Belgian Grand Prix: June 4, 1972

Emerson Fittipaldi (Lotus-Ford) was on pole ahead of Clay Regazzoni (Ferrari) and Denny Hulme (McLaren-Ford). Jean-Pierre Beltoise was sixth in the leading BRM, and Howden Ganley, Peter Gethin, and Helmut Marko were 15th, 17th and 23rd respectively. Vern Schuppan was denied the opportunity to drive a BRM, as Gethin required the fifth car after he crashed his during practice.

Regazzoni was followed by Fittipaldi at the start of the race, and these two led Jacky Ickx (Ferrari),

Hulme and François Cevert (Tyrrell). On lap nine the JPS Lotus took the lead, and stayed there until the end, with Cevet second and Hulme third. Ganley and Marko were eighth and tenth, while Beltoise and Gethin retired on laps 15 and 27 due to mechanical problems.

The French Grand Prix: July 2, 1972

Chris Amon was fastest in Clermont-Ferrand in his Matra-Simca. Helmut Marko was in sixth place and Reine Wisell 18th in their BRMs. Jean-Pierre Beltoise had to start at the back of the grid, not having had time to practice in his P160B after the driveshaft had broken on his P180.

Amon, Denny Hulme (McLaren) and Jackie Stewart (Tyrrell) led, while Marko retired when a stone flew up and pierced his eye. Sadly, this incident ended his racing career.

After Amon and Hulme dropped back the race was won by Stewart, with Emerson Fittipaldi's Lotus second and Amon third. Beltoise finished in 15th place, a lap behind. Wisell retired on lap 25.

The British Grand Prix: July 15, 1972

Jackie Oliver was back in a BRM for the British Grand Prix at Brands Hatch. Jacky Ickx (Ferrari) was on pole with Emerson Fittipaldi (Lotus) next to him. Of the other BRM drivers, Jean-Pierre Beltoise was sixth, Oliver 14th and Peter Gethin 16th.

Beltoise made a brilliant start, running third behind Ickx and Fittipaldi, but he dropped back as the race proceeded and finished in eleventh place. Ickx retired on lap 49 due to failing oil pressure, and the honours finally went to Fittipaldi, who was followed across the line by Jackie Stewart's Tyrrell and Peter Revson's McLaren-Ford. Gethin retired on lap six with engine trouble and Oliver on lap 37 due to suspension failure.

Dr Helmut Marko driving the P160B BRM in the 1972 French Grand Prix.

Emerson Fittipaldi in the JPS Lotus 72D during the 1972 French Grand Prix.

The German Grand Prix: July 30, 1972

Jacky Ickx (Ferrari) and Jackie Stewart (Tyrrell) were on the front row at the Nürburgring. Jean-Pierre Beltoise, Reine Wisell and Howden Ganley stood in 13th, 17th and 18th on the grid in their BRMs.

Ickx, Ronnie Peterson (March) and Clay Regazzoni (Ferrari) headed the field in that order – Stewart was delayed when he touched Peterson's car. Emerson Fittipaldi (Lotus) rose to second place with Peterson, Regazzoni and Stewart behind him. Fittipaldi's car caught fire on lap 11, and on lap 13 Stewart and Regazzoni touched wheels while travelling side-by-side, putting an end to the Tyrrell's race. Ickx went on to win, followed by Regazzoni, Peterson and Ganley. Beltoise finished in ninth position after stopping with a broken battery mount, Wisell having retired because of engine trouble on lap four.

The Austrian Grand Prix: August 13, 1972

Emerson Fittipaldi's Lotus was fastest in practice, followed by Clay Regazzoni's Ferrari, Jackie Stewart's Tyrrell-Ford and Peter Revson's McLaren-Ford. The BRMs of Howden Ganley, Peter Gethin and Jean-Pierre Beltoise were tenth, 16th and 21st on the grid, Beltoise having been beset with engine failures in the course of practice.

Stewart led from Regazzoni and Fittipaldi, but as the race progressed his car developed oversteer and he was passed by Fittipaldi and Denny Hulme (McLaren-Ford). The race went to Fittipaldi with Hulme just over a second behind him. Revson was third, Ganley sixth, Beltoise eighth and Gethin 13th.

When I sent Ken Tyrrell a painting of Jackie Stewart's car in this race, he wrote: "No wonder Jackie complained of an oversteer!"

The Italian Grand Prix: September 10, 1972

Jacky Ickx won pole position with his Ferrari from Amon's Matra-Simca by just 0.04 of a second. The BRMs of Reine Wisell, Peter Gethin, Jean-Pierre Beltoise and Howden Ganley were tenth, 12th, 16th and 17th on the grid, Beltoise driving the new P180 and the others P160Cs.

The clutch of Jackie Stewart's Tyrrell failed at the start, so, to the delight of the crowd, the race was led by the Ferraris of Ickx and Clay Regazzoni. The two changed places, but Regazzoni had to retire after touching Carlos Pace's spinning March. The race developed into a duel between Ickx and Emerson Fittipaldi's Lotus until the Ferrari lost all power, leaving Fittipaldi a clear winner from Mike Hailwood in a Surtees-Ford. Gethin was sixth, Beltoise eighth, Ganley 11th and Wisell 12th.

The Canadian Grand Prix: September 24, 1972

Peter Revson (McLaren), Denny Hulme (McLaren) and Ronnie Peterson (March) were at the front of the grid at Mosport, with the BRMs of Peter Gethin, Howden Ganley, Jean-Pierre Beltoise and Bill Brack in 12th, 14th, 20th and 23rd places.

At the start it was Peterson in front, followed by Jackie Stewart (Tyrrell) and Revson. Stewart then overtook Peterson and held his lead thereafter. As Peterson dropped back Revson and Hulme claimed the next two places at the end of the race. Ganley finished in tenth place but the other three BRM's retired: Brack following a spin and Beltoise with an oil leak, both on lap 21; Gethin on lap 26 due to suspension problems.

United States Grand Prix, October 8, 1972

The BRM team ended a rather dismal season, Monaco apart, firmly entrenched in the lower-half of the starting grid. Jackie Stewart's Tyrrell, Peter Revson's McLaren and Denny Hulme's McLaren were at the front at Watkins Glen, while Howden Ganley was 16th, Jean-Pierre Beltoise 17th, Brian Redman 23rd and Peter Gethin 26th.

Stewart led from start to finish, and his teammate François Cevert held second place from halfway through the race, with Hulme finishing third. The BRMs all retired with mechanical problems: Redman on lap 35, Beltoise on lap 44, Ganley on lap 45 and Gethin on lap 48.

The 1972 World Championship

Emerson Fittipaldi won the World Championship with 61 points. Beltoise was 11th with nine points,

Ganley 13th with four. Redman scored four with his drives for BRM and McLaren. Peter Gethin, scoring just one point, was 20th.

The Constructors' World Championship was won by JPS Lotus with 61 points. BRM came seventh with 14.

1973

Another year with the P160s
BRM had lost faith in the P180, and so the P160C, D and E appeared with increased output from the V12 engine, achieved by Peter Windsor-Smith. The cars had new rear aerofoils with large side plates, and full-width nose cowlings. Niki Lauda and Clay Regazzoni joined Jean Pierre Beltoise in the BRM team.

Also in 1973, James Hunt drove Lord Hesketh's March, and Gordon Murray became Bernie Ecclestone's designer at Brabham, producing the Brabham BT42. Ken Tyrrell further developed his cars, and Enzo Ferrari produced a full monocoque for his flat-12 engine, designated the 312B/3.

The Argentine Grand Prix: January 28, 1973
Clay Regazzoni's BRM was on pole position for the Argentine Grand Prix, with Emerson Fittipaldi's Lotus-Ford second on the grid. Jean-Pierre Beltoise was seventh, and Niki Lauda 13th in the remaining BRMs.

Regazzoni and Fittipaldi were side-by-side into the first bend, François Cevert then passing them briefly before the BRM was in front again, with Lauda in fifth place. On lap 29, Regazzoni, after giving BRM supporters a brilliant display at the front, had to surrender his position due to failing tyres. Lauda and Beltoise retired due to engine trouble on laps 67 and 80, and Regazzoni eventually finished down in seventh place – the race being won by Fittipaldi.

The Brazilian Grand Prix: February 11, 1973
Clay Regazzoni was fourth fastest behind the Lotus-Fords of Ronnie Peterson and Emerson Fittipaldi, and Jacky Ickx's Ferrari. Jean-Pierre Beltoise was tenth and Niki Lauda 13th in their BRMs.

Fittipaldi and Carlos Pace (Surtees-Ford) made magnificent starts, but Jackie Stewart (Tyrrell-Ford) moved up to second place on lap two, and Pace was also overtaken by Peterson until he spun, breaking a rear wheel. Ickx, who was now in front of Pace, inherited third place, while Beltoise and Clay Regazzoni were in fourth and sixth. Beltoise pulled out with electrical problems on lap 24, and was

Clay Regazzoni: a welcome addition to the BRM line up.

Regazzoni in his BRM.

Clay Regazzoni leading the 1973 Argentine Grand Prix before dropping back due to tyre wear.

classified as eighth. The race was won by Fittipaldi, Stewart and Hulme (McLaren-Ford) taking second and third. Lauda finished in eighth place.

The South African Grand Prix: March 3, 1973
Clay Regazzoni was again on the second row of the starting grid, behind Denny Hulme (McLaren), Emerson Fittipaldi (Lotus) and Jody Scheckter (McLaren). Jean-Pierre Beltoise was seventh and Niki Lauda tenth in the cars from Bourne.

Fittipaldi led from Hulme and Scheckter, but soon dropped behind them. After this, Stewart (Tyrrell-Ford) improved his position, and eventually took the lead to win. Peter Revson (Lotus) was second and Emerson Fittipaldi third. On lap three Regazzoni was involved in a multiple car pile-up, and his BRM to caught fire. He was dragged, unconscious, from the car by Mike Hailwood, whose Surtees had started

the incident when it crashed into Reutemann's sliding Lotus. Beltoise retired on lap five (clutch) and Lauda on lap 27 (engine).

The Spanish Grand Prix: April 29, 1973
Ronnie Peterson (JPS Lotus-Ford) and Denny Hulme (McLaren-Ford) secured the front row of the starting grid at Montjuïc Park. Clay Regazzoni, Jean-Pierre Beltoise and Niki Lauda were eighth, tenth and 11th in their BRMs.

The order after the start was Peterson, Hulme, Jackie Stewart (Tyrrell), François Cevert (Tyrrell), and Beltoise. Stewart overtook Hulme, and Emerson Fittipaldi (Lotus) overtook Beltoise, while Lauda was just behind him. Peterson maintained his lead, but the Tyrrells were next up when Hulme came in to change a wheel. Fittipaldi overtook Cevert on lap 27, just before the latter went to the pits with a puncture, and Peterson dropped out of the race due to gearbox trouble on lap 57. The race ended in a win for Fittipaldi, followed by Cevert, George Follmer (Shadow-Ford), Peter Revson (McLaren) and Beltoise. Regazzoni finished ninth; Lauda had retired on lap 28.

The Belgian Grand Prix: May 20, 1973
Ronnie Peterson (Lotus) and Denny Hulme (McLaren) were fastest in practice at Spa. Jean-Pierre Beltoise was fifth in the leading BRM, Clay Regazzoni 12th and Niki Lauda 14th.

François Cevert (Tyrrell) established an early lead from Peterson, while Beltoise ran in the first five until delayed by failing brakes. Cevert then lost several places through a spin, and Jackie Stewart (Tyrrell) made progress, overtaking Emerson Fittipaldi's Lotus to lead the race. Cevert made up ground again to take second place behind Stewart.

At the end the order was Stewart first, Cevert second and Fittipaldi third. Lauda finished fifth and Regazzoni tenth. Beltoise was seven laps behind the leader, and therefore unclassified.

The Monaco Grand Prix: June 3, 1973
Jackie Stewart recorded the fastest time in practice with his Tyrrell, and was placed alongside

Ronnie Peterson's Lotus, which was only 0.2 seconds slower. Niki Lauda's BRM was sixth, Clay Regazzoni's eighth, and Jean-Pierre Beltoise's 11th.

François Cevert's Tyrrell led the race until delayed by a puncture, when the order became Peterson, Regazzoni, Stewart, Emerson Fittipaldi (Lotus) and Lauda. Regazzoni retired with failing brakes on lap 16, and Peterson was overtaken by both Stewart and Fittipaldi. Cevert recovered to take fourth place after Peterson and Stewart won the race from

Fittipaldi, Peterson and Cevert. Lauda retired on lap 29 due to gearbox trouble, and Beltoise on lap 40 after a crash.

The Swedish Grand Prix: June 17, 1973

François Cevert was marginally faster than his team-mate in practice at Anderstorp, coming second to Ronnie Peterson's Lotus on the starting grid. Jean-Pierre Beltoise, Clay Regazzoni and Niki Lauda were ninth, 12th and 15th in the BRMs.

Clay Regazzoni's Marlboro BRM leading Jackie Stewart's Tyrrell-Ford during the 1973 Monaco Grand Prix.

Another view of Regazzoni and Stewart at Monaco.

Emerson Fittipaldi (JPS Lotus-Ford) made a good start to lead Peterson, Jackie Stewart, Cevert and Denny Hulme (McLaren-Ford). Stewart closed on the two Lotus drivers, and Hulme caught up to him, now ahead of Cevert. Then, on lap 69, Fittipaldi slowed due to failing brakes – Stewart suffered the same problem on the last lap. The race went to Hulme, who passed Peterson – slowed with a deflating tyre – on the last lap. Cevert was third, Regazzoni ninth and Lauda tenth. Beltoise had retired because of engine trouble on lap 58.

The French Grand Prix: July 1, 1973

Ford engines filled the first eight places on the starting grid, led by Jackie Stewart's Tyrrell. Clay Regazzoni was ninth in practice, Jean-Pierre Beltoise 15th and Niki Lauda 17th in the three BRMs.

Jody Scheckter led the race in his McLaren-Ford, followed by Jackie Stewart. Emerson Fittipaldi (Lotus) took up the chase and, as he attempted to pass Scheckter, the two cars touched, and consequently, both were out of the race. This left Peterson with a clear lead over Cevert and Carlos Reutemann (Brabham-Ford), and they held their positions to the end. Lauda finished ninth, Beltoise 11th and Regazzoni 12th.

The British Grand Prix: July 14, 1973

Behind the front three rows of Ford-engined Lotuses, McLarens, Tyrrells and Brabhams, the BRMs of Niki Lauda and Clay Regazzoni were in ninth and tenth positions, while Jean-Pierre Beltoise was further back in 17th spot.

Lauda's car's driveshaft failed on the grid, rekindling memories of Silverstone in 1950, and his car was shunted by Oliver's Shadow-Ford. A multiple car pile-up on the first lap then caused several retirements, including that of Beltoise. The most serious injury, however, was Andrea de Adamich's broken ankle.

When the race was re-started, Ronnie Peterson (Lotus) led from a hastily repaired BRM, Lauda having made a fantastic spurt from the third row. Jackie Stewart (Tyrrell) then overtook Lauda, but immediately spun off into the long grass. Lauda continued to lose position, and Peterson led from Emerson Fittipaldi (Lotus), Peter Revson (McLaren) and Denny Hulme (McLaren). Fittipaldi retired due to transmission trouble ,and Revson overtook Peterson to win the race. Regazzoni finished seventh and Lauda 12th.

The Dutch Grand Prix: July 29, 1973

The front line of the grid consisted of Ronnie Peterson, Jackie Stewart and François Cevert. Jean-Pierre Beltoise was ninth, Niki Lauda 11th and Clay Regazzoni 12th in the BRMs.

Peterson went into an immediate lead at the start of the race, while Lauda was shunted off the circuit by Howden Ganley's Williams-Ford. Jackie Stewart (Tyrrell) was in pursuit of Peterson for second place, when Roger Williamson's March hit the barriers, landed upside-down, and caught fire. Tragically, Williamson died, in spite of the superhuman efforts of David Purley to save him.

The race continued, the cars passing the burning wreckage through a screen of black smoke. Stewart went on to win, with Cevert finishing second and Hunt third. Beltoise took fifth place and Regazzoni eighth. Lauda had retired on lap 52 because of a failed fuel pump.

The German Grand Prix: August 5, 1973

A ban on tobacco advertising in Germany at this time caused BRM and others to cover their sponsors' prominent logos. Jackie Stewart (Tyrrell) and Ronnie Peterson (Lotus) shared the front row at the Nürburgring. The BRMs of Niki Lauda, Jean-Pierre Beltoise and Clay Regazzoni were fifth, ninth and tenth.

Stewart and François Cevert led after Peterson's engine failed on the first lap. The Tyrrells were pursued by Ickx and Lauda, until Lauda crashed on lap two when one of his tyres deflated. Beltoise stopped at the pits on lap two with the same problem.

Stewart, Cevert and Ickx managed to maintain their positions to the end. Beltoise retired on lap five due to gearbox problems, and Regazzoni's engine failed on lap eight.

The Austrian Grand Prix: August 19, 1973

The Lotus-Fords of Emerson Fittipaldi and Ronnie Peterson were at the front of the grid at the Österreichring, while the BRMs of Jean-Pierre Beltoise and Clay Regazzoni, now with their more conspicuous air boxes, were back in the seventh row. Niki Lauda withdrew from the race with an injured wrist.

At the start the order was Peterson, Denny Hulme (McLaren-Ford) and Fittipaldi, pursued by Arturo Merzario's Ferrari. Cevert's race ended when he touched the rear wheel of Scheckter's McLaren-Ford – both retired. Hulme pitted due to a misfiring engine and Carlos Pace (Surtees-Ford) challenged Stewart (Tyrrell-Ford) for second place. The result was another win for Peterson, and the BRMs of Beltoise and Regazzoni taking fifth and sixth.

The Italian Grand Prix: September 9, 1973

Ronnie Peterson (JPS Lotus-Ford) was fastest at Monza, with Peter Revson (McLaren-Ford) next to him on the grid. BRM drivers Jean-Pierre Beltoise, Niki Lauda and Clay Regazzoni were 13th, 15th and 18th.

Peterson and Emerson Fittipaldi in JPS Lotus-Fords established an immediate lead from Jackie Stewart (Tyrrell-Ford) and Denny Hulme (McLaren-Ford). Stewart stopped at the pits with a puncture, allowing Hulme to take third place. The two John Player Specials held their positions to the end, but Revson ultimately took third after Hulme was slowed due to brake trouble.

Beltoise finished 13th, a lap behind the leaders, while Regazzoni retired on lap 31 with engine trouble and Lauda dropped out on lap 34 when a defective tyre sent his car into the guard rail.

The Canadian Grand Prix: September 23, 1973

Ronnie Peterson (Lotus) and Peter Revson (McLaren) were again on the front row at Mosport with Carlos Reutemann (Brabham) and Jody Scheckter (McLaren) immediately behind them. The BRMs of Niki Lauda, Jean-Pierre Beltoise and Peter Gethin were eighth, 16th and 25th. Clay Regazzoni was also present, but without a drive.

In extremely wet conditions, Lauda took the lead from Peterson and Scheckter on lap three, quickly

Niki Lauda leading the 1973 Canadian Grand Prix with his V12 BRM, shod with wet weather Firestone tyres.

stretching it to 20 seconds thanks to his Firestone tyres. Peterson left the circuit on lap 17 when his rear suspension collapsed, and Scheckter dropped back as the circuit began to dry out. Lauda lost time changing to intermediate tyres on lap 20, and the race was then led by Emerson Fittipaldi (Lotus). François Cevert (Tyrrell) and Jody Scheckter crashed without personal injury, triggering the first use of a pace car in a Formula One Grand Prix, which gave rise to some confusion at the end of the race. Revson was declared the winner and Beltoise was fourth, Gethin and Lauda having retired on laps six and 33 respectively, both because of mechanical problems.

The United States Grand Prix: October 7, 1973

Ronnie Peterson (Lotus) was fastest in practice at Watkins Glen, with Carlos Reutemann (Brabham) sharing the front row. Jean-Pierre Beltoise, Clay Regazzoni and Niki Lauda were 14th, 15th and 21st on the grid in their BRMs.

Practice was marred by François Cevert's fatal accident in his Tyrrell-Ford. It was an immense personal loss for Ken Tyrrell, who often spoke to me about him, and who firmly believed that he would have been a future World Champion.

Peterson led the race from Reutemann and James Hunt (March-Ford). Hunt passed Reutemann early on, and that was how the race ended. Regazzoni was eighth and Beltoise ninth, Lauda having retired on lap 36 because of a faulty fuel pump.

1973 World Championship

Jackie Stewart won his third World Championship with the Tyrrell-Ford, having achieved 71 points. Beltoise was tenth with nine points, while Lauda and Regazzoni were joint 17th with two points each.

In the Constructors' Championship JPS Lotus was the winner with 92 points. BRM came sixth, equal to Ferrari, with 12 points.

Jackie Stewart's third World Championship.

3.3

The last years and the Stanley-BRM

STANLEY-BRM

The P201 in 1974

Mike Pilbeam first joined BRM back in 1962 as a stress engineer working for Tony Rudd and, after a spell with Colin Chapman working on the Lotus 72, and another with Surtees, he returned to BRM to assist Tony Southgate in developing the P160. He then took over when Southgate left BRM in 1972, and was therefore responsible for the entirely new P201: introduced at the beginning of 1974.

The V12 P201 monocoque had sides which sloped inwards towards the cockpit, rather like the Brabham BT42. A large air-box was positioned above the driver, and the car had four inboard mounted brakes. With the financial support of a French company, Jean Pierre Beltoise was joined by Henri Pescarolo and François Migault. Sadly, Sir Alfred Owen died in 1974.

The 312B Ferraris were considerably revised for 1974, Ken Tyrrell signed Jody Scheckter and Patrick Depailler, and James Hunt drove the new Hesketh-Ford painted patriotically in red, white and blue. Marlboro now sponsored McLaren, leaving French firm Motul Oil as BRM's only sponsor.

The Argentine Grand Prix: January 13, 1974

Ronnie Peterson was fastest in practice in his Lotus while Clay Regazzoni was second in the new Ferrari. The P160 BRMs of Jean-Pierre Beltoise,

Henri Pescarolo and François Migault were 14th, 21st and 22nd.

Peterson led the race from Carlos Reutemann (Brabham-Ford) and Emerson Fittipaldi (McLaren-Ford) but Reutemann soon took the lead with Denny Hulme (McLaren-Ford) taking up the chase as Reutemann dropped out of contention, his Brabham only firing on seven cylinders. Peterson lost ground after lap nine, and it was Hulme who won the race, followed by the Ferraris of Niki Lauda and Clay Regazzoni. Beltoise was fifth, Pescarolo ninth, while Migault retired due to engine trouble on lap 32.

The Brazilian Grand Prix: January 27, 1974

Emerson Fittipaldi's McLaren-Ford and Carlos Reutemann's Brabham-Ford were the front-runners at Interlagos, while, in last year's BRMs,

Jean-Pierre Beltoise was 18th, Henri Pescarolo 21st and François Migault 24th.

Reutemann took an immediate lead from Ronnie Peterson (JPS Lotus) and Fittipaldi, but dropped behind them on lap four. Fittipaldi then overtook Peterson on lap 16, and managed to stave off the Swedish driver, who eventually stopped at his pit because of a puncture. This left Fittipaldi a clear winner from Clay Regazzoni's Ferrari and Jacky Ickx in the JPS Lotus. The BRMs of Beltoise, Pescarolo and Migault finished tenth, 14th and 16th.

The South African Grand Prix: March 30, 1974 – an encouraging debut for the P201

Jean-Pierre Beltoise had the new Mike Pilbeam-designed P201 BRM at Kyalama, and managed 11th place on the grid. Henri Pescarolo and François Migault were 21st and 25th in P160Es. At

Jean Pierre Beltoise driving the new P201 BRM ahead of Carlos Reutemann's Brabham, to finish second in the 1974 South African Grand Prix.

the front of the grid were Niki Lauda's Ferrari and Carlos Pace's Surtees-Ford.

It was Lauda who led at the start, but he was overtaken by Carlos Reutemann's Brabham on lap ten, with Beltoise in 11th place. The new BRM then overtook Denny Hulme (McLaren), Jody Scheckter (Tyrrell) and Patrick Depailler (Tyrrell) and, by lap 65, was lying third behind Reutemann and Lauda. After Lauda slowed due to falling oil pressure, Beltoise moved up to secure second place with the P201 on its first outing. Migault was 15th and Pescarolo 18th.

The Spanish Grand Prix: April 28, 1974
Jean-Pierre Beltoise was 11th on the starting grid with the P201, while Henri Pescarolo and

François Migault lined-up in 20th and 22nd places in the earlier cars. Niki Lauda's Ferrari and Ronnie Peterson's JPS Lotus-Ford were in the front row.

The P201 broke a valve on lap three, taking it out of the race. Migault retired on lap 28 due to engine trouble, and Pescarolo finished in 12th place. The race went to Lauda, with Regazzoni's Ferrari finishing second, and Emerson Fittipaldi's McLaren third.

The Belgian Grand Prix: May 12, 1974
Clay Regazzoni (Ferrari) and Jody Scheckter (Tyrrell) lined up at the front of the grid at Spa, while the BRMs of Jean-Pierre Beltoise, Henri Pescarolo and François Migault were seventh, 15th and 25th.

After the start, Regazzoni was followed by

Jean Pierre Beltoise in the P201 BRM at the congested start of the 1974 Monaco Grand Prix.

Scheckter, but then Emerson Fittipaldi (McLaren) passed the Tyrrell, and Regazzoni lost time in a brief excursion from the course. Niki Lauda (Ferrari) made up ground through the course of the race to finish second to Fittipaldi, with Scheckter and Regazzoni third and fourth. Beltoise was fifth in the P201, while Migault finished in 16th place. Pescarolo had retired on lap 13 after a Guy Edwards' Lola shunted him off the course.

The Monaco Grand Prix: May 26, 1974
Jean-Pierre Beltoise was 11th on the grid with his P201, while François Migault was 22nd and Henri Pescarolo 27th in the earlier cars. The Ferraris of Niki Lauda and Clay Regazzoni were on the front row.

Regazzoni led from Lauda at the start. Behind them, on the first lap Denny Hulme (McLaren) and Beltoise touched wheels, and a number of cars quickly became involved in the incident. It meant the end of the P201's race, and, after ramming the barriers on lap five, Migault was to follow. Pescarolo retired due to gearbox trouble on lap 63 and the race eventually went to Ronnie Peterson (Lotus), with Jody Scheckter (Tyrrell) second and Jean-Pierre Jarier (Shadow-Ford) third.

The Swedish Grand Prix: June 9, 1974
The Tyrrells of Patrick Depailler and Jody Scheckter monopolised the front row at Anderstorp, while the two P201 BRMs of Jean-Pierre Beltoise and Henri Pescarolo were 13th and 19th.

Scheckter led the race from Ronnie Peterson (Lotus) and Depailler, but Pescarolo's P201 caught fire and retired on lap one. Beltoise also had to retire on lap three due to engine trouble. After Peterson stopped because of a broken driveshaft on lap nine, the two Tyrrells went on unchallenged, finishing first and second, with James Hunt in the new Hesketh-Ford following in third place.

The Dutch Grand Prix: June 23, 1974
Jean-Pierre Beltoise and François Migault had the P201 BRMs at Zandvoort while Henri Pescarolo drove a P160E.

The Ferraris of Niki Lauda and Clay Regazzoni were at the front of the grid and Beltoise, Pescarolo and Migault were 16th, 24th and 25th.

The order on lap one was Lauda, Mike Hailwood (McLaren), Patrick Depailler (Tyrrell) and Regazzoni, but the two Ferraris were soon together out in front. At the end it was Emerson Fittipaldi (McLaren) who took third place behind Lauda and Regazzoni. Pescarolo withdrew from the race on lap 15, while both Beltoise and Migault retired because of gearbox problems on laps 19 and 60.

The French Grand Prix: July 7, 1974
Niki Lauda's Ferrari was again fastest in practice at Dijon, but Ronnie Peterson's Lotus and Pryce's Shadow were ahead of Clay Regazzoni's Ferrari. The BRMs of Jean-Pierre Beltoise, Henri Pescarolo, now in the second P201, and François Migault were 17th, 19th and 21st on the grid.

Tom Pryce (Shadow), Carlos Reutemann (Brabham) and James Hunt (Hesketh) collided at the start of the race, and it was Lauda who led from Peterson and Regazzoni. Peterson overtook Lauda and soon drew away. The race ended with the three cars in that order. Beltoise was tenth, and Migault 14th, while Pescarolo had retired because of a defective clutch on the first lap.

The British Grand Prix: July 20, 1974
Niki Lauda (Ferrari) and Ronnie Peterson (Lotus) were fastest at Brands Hatch and the BRMs of François Migault (P160E), Henri Pescarolo (P201) Jean-Pierre Beltoise (P201 with a new short stroke V12) were 14th, 23rd and 24th on the grid.

Lauda immediately established a good lead from Jody Scheckter (Tyrrell) and Clay Regazzoni (Ferrari). Hans Stuck's March crashed on lap 36, and the circuit was littered with debris. As a result, Peterson and Regazzoni were delayed on lap 37 with punctured tyres, and the order became Lauda, Scheckter and Emerson Fittipaldi (McLaren). It then transpired that Lauda also had a slow puncture, causing him to drop back, and resulting in a win for Scheckter, with Fittipaldi and Jacky Ickx (Lotus) second and third. Beltoise was 12th, three laps behind the winner, and Migault finished a further nine laps back. Pescarolo had retired on lap 65 due to engine trouble.

The German Grand Prix: August 4, 1974

For the first time ever, three P201s were set to race, but engine failures reduced BRM's entries at the Nürburgring to two. Niki Lauda and Clay Regazzoni were on the front row with their Ferraris, while Jean-Pierre Beltoise and Henri Pescarolo were 15th and 24th in the BRMs.

As the race began, Regazzoni led from Jody Scheckter (Tyrrell-Ford) and Lauda, until the latter crashed after making contact with the Tyrrell. The two leading cars consolidated their positions through the race, and Reutemann finished in third place. Beltoise retired on lap five due to mechanical troubles and Pescarolo finished tenth.

The Austrian Grand Prix: August 18, 1974

Only one BRM made it to the Österreichring, driven by Jean-Pierre Beltoise. Niki Lauda was fastest in practice, with Carlos Reutemann alongside him at the front of the grid in the second Ferrari. Beltoise was 18th in his P201 BRM.

Reutemann (Brabham) led the race from Lauda and Regazzoni, with James Hunt in fourth place in the Hesketh-Ford. Lauda retired on lap 17 because of engine trouble, and Regazzoni dropped back with a puncture after lap 40. Reutemann led throughout to win, with Denny Hulme (McLaren) second and Hunt third. Beltoise retired on lap 22 due to engine trouble.

The Italian Grand Prix: September 8, 1974

The three P201s of Jean-Pierre Beltoise, François Migault and Henri Pescarolo were placed 11th, 24th and 25th on the grid, with Niki Lauda (Ferrari) and Carlos Reutemann (Brabham) on the front row.

All three BRMs were soon out of the race, Beltoise with electrical problems and Migault with a gearbox failure, both on lap one, and Pescarolo with engine trouble on lap four. The race went to Ronnie Peterson (JPS Lotus-Ford), with Emerson

Jody Scheckter's Tyrrell-Ford during the 1974 German Grand Prix.

Fittipaldi (McLaren-Ford) taking second and Jody Scheckter (Tyrrell-Ford) third. The Ferraris of Lauda and Regazzoni retired due to engine failures after leading the race at an early stage of the race.

The Canadian Grand Prix: September 22, 1974

Emerson Fittipaldi (McLaren) and Niki Lauda (Ferrari) formed the front row of the grid at Mosport. Chris Amon drove the latest of the P201 BRMs, but was at the back of the grid, complaining about his car's handling. Jean-Pierre Beltoise was 17th, but Henry Pescarolo and François Migault had both been released by BRM to reduce costs.

The order at the start of the race was Lauda, followed by Fittipaldi and Clay Regazzoni (Ferrari), with Jody Scheckter (Tyrrell) in fourth position and James Hunt (Hesketh) fifth. Scheckter crashed without injury when his brakes failed on lap 49. Lauda also crashed on lap 68. It was Fittipaldi who eventually led Regazzoni, Peterson and Hunt across the line. Amon and Beltoise were unclassified, finishing ten and 20 laps respectively behind the winner.

The United States Grand Prix: October 6, 1974

Chris Amon drove the sole BRM to compete at Watkins Glen, as Jean-Pierre Beltoise injured his foot when he crashed during practice. Amon was 12th on the grid, four rows behind Carlos Reutemann's Brabham and James Hunt's Hesketh.

Reutemann and Hunt were out in front at the start of the race, with Carlos Pace (Brabham) running in third. Sadly, Helmuth Koinigg was killed when his Surtees-Ford left the circuit on lap ten. Hunt lost contact with Reutemann, and was overtaken by Pace – this was the order in which they finished the race. Amon finished in ninth place, two laps behind the winner.

1974 World Championship

Emerson Fittipaldi won the World Championship with 55 points. Beltoise was 13th with 10 points. The Constructors' Championship was won by McLaren with 73 points. BRM was seventh with 10 points.

Emerson Fittipaldi winning his second World Championship in his McLaren-Ford.

1975

The Stanley-BRMs in 1975

In 1975, following the death of Sir Alfred Owen and the collapse of Rubery Owen, Louis Stanley became the Team Principal of Stanley-BRM with his wife Jean, the car being rudely called by some the 'Stanley Steamer.' Aubrey Woods became the team's designer in place of Mike Pilbeam, and Alan Challis took over Tim Parnell's role as team manager. The P201 was painted red, white and blue. A revision of the V12 unit proved to be unsuccessful, so, that, apart from the colour, the car was essentially unchanged from the previous year. Only one car ran, its driver for the first two races being Mike Wilds, and after that Bob Evans.

The Argentine Grand Prix: January 12, 1975

Practice was limited for Mike Wilds, as the Stanley-BRM had a persistent fuel leak and a split oil tank, and it placed 22nd of 23 cars on the starting grid. Handicapped at the start by a blocked fuel pipe, Wilds eventually retired his car on lap 25 with a seized scavenger pump. The race was won by Emerson Fittipaldi's McLaren-Ford.

The Brazilian Grand Prix: January 26, 1975

Mike Wilds crashed in practice at Interlagos, but

RAYMOND MAYS

TELEPHONES:
BOURNE 2131 (OFFICE)
BOURNE 2017 (EASTGATE HOUSE)

Eastgate House
BOURNE
LINCOLNSHIRE
PE10 9LB

The Revd. Bryan G. Apps,
125 Paynes Road,
Freemantle,
Southampton.

6th January, 1975

Dear Bryan,

Thank you so much for your letter, and for the excellent phtograph. Certainly model cars will be an economy in petrol over the other kind, and it must be an extremely interesting hobby.

Sir Alfred Owen has been too ill to take any active part in B.R.M. for some years, and the firm has been under the direction of Mr. and Mrs. Louis Stanley. However, this autumn Rubery Owen felt obliged to draw out, and B.R.M. went into voluntary liquidation. It has now been reformed under the name of Stanley B.R.M., and is continuing on a reduced scale in the same premises here. With the reorganisation I felt that I did not any longer want to take any active part, and therefore I resigned from my directorship. At the same time all my own family businesses were sold, so I have had to get used to a very different way of living. However I am gradually settling down, and I hope to be able to attend a few races this coming season.

The prospects for Formula I racing do not look too good, as the costs are so enormous, both for running the cars and for organising the race meetings. How well B.R.M. will do now it is impossible to say. They are competing with one car in the Argentine G.P. on 12th January. You are right: there has never been a car to equal the V-16 if only there had been time to have developed reliability before the change of Formula.

I hope things are going well with you, and may I now send my best wishes to you and your wife for 1975

Yours ever,

Raymond Mays

Raymond Mays commenting on my interest in antique tin plate toy cars, and bringing me up to date with regard to Sir Alfred Owen, Louis Stanley, BRM, and his own changed circumstances.

his car was straightened out in time to take up position on the grid in 22nd place, ahead of Rolf Stommelen's Lola-Ford. His race ended on lap 23 due to an electrical fault, and the winner was Carlos Pace's Brabham-Ford.

The South African Grand Prix: March 1, 1975
Bob Evans drove the Stanley-BRM at Kyalami, but

he experienced fuel starvation and an oil leak in practice, and was 24th of 27 on the grid. He ended the race in 15th place, two laps behind the winner, Jody Scheckter's Tyrrell-Ford.

The Spanish Grand Prix: April 27, 1975
Bob Evans was in the 12th row on the starting grid in the Stanley-BRM, and was 23rd of 25 cars. He

Niki Lauda winning the 1975 Swedish Grand Prix for Ferrari.

Carlos Reutemann winning the 1975 German Grand Prix.

Bob Evans driving the P201 Stanley-BRM at Monza in 1975.

retired on lap eight with fuel feed problems. The race went to Jochen Mass' McLaren-Ford.

The Belgian Grand Prix: May 25, 1975
Nearly four seconds slower than the pole setter, Bob Evans failed to qualify the Stanley-BRM at Monaco, but at Zolder for the Belgian Grand Prix, he was 18th on the grid. He finished the race in ninth place, two laps behind winner Niki Lauda in a Ferrari 312T.

The Swedish Grand Prix: June 8, 1975
The Stanley-BRM was a lowly 23rd on the starting grid at Anderstorp, and Bob Evans finished in 13th place, two laps behind the winning Ferrari, again driven by Niki Lauda.

The Dutch Grand Prix: June 22, 1975
Bob Evans was in 20th place in the spare Stanley-BRM, having experienced engine problems with the car intended for the race. He retired on lap 24 with a broken crown wheel and pinion. The popular winner was James Hunt in the Hesketh-Ford.

The Austrian Grand Prix: August 17, 1975
In an effort to make it more competitive, The Stanley-BRM did not appear at Silverstone or the Nürburgring while mechanics worked on the car. It was, however, brought to the Österreichring, and Bob Evans took 24th place on the grid, again having to resort to the spare car. He pitted on lap two and retired after one more lap with engine trouble. The winner was Vittorio Brambilla in a March-Ford.

The Italian Grand Prix: September 7, 1975
This proved to be the last race of the year for the Stanley-BRM, as it would not appear at Watkins Glen, and Bob Evans only managed 20th place on the starting grid, and retired on lap one because of electrical problems. The winner of the race was Clay Regazzoni in a Ferrari.

1975 World Championship
Niki Lauda won the World Championship with 64½ points, and Ferrari won the Constructors' Championship with 72½. Sadly, the Stanley-BRM failed to achieve any points.

1976 AND THE LAST GASP OF THE P201

The Brazilian Grand Prix, January 25, 1976
Without a sponsor, the P201 Stanley-BRM made one last appearance in 1976 at the Brazilian Grand Prix Interlagos, with Ian Ashley at the wheel. Modifications to the radiators and brakes had been carried out over the course of the winter, and a revised crankcase layout had been adopted. However, the car was on the back row of the grid after its practice was plagued with troubles relating mainly to the gearbox and oil pump belt.

The powerplant of what was called the P201B had been changed, as the preferred engine had blown up in practice, and the Stanley-BRM was still being coaxed into life after the field had left. On lap three, Ashley brought it back to the pits with another broken oil pump belt, and that was that.

For the record, the race was won by Niki Lauda's Ferrari, and the World Championship went to James Hunt in a McLaren-Ford.

A footnote to 1977

In 1977 the P207 BRM, designed by Len Terry, appeared, with the comparatively meagre sponsorship of Rotary Watches. It was of conventional design, with an aluminium monocoque, and had longitudinal radiators. The faithful but uncompetitive V12 engine was used as a stressed member. Larry Perkins, Conny Andersson and Teddy Pilette were all on-hand as potential drivers, but in the financial climate of Formula 1 in 1977, it couldn't even become an also ran, as it wasn't fast enough to qualify in any of its eight appearances. Thus ended the last brave attempt to keep the 'British Ferraris' running on the circuits of Europe alongside the multitude of Ford-engined cars.

The P207 BRM.

Postscript

RAYMOND MAYS – BRDC MEMBER 1929-1980

A second visit to Raymond Mays at Eastgate House

Raymond Mays suffered a coronary thrombosis in February 1977, a set-back which was followed by a slight stroke. In spite of this, he was able to write to me in March 1978. Sadly, I had missed the *World of Difference* programme he mentions, in which he had featured.

RAYMOND MAYS

TELEPHONE·
(077 82) 2017

EASTGATE HOUSE
BOURNE
LINCOLNSHIRE
PE10 9LB

The Revd. Bryan G. Apps,M.A. B.A.
126 Payne Road,
Southampton.

2nd March, 1978

Dear Bryan,

    Thanks so much for your letter and for the most interesting booklet which I was delighted to have.

    Did you see my programme on BBC2 on 7th February last, in the World of Difference series? It was very good, and I have had many letters about it. I regret to say I have been ill with a coronary thrombosis last year and a slight stroke this year, but I am hlad to say I am gradually improving.

    My best wishes to you and your wife,

        Yours ever,

RAYMOND MAYS C.B.E.

TELEPHONE:

(077 82) 2017

EASTGATE HOUSE
BOURNE
LINCOLNSHIRE
PE10 9LB

The Revd. Bryan G. Apps,
14 Stourwood Road,
Southbourne,
Bournemouth. BH6 3QP

5th July, 1979

Dear Bryan,

It was very nice to have your letter and to hear all your
news. I do so much appreciate all your remarks, and many of
them bring back many happy memories to me of the past, but
what a sad state B.R.M. is in now - I do not like thinking
about it or even writing about it.

So glad you have had such nice holidays in Cornwall, but
I am sure you will have a lovely time in your rented cottage
in the Lakes. Yes, thank you, I have improved since my coronary
thrombosis and stroke, but of course not anything like I was
before, and after all I am 80 next birthday. It would be
nice to see you again.

With every good wishes,

Yours ever,

Raymond Mays

On the July 5 the following year, he wrote of his profound sadness at the state of BRM, but was also able to report a
further improvement in his health.

RAYMOND MAYS C.B.E.

TELEPHONE:
(077 82) 2017

EASTGATE HOUSE
BOURNE
LINCOLNSHIRE
PE10 9LB

The Revd. Bryan G. Apps,
14 Stourwood Road,
Southbourne,
Bournemouth.
Dorset. BH6 3QP

7th August, 1979

Dear Bryan,

Your letter of 3rd has only just come to hand. I note your remarks, and all being well I will make a point of being here on Friday afternoon, 17th, as it would be nice to see you.

Please let me know what time you will be calling. I have been none too well recently.

Best wishes,

Yours ever,

Raymond Mays!.

We arranged to visit him at Eastgate House later that year, and Raymond wrote to ask me to let him know the precise time that we would call.

We found him to be in remarkably good spirits. He was delighted to see us again, and showed little sign of his age, or of his decline in health.

Raymond Mays in good form.

Time had, of course, finally run out for BRM – the Stanley BRMs were uncompetitive and underfunded (the cars would be sold by Christies on October 22, 1981) – and Raymond told me that he wished they would remove the large BRM roundel on the building next door to the house and put an end to it altogether.

I wrote to him that September, and enclosed a promotional booklet of caricatures of racing drivers by Brockback, produced by Shell. It included one

RAYMOND MAYS C.B.E.

TELEPHONE:
(077 82) 2017

EASTGATE HOUSE
BOURNE
LINCOLNSHIRE
PE10 9LB

Revd. Bryan G. Apps,
14 Stourwood Road,
Southbourne,
Bournemouty.
Dorset. BH6 3QP

21st September, 1979

Dear Bryan,

Thank you very much for your letter of 3rd September, which I received on my return home this week, and also many thanks indeed for the book of caricatures, which I am so glad to have, and which will give me much pleasure.

I have just come back from Switzerland, from where I went to Milan for the Italian Grand Prix, which I enjoyed, but the present cars and drivers are nothing to the earlier days. I do so appreciate all you say about B.R.M., it is nice to hear of such enthusiasts as yourself.

I very much enjoyed your visit, and my very best wishes to all of you, and again my thanks for the book,

Yours sincerely,

Raymond Mays!

of Mays alongside his beloved ERA and he was very pleased with it. He wrote that "... the present cars and drivers are nothing to the earlier days."

Raymond Mays passed away at the age of 81 on January 6, 1980. He had been awarded the CBE in 1978 in recognition of his services to motor racing.

In his book about the BRM, published by Cassell in 1962, Ray was able to look back upon what it had achieved with justifiable satisfaction. He wrote: "BRMs may not have been the cars that took Britain to the front, but I think I can claim that it was the BRM which largely provided the incentive to other manufacturers, and that it was the BRM (still the only car that is considered by spectators to be representatively British) that first interested the general public of Britain in the sport."

Louis and Jean Stanley at the Old Mill House in 1990

Louis Stanley's distinguished presence led many foreigners to think that he was an English Lord. He was often called 'Big Lou' in the paddock, but never to his face, and is said to have been the son of Herbert Asquith, the former Prime Minister. For many years he was the Managing Director of the Dorchester Hotel. Through his marriage to Jean Owen, the sister of Sir Alfred Owen, he became closely connected with BRM, and took full control of the company in 1974 after Alfred's death.

Intensely shocked by the death of Jochen Rindt during practice at Monza in 1970, Stanley accompanied his body to an Italian hospital, and then started a public subscription for the provision of a Mobile Grand Prix Medical Unit, to ensure that injured drivers would be given expert medical help as soon as possible. This vehicle was driven to every World Championship race throughout 1971, and beyond, until helicopters were placed on standby at each circuit ready to fly injured drivers to the nearest suitable hospital. After the horrific death of Jo Siffert in a BRM at Brands Hatch in 1971, Louis and Jean stayed up all night with his distraught widow. He was the Honorary Secretary and Treasurer of the

Louis Stanley.

Grand Prix Drivers' Association, Chairman of the Siffert Council, Trustee of the Jim Clark Foundation, and the author of nearly 100 books.

I first wrote to Louis Stanley in May 1986, when I sent him a painting of Graham's BRM at Monaco in 1962, and he characteristically associated Jean with his reply.

He enclosed a signed copy of his book *Behind the Scenes,* in which he describes the last time he met Raymond Mays:

"Our last meeting was in Stamford hospital a few days before he died. Even then his vitality did not suggest the outlook of an octogenarian. He was still a keen observer of the racing scene and his comments on current events were pertinent.

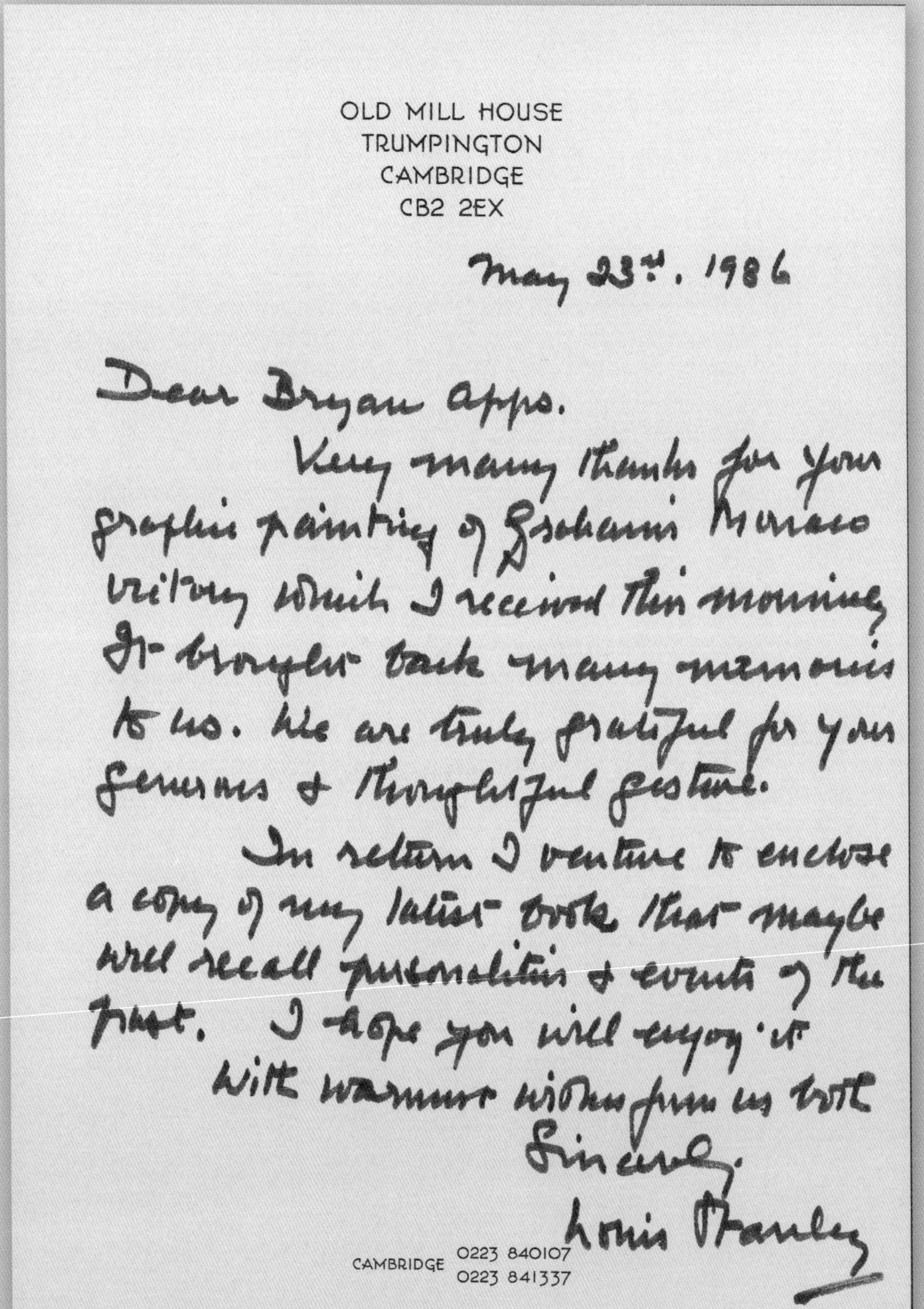

OLD MILL HOUSE
TRUMPINGTON
CAMBRIDGE
CB2 2EX

May 23rd. 1986

Dear Bryan Apps.

Very many thanks for your graphic painting of Grahams Monaco victory which I received this morning. It brought back many memories to us. We are truly grateful for your generous & thoughtful gesture.

In return I venture to enclose a copy of my latest book that maybe will recall personalities & events of the past. I hope you will enjoy it.

With warmest wishes from us both

Sincerely,

Louis Stanley

CAMBRIDGE   0223 840107
            0223 841337

Louis Stanley's letter.

He enjoyed life in his own distinctive way, always courteous and responsive to detail. Shortly before, I had enquired if there was anything he wanted. The answer was simple and typical. Could I locate any tins of watercress soup, a favourite that no one could find in Bourne or Stamford. Eventually a supply was found at his favourite London shop, Fortnum and Mason. Thus armed, I arrived at his bedside. His reaction was one of almost childish delight."

Stanley also wrote that one of Raymond Mays' achievements was that he lived on his nerves for so long without getting on others, adding that, while he was never selfish, he managed to whittle life to his dimensions with discriminating taste.

The Old Mill House, Trumpington: March 15, 1990

Kath and I visited Louis and Jean Stanley in their home in Cambridge with our son, Michael. We were shown into the living room, where my painting of Jackie Stewart driving a BRM at Spa during the 1965 Belgian Grand Prix was prominently displayed. A staunch Anglican, Louis Stanley was delighted that I was both a cleric and a motor racing enthusiast, saying that most of the cathedral clergy in Cambridge looked as though they were incapable of completing a lap around its aisles!

Over afternoon tea, Louis and Jean produced an enormous photograph album, which recorded a multitude of paddock scenes and included many of the famous people they had met over the years. We were reminded of an album of similar proportions, which Manfred and Lieselotte von Brauchitsch had shown us in their home in eastern Germany.

Louis and Jean were both intensely interested in seeing my BRM scrapbooks, and it was then that they signed them.

I reminded Jean of the incident, related by Raymond Mays and recorded in my introduction, which occurred during the 1959 Italian Grand Prix, when an Italian policeman ordered Raymond to leave the pit lane. He had stoutly refused, and was about to be carried away by six stalwart policemen, when Jean snatched the helmet off the head of one of them and ran away "... bowling it down the pit area." By the time they caught up with the helmet, Jean was no longer to be seen!

Jean and Louis then took us upstairs to their trophy room where, inside a large glass-fronted cabinet, my painting of Graham Hill's BRM at Monaco had been propped up against the impressive silver cup which had been won there.

In 2001, Louis invited us to the launch of his latest book, *Vignettes & Memories,* at the Dorchester Hotel. It was in the evening of the day of Michael's graduation ceremony at Colchester, and amongst

The Old Mill House, Trumpington.

My painting of Jackie Stewart at Spa in 1965.

the guests were Lord Montagu of Beaulieu and Sir Jack Brabham. We were all given a signed copy of the book. Sadly, Jean was too ill to attend, and Louis later phoned me to say that he had placed one of my paintings by her bedside, where she was able to enjoy it. After her death, he phoned me on a number of occasions to talk of personal matters that troubled him greatly.

Louis had established a publishing firm with the object of producing two books. One was to have been his 100th title, and the other would have been based on my BRM scrapbooks. There wasn't time for either book to be published before he died, but this volume has grown out of the scrapbooks which he and Jean had signed in their home.

Louis Stanley at Trumpington.

Jean Stanley.

My painting of Graham Hill at Monaco.

Louis Stanley is remembered by many for his brief, but perceptive, biographies of the famous people he met and came to know over the course of his life. He didn't spare anyone while they lived, but declined to sign my copy of Doug Nye's brilliant book, *BRM: The Saga of British Racing Motors*, because he took exception to the writer's adverse comments about a late relative of Raymond Mays.

A final word.

There is a worthy memorial in stone to Raymond Mays in Bourne, but the most fitting memento to this great motor racing patriot is the original V16 BRM, which, in 1950, was demonstrated by Mays himself at Silverstone at the British Grand Prix meeting in May; failed on the line at the beginning of the International Trophy Race in August; won the two races at Goodwood in the hands of Reg

Parnell in September; briefly shone at the Peña Rhin Grand Prix in October, and is now to be seen in the National Motor Museum at Beaulieu. It was the product of Ray's magnificent obsession, and remains an awesome machine by any standards.

In addition, the other two Mark I V16 cars have been painstakingly restored, and later BRMs, including the World Championship winning 'Old Faithful,' can be seen at historic racing car events, to say nothing of the ERAs, all but one of which I believe still survive and continue to give pleasure to those who encounter them.

I still recall the thrill of receiving my first letter from Raymond Mays in 1952, and my pleasure in meeting him in person 11 years later. His kindness and patience never failed, over so many years responding to the letters of someone who was something of an obsessive about the BRM himself.

Appendix

Directors: F. B. Wheatcroft K. Wheatcroft

WHEATCROFT & SON LTD

THE FARM · LUTTERWORTH ROAD · ARNESBY
LEICESTERSHIRE · LE8 5UT
Telephone: 0116 247 8899 · Fax: 0116 247 8906
Email: info@wheatcrofts.co.uk

Registered in England No. 526780

Ref.6927/WS/m

The Revd. Bryan Apps M.A.
14 Barlett Drive
Castledean Park
Bournemouth
BH7 7JT

3 May 2006

Dear Reverend Apps,

Further to your letter of 13 April.

Firstly, I hope you are keeping well. Of course I remember you and your paintings are still hanging within the Donington Grand Prix Collection. I was very interested to read of your BRM book and will try and help solve some of the queries you raised in your letter.

Our Mk 1 is based on the remnants of Ken Wharton's Albi car. Some of the original remains of this car were dug up at the back of the old BRM test sheds at Folkenham Airfield and we bought a lot of parts from the BRM sale back in the 1980's. The car was put together from these various parts.

Our Mk 2 was bought complete from the BRM sale.

It was indeed our Mk 1 finished in light green that you saw Froilan Gonzales driving at Goodwood in 1998. Whether that car had ever previously crashed at Goodwood I don't know, certainly not under our ownership. This one carries the chassis number 1/02, therefore, 1/01 was the complete car sold at Earls Court.

We did, in fact, buy a second Mk 2 V16 which was originally bought at a Christies sale by Nick Mason of Pink Floyd. We bought this car from him just over a year ago and for a short time it sat with its two sisters in the Donington Grand Prix Collection before being sold to Bernie Ecclestone in whose ownership it remains to this day.

I hope the above information helps you a little and I would be very pleased to read a copy of your book when finished.

Yours sincerely,

M. fearn

Kevin Wheatcroft

Rl

(Dictated by KW and signed in his absence)

In association with

The Heart of British Motorsport

Kevin Wheatcroft explains what eventually happened to the two Mark 1 V16 BRMs 1/02 and 1/03.
1/01 can be seen in the National Motor Museum at Beaulieu.

THE GOODWOOD FESTIVAL OF SPEED

BRM photographs taken by the author at the 1990 Goodwood Festival of Speed.

Three views of the Donington-owned P15 V16 car in pale green, which was driven by Froilán González.

The two Mark II Sprint cars.

A 1964 P261 BRM.

A P83 H16 BRM.

A V12 P133 BRM.

THE ORIGINAL BRM IN THE NATIONAL MOTOR MUSEUM, BEALIEU

The author at the wheel of the original BRM – The V16 Mark I, chassis no 1/01 – which was driven by Sommer at Silverstone in 1950, and by Parnell, Fangio and Gonzales in the years that followed.

The engine of the P15/01 Beaulieu car exposed.

Back behind the wheel – the author revisits the Beaulieu BRM in 2015.

THE B.R.M.

— a unique record compiled by a genuine enthusiast.

Louis T. Stanley.
Jean Stanley.

Pit scene, mid-race! Parnell's B.R.M. is refuelled while Walker's accelerates out of the crowded pit area. Visible on the right of the photograph are Raymond Mays and John Bolster in front of the policeman.

THE
BRITISH RACING MOTOR

The title page of the scrapbook with the signatures of Louis and Jean Stanley.

Also available from Veloce Publishing –

Few racing cars of any kind have a more exotic and exciting reputation among enthusiasts than
the first BRM, a 16-cylinder wonder machine that was a bright beacon of promise in Britain's drab
postwar years. Packed with photos from the author's collection, this is the story of a bold but ultimately
misguided venture that delivered too much, too late.

ISBN: 978-1-845840-37-2
Hardback • 25x25cm • £17.99* UK/$$34.95* USA • 96 pages • 161 colour and b&w pictures

For more info on Veloce titles, visit our website at www.veloce.co.uk
• email: info@veloce.co.uk • Tel: +44(0)1305 260068
* prices subject to change, p&p extra

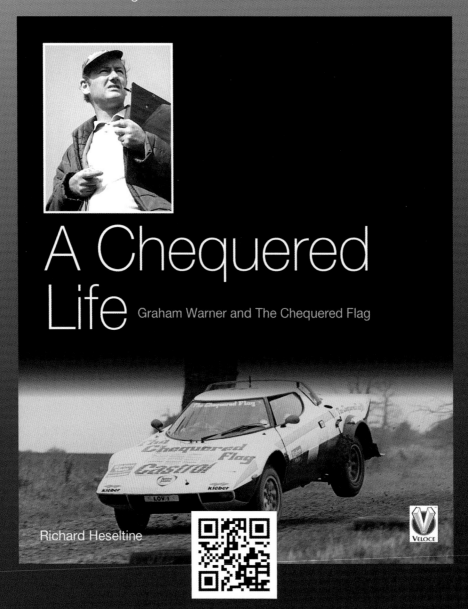

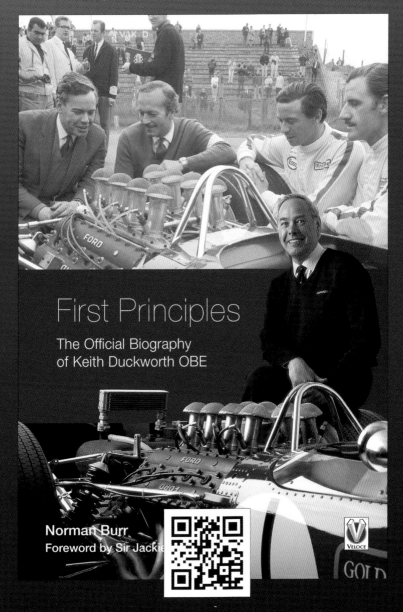

Available from Veloce Digital –

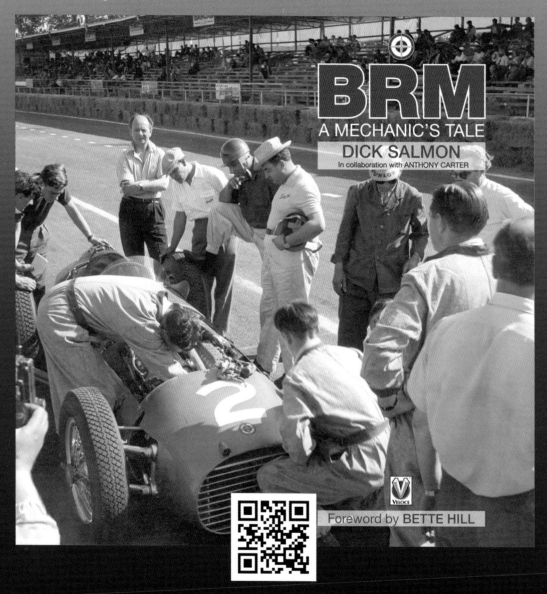

Index

RAHAM JOINS TH
WORLD CHAMPION

DUTCH

MONZA.

TWO BRMs ARE TO RACE IN ITALY

TWO B.R.M. cars will race in the Italian Grand Prix at Monza on September 16, Mr Raymond Mays, originator of the £200,000 B.R.M. venture, announced yesterday. Reg Parnell will drive one of them.

He got the low green car up to 182 miles an hour—the fastest it has ever shown.

Italy's top race may give BRM man his chance

By KAY PETRE, Daily Graphic Motoring Correspondent

FOR three years a lean man of 40 has nursed the £200,000 B.R.M. cars through their teething troubles, driven them for hundreds of test miles—and had an ambition to drive one in a race.

He is Ken Richardson, B.R.M. test driver and chief mechanic.

And his ambition may be fulfilled on September 16. Two B.R.M.s have been entered for the Italian Grand Prix at Monza.

Reg Parnell is nominated as number one driver. But no one has been named for the second car.

Ken Richardson

An official said last night that the second driver's name was being kept secret. My forecast is that it will be Richardson.

1,000-mile hustle

After competing in the Ulster Tourist Trophy race at Dundrod yesterday, young Londoner Lesley Johnston made a 1,000-mile car-and-air dash to Italy to be in reserve as a B.R.M. driver for the races at Monza. Britain's B.R.M. No. 2, driven by Ken Richardson, lapped at 112 m.p.h. in the speed trials. An Alfa-Romeo averaged 125 m.p.h.

After mechanics had worked all night to lower the gear ratios, 40-year-old Ken Richardson took it out for practice lapping.

Taking a third corner, he tried to change down into third gear, but the selectors jammed, and he was left in no gear at all.

Without the engine to act as a brake, the car drifted off the track into the straw bales.

The bump was not serious, but the front of the car was dented. Meanwhile Reg Parnell in the other B.R.M. was going splendidly. He put in a lap at 2mins. 2secs., which is within 2secs. of the lap record.

Italian experts are openly forecasting that the 1½-litre B.R.M.s which cost £200,000 to build, will be in the first three in the race.

MONZA CIRCUIT
START: DOUBLE-BEND.
1¼ MILE STRAIGHT.
DOUBLE-BEND.
¾ MILE STRAIGHT.

NEXT YEAR OPPOSITION MAY COME FROM MERCEDES.

SNEERS AS BRM CARS FLOP AGAIN

THE B.R.M.s' challenge to the supremacy of continental racing cars resulted in another humiliating failure yesterday.

Both entries were withdrawn from the Italian Grand Prix at Monza with gear-box trouble a few hours before the race.

The announcement, made through loudspeakers, brought a wave of sneers from the 100,000 spectators, who had expected a tough British-Italian contest.

Almost in tears

Reg Parnell, who was to have driven one of the £200,000 B.R.M.s, was almost in tears.

"Well, it can't be helped," he said. "It's better for things to go wrong before the race than during it.

"This is just one of those scurvy tricks fate plays from time to time."

Reg Parnell sits at the wheel of one of the "world beater" BRMs as a mechanic starts up the engine for a practice run

Said Raymond Mays, "father" of the B.R.M.: "It is one of the biggest blows we have had. The race experience to-day would have been invaluable.

"There is only one thing for us to do to save the name of British motoring.

"We shall stay here with one B.R.M. car, the gearbox of which will be put in order before Tuesday, and we shall engage drivers of international fame now assembled at Monza.

"They will drive the B.R.M. the same distance and under the same conditions as prevailed in the Grand Prix to-day, and we hope it will do even better than the cars of Italy's great motoring industry did."

Record beaten

That means beating the average speed of 115.5 m.p.h. with which Alberto Ascari, the Italian ace, won the race in a Ferrari.

He set up a new record for the 313-mile course.

Froilan Gonzales (Argentina), also in a Ferrari, was second and Giuseppe Farina (Italy), in an Alfa-Romeo, third.

Reg Parnell noticed the gearbox trouble when he brought the No. 1 B.R.M. back to the pit after a final practice run.

The trouble in the other B.R.M. was discovered about the same time by Hans von Stuck, the German appointed to partner Parnell because Ken Richardson was refused R.A.C. permission to drive in the race.

THE "MOTOR" SPEAKS WELL OF THE B.R.M.
REFERING TO THE SECOND LAP "THE B.R.M. WOULD HAVE SHONE AGAINST ITALY"

B.R.M. "uncertain"

A